Leave If You Can

California Series in Public Anthropology

The California Series in Public Anthropology emphasizes the anthropologist's role as an engaged intellectual. It continues anthropology's commitment to being an ethnographic witness, to describing, in human terms, how life is lived beyond the borders of many readers' experiences. But it also adds a commitment, through ethnography, to reframing the terms of public debate—transforming received, accepted understandings of social issues with new insights, new framings.

Leave If You Can

MIGRATION AND VIOLENCE IN
BORDERED WORLDS

Amelia Frank-Vitale
Foreword by Jason De León

UNIVERSITY OF CALIFORNIA PRESS

University of California Press
Oakland, California

Library of Congress Cataloging-in-Publication Data

Names: Frank-Vitale, Amelia author | De León, Jason, 1977- writer
of foreword
Title: Leave if you can : migration and violence in bordered worlds /
Amelia Frank-Vitale ; foreword by Jason De León.
Other titles: California series in public anthropology 62.
Description: Oakland, California : University of California Press,
[2026] | Series: California series in public anthropology ; 62 |
Includes bibliographical references and index.
Identifiers: LCCN 2025045830 (print) | LCCN 2025045831 (ebook) |
ISBN 9780520421349 cloth | ISBN 9780520421356 paperback |
ISBN 9780520421363 ebook
Subjects: LCSH: Deportation—United States | Hondurans—United
States—Social conditions | Hondurans—Mexico—Social
conditions | Caravans—Central America | Honduras—Emigration
and immigration | United States—Emigration and immigration—
Government policy
Classification: LCC JV7419.F73 2026 (print) | LCC JV7419 (ebook) |
DDC 304.80973--dc23/eng/20251113
LC record available at https://lccn.loc.gov/2025045830
LC ebook record available at https://lccn.loc.gov/2025045831

GPSR Authorized Representative: Easy Access System Europe,
Mustamäe tee 50, 10621 Tallinn, Estonia, gpsr.requests@easproject.
com

35 34 33 32 31 30 29 28 27 26
10 9 8 7 6 5 4 3 2 1

Contents

Foreword

I was once asked in a marketing meeting whether we should include "Honduras" in a forthcoming book's title. I noted that we should do that only if we don't want Americans to read it. The sad fact is that many of my fellow citizens don't care about Central America and a good number of them probably think Honduras is a beach town in Mexico. However, this has not always been the case. We have sporadically—and fleetingly—cared about the country of ten million wedged between Guatemala and Nicaragua, mostly when it concerns our own well-being. Some folks could find Honduras on a map in the 1980s. This is because we considered the country an important military ally in the fight to stop the spread of communism across the Northern Triangle. As I write these words, some Americans are looking up El Salvador on Google Earth to see where America's newest immigration detention prison is located.

In 1998, President Bill Clinton surprisingly let in one hundred thousand *catracho* (Honduran) refugees displaced by Hurricane Mitch, a fleeting moment of American recognition that migration and extreme weather are inextricably linked. Sixteen years after that Category 5 hurricane devastated the country (a preview of what would later become normalized by climate change), Americans once again became aware of Honduras when thousands of unaccompanied minors came knocking on our southern border door. Images of children locked up for the crime of trying not to be killed by the potent cocktail of violence and late-stage capitalism in places like La Planeta, or San Pedro Sula, were shocking to readers of *The New York Times*. That shock lasted about fifteen minutes, until the Obama administration started newly paying and training Latin American governments to stop migrants before they could reach our border. Desperate Hondurans are easier to ignore if they are detained, kidnapped, extorted, and/or killed in Mexico or simply incorporated into that country's growing undocumented labor force.

For decades, the news media and many social scientists have sought to understand migration (especially the Central American brand) primarily by standing at the US-Mexico border and taking notes. This is why you can't throw a rock in the Sonoran Desert of Arizona without hitting a reporter or an anthropologist. But the migration story can only partly be understood at that geopolitical boundary. If we really want to understand the global migration crisis we are living in, we need to go to the starting point, the "home" countries that people can no longer call home. This is the powerful view that *Leave If You Can* gives us. But the ethnographic data presented in the next several hundred pages make it clear that it is no easy task to work in the original Anchuria.

Honduras is a beautiful country rich in resources, culture, and history. Unfortunately, it is also a laboratory to study the relationship among poverty, violence, (dis)organized crime, corruption, climate change, displacement, migration, and deportation in this current political moment. The story told in this book feels like a window into the future of many countries in the global south grappling with growing inequalities, political instability, and a citizenry increasingly seeking refuge anywhere but home. Leave if you can indeed.

Amelia Frank-Vitale makes a compelling ethnographic case for the importance of Honduras not just as a locale to study a growing migration catastrophe but also as the home of millions of people caught between a rock and a hard place. Honduras is a country many catrachos love but also a place they no longer feel welcome or safe. It is clear that Frank-Vitale has deep compassion for the young people she introduces us to in this important book. As she poignantly shows, they don't want the American dream. They want to escape the Honduran nightmare that the United States has helped create for over one hundred years. Now more than ever, we need to understand what is happening in places where the only viable option is to run north no matter how many times we deport them back "home."

Jason De León
Los Angeles, California

Prologue

He's still wearing the blue canvas shoes they give you in detention.

Manuel was deported from the United States just a few days before we sit down to talk and record an interview. He's staying at his sister Alma's house in Villanueva, Cortés, on the outskirts of San Pedro Sula. Manuel introduces me briefly to Alma and her household. She is kind and warm but drawn, exhausted. She's clearly fond of her little brother, but his presence is an added burden, both in terms of having another mouth to feed, another body to squeeze into an already stretched-to-capacity space—the house is tiny, basically a hallway and two small rooms—and in terms of his being an unfamiliar young man newly arrived in this neighborhood. His presence puts everyone on edge.

"I can't really stay here," he tells me. "They have to know you here to be able to enter the neighborhood. When I arrive, they have to go pick me up and bring me to the house. I can't just come in and out."

We go for a walk so that he and I can talk alone. Manuel doesn't want Alma to be present for the interview, but there wouldn't be space in the home for quiet anyway. We make our way to the edge of the neighborhood and find what is supposed to be a park but is really more of an abandoned field. The sun is brutal, the earth dry and cracked. The lush, suffocating humidity of San Pedro Sula seems to give way to desert-like aridity. A graffiti-covered bench waits for us. There's a bit of shade, but it doesn't provide much relief. Manuel tries to show me photos on his phone, but the sun is too bright. Still, there's a peacefulness here with no one else around.

I am unsure of how to run this interview. Usually I do this with people with whom I have already had the chance to build at least a bit of rapport; often I already know their "story" long before I ask to turn on the voice recorder. I don't know this young man very well, though, so I am cautious, gentle, tentative. Manuel, however, wants to talk. He had reached out to me, asked me to come visit him, to record his story. He doesn't seem to know *how* to talk, but he's emphatic that he wants to. He fights to hold back tears, explaining, almost apologizing, "Soy muy sensible." (I'm very sensitive.) His voice breaks, there are long pauses, and I offer to wrap up the conversation several times. But he keeps going.

Twenty-two-year-old Manuel grew up in Tegucigalpa, the country's capital city, about four hours away from where we are seated now. His mother had ten children, but only five of them are still alive, or at least he is only sure that five are living. One of his sisters died from an asthma attack when Manuel was a baby; another sister was murdered about two years earlier, in Tegucigalpa. Two brothers disappeared in Mexico, one seventeen years ago, one more recently. His other living brother left for Mexico while Manuel was in detention, waiting to be deported. Manuel has worked since he was seven years old, selling things, landscaping, minor electrical work, whatever opportunity arose. He has a son of his own now, just two years old, living with the boy's mother in Tegucigalpa. He catches himself from crying when he mentions his son.

Before he left Honduras, Manuel was selling *productos del horto*, garden produce and the products made from it, on buses. Fighting against the glare, he proudly pulls up a photo of the *atol de elote*, the sweet, hot cornmeal drink he would sometimes sell. It's a common scene in Central America. Vendors get on a bus with a large basket of goods: pastries, fruit, chips, bottles of soda, bags of juice. Sometimes they'll just sell what they can while the bus is idling, waiting for stragglers to board. Often, especially when they have a good relationship with the driver on the route, they'll ride along for a few stops, sell what they can, get off, find another bus, then sell to other passengers going the other way. Doing this kind of mobile work, however, is what put Manuel in so much danger that he felt he had to leave the country.

Manuel tries to explain:

A mí me querían meter en el negocio. . . . Para ellos es más fácil . . . porque uno camina su canasto . . . y ahí meter las cosas. . . . Y el trayecto donde trabajo yo . . . como yo trabajaba vendiendo arriba de los buses. Yo me subí al bus y a los vendedores . . . no nos revisa la policía. La primera vez pasé . . . como la única vez . . . pasé como unos tres cuatro kilos. Ellos querían . . . como vieron que funcionó . . . querían obligarme después.

They wanted to get me into the business. . . . It is easier for them . . . because you carry a basket . . . to put things in there. . . . And the route I work . . . since I worked selling on board the buses. I would get on the bus and the vendors . . . the police don't check us. The first time I moved . . . well the only time . . . I moved about three or four kilos. They wanted . . . since they saw that it worked . . . they wanted to force me afterward.

Manuel recounts this run-in with gangs in Tegucigalpa without specific details; he never names the gang or even uses the word; he does not say the word *drugs* either; he also never elaborates on what the threats were, exactly, when he refused to keep transporting drugs in his basket. Or what they did to convince him to do it that first time.

Like so many young Hondurans, he's practiced at speaking around life-threatening situations, letting me know what he means without saying too much. His words alone do not capture the gravity of the terror he feels, but it comes through in the halting way he speaks, the pauses he interjects between half-finished sentences. By the time I sit down with Manuel, I've interviewed hundreds of migrants, asylum seekers, deportees. He seems more fragile than almost anyone I've spoken with. Manuel seems heartbroken, crushed, without any of the whimsical affect, the joking demeanor, or the tough guy bravado that so many people put on when they're talking with me. There is no silver lining for him. He's too raw, too sad, too defeated to pretend otherwise.

When the asylum officer interviewed him in the United States, Manuel told him the same thing he told me. Like so many, though, he did not pass his credible fear interview, the first step toward being able to seek asylum in the United States. I don't have the transcript of the interview; I don't know exactly what was said to the officer who was judging whether or not he had a real fear of being sent back to Honduras. But I have seen few young men from Honduras so clearly terrified, so openly broken, when they talk about what had happened to them at home. Manuel appealed the first decision, repeated his story, and was once again denied. Then deported.

During nearly three months in detention (just nine days short, he tells me), he was moved around frequently, bused from place to place, almost deported multiple times, and made to spend hours on end—one time, a full twenty-four hours—in shackles. *Enchachado.*

Reflecting on this, he says, "Yo me preparé un poco, va, porque dije, es como una prueba psicológica la que lo hacen a uno. Para que uno no vuelva, eso es lo que quieren hacer. Para que uno no vuelva arriba." (I prepared myself a bit, you know, because I said, it's like a psychological test that they subject you to. So that you don't come back, that's what they want to do. So that you don't go up again.)

I ask him, "Even so, you're thinking about trying again?"

"Ellos pueden hacer lo que quieran," he replies, "pero uno siempre regresa para arriba." (They can do whatever they want, but you always go back up [North].)

He would like to visit his baby boy before he leaves the country again, but he's not sure if that's a good idea. He doesn't have the money for the bus to Tegus, on the one hand, and, on the other, he's not sure his child's mother would let him near his son. His presence puts everyone at risk. He would also very much like to hug his own mother once more before he goes. And he knows he cannot stay with Alma and her family for very long.

Manuel gets together a few hundred lempiras for the journey—enough to start out but not even enough for the bus ticket to cross Guatemala—and he leaves Honduras again just a few days after we speak, wearing the only shoes he has, the pair they gave him in detention. He had asked to keep the whole uniform, but they wouldn't let him.

Before we say goodbye, I ask Manuel what he was thinking when he was in the airplane, on his way back to Honduras.

"Yo pensaba regresar el mismo día." (I was planning to go back [to the United States] that same day.)

Introduction

Field Notes

La Libertad. Interview with Pedro. After a while other guys start to come by, most of whom I know by now. Anderson sits down next to me and starts riffing. One of the other ex-*pandilleros* (maybe current *pandilleros?*) kind of sidles up and mostly keeps quiet but hangs. Ramón comes by and Checho and we're all just kind of sitting around, chatting, telling stories. It is a chill, jovial atmosphere. I buy everyone coke and potato chips. At one point Ramón stops and says, "Look! Everyone here is *deportado*. All *deportados! Deportado, deportado, deportado*," pointing at each person in our little circle. Except for the seventeen-year-old kid; he's the lone outlier. The rest of them have all been deported, at least once, many of them multiple times.

. . .

La Libertad is the pseudonym I've given to a small neighborhood on the edge of the sprawling Rivera Hernández sector of San Pedro Sula, the economic and industrial capital of Honduras. It is not a particularly out-of-the-ordinary neighborhood; La Libertad could be any number of the neighborhoods built up around the urban centers

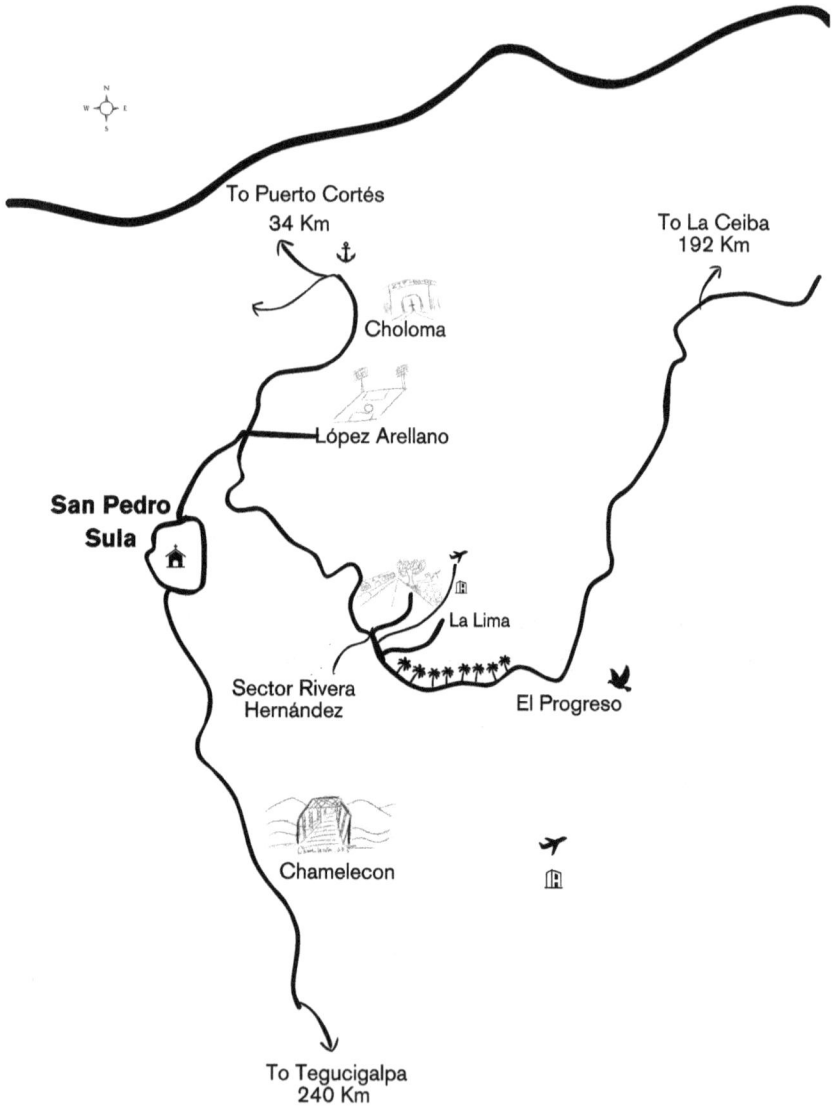

MAP 1. Map (not to scale) of key neighborhoods in the Sula Valley, Honduras. Designed by Catherine Calderón of *ContraCorriente*. ©Author

across the Sula Valley and along Honduras's northern coast. Mostly single-story, concrete block houses line the packed dirt streets. When painted, the houses sport light colors, cream, peach, yellow, beige, chosen in hope of offsetting the unrelenting sun. *Pulperías* (corner stores) occupy the front rooms of a handful of the homes; a church sits off the main road; faded murals cover some of the walls. The working-class residents have been here for a few generations; they mostly know each other, each other's families. Skinny teens on bicycles make the rounds, watching out for anyone or anything that seems to be out of place. Just like in most comparable neighborhoods, La Libertad is controlled by a street gang, a *pandilla*, made up of many of the sons (and some daughters) of those families.

And just like the other neighborhoods, La Libertad is full of people who have been deported.

The Ordinariness of Deportation

Sitting around in La Libertad that day, I was struck by how casual the label "deportado" had become. It was not an insult; Ramón's pointing at each of them (and including himself) did not inflict shame, did not provoke ridicule. They laughed together, chuckling at the coincidence that they had all been deported. Enunciating this shared experience among them was done for my benefit; being deported became a topic of conversation and identification only because of my presence. I was in Honduras to study deportation. Ramón knew this, and the realization came to him in the moment—that all these young men who happened to be gathered around, save one, had already been deported. For them it was incidental, an amusing coincidence. For me, it was emblematic of a kind of relationship to deportation that I saw emerging in Honduras.

Deportation is often written about as a violent process that sends people back to "home" countries that they do not know well and where they are not equipped to live, breaking apart families and communities in the process. A substantial ethnographic contribution to deportation studies has been documenting and theorizing the experience of people who lived most of their lives in the United States and were then sent back to countries of citizenship that were essentially unfamiliar to them.[1] Scholars have likened this experience to exile and banishment, revealing deportation as a process of violent rending.[2] The experience of exile chronicled in these works is twofold, when people are made to leave their country of origin in the first place and again when they are made to leave the country they had come to know as home.

There has been good reason for this focus. Changes to the law in the mid-1990s in the United States made more immigrants with legal status deportable. This ushered in an era of deportation-as-exile, where people who had mostly grown up in the United States were sent to countries of first citizenship that they had not seen since they were children. This focus on deportation has also been essential to push against an enduring legal fiction baked into US law: that deportation is not about punishment for crimes but an administrative fix for civil infractions. Legally, deportation is constructed as restoring order, sending people back to their supposedly rightful place; the scholarship that focuses on the legal violence of deportation and the damage it causes to those it exiles reveals how disordering deportation actually is.

Much of this literature emerges in the context of people sent from the United States to the Caribbean and Central America, with El Salvador and Guatemala figuring prominently. I went to Honduras, then, expecting to find people deported from the United States who were dealing with confounding rupture, out of place in their country of citizenship, longing for families and communities left behind in New York and New Orleans and Miami and Houston. I found some people in that situation, but I also found a lot of people like the guys in La Libertad.

Their experience, one in which deportation is ordinary rather than an extraordinary kind of rupture, is the core story of this book. By "ordinary," I mean to indicate three things: First, deportation has become commonplace within communities in Honduras's urban margins today; second, a single person, like Ramón, increasingly experiences deportation multiple times; and third, the awfulness of deportation, the criminalization and the constraints on a person's mobility that it entails, is not drastically different from a young man's everyday experience in Honduras. In the context of young people in urban Honduras, deportation can feel particularly mundane, not because it is unobjectionable or readily accepted, but because their lives at home are also shaped by the life-threatening micropolitics of containment and a society that constructs them as suspicious, dangerous, potentially criminal, and expendable.[3] None of this is to say that familiarity with deportation renders it less than violent. To the contrary, this book aims to illustrate the continuities of violence embedded in the ordinariness of deportation.

Deporting Honduras

Honduras juts out into the Caribbean from the Central American isthmus, bordering Guatemala, El Salvador, and Nicaragua. It is home to Copán, one of the most important sites of the ancient Maya civilization; the second largest coral reef in the world; pristine beaches; exceptional varieties of coffee; award-winning cigars and chocolate; a large Afro-Indigenous Garifuna population and at least seven other recognized Indigenous groups; and the largest port in Central America, Puerto Cortés. Honduran Francisco Morazán was a founding hero of Central American independence and a reference point for liberal democracy in the region.

Honduras also served as the staging ground for US counterinsurgency operations in Central America during the Reagan era and continues to house one of the United States's largest military bases in the hemisphere; lived through a military coup d'etat in 2009; saw the assassination of prominent Indigenous and environmental activists, including Bertha Cáceres in 2016 and Juan López in 2024; and has had some of the highest rates of homicide in the world. O. Henry's depiction of the fictional Republic of Anchuria, which coined the term "banana republic," was based on his time in Honduras. Now most of the cocaine consumed in the United States passes through here; many Honduran businessmen, police officials, and politicians are serving lengthy sentences in US prisons for crimes related to narcotrafficking, including the country's former president, Juan Orlando Hernández Alvarado (2014–22).

Many analysts, commentators, scholars, and activists who have become focused on Honduras in recent years point to the 2009 coup as the root cause of the nation's current problems, including violence and migration. I think, however, that the coup is one inflection point—albeit a critical one—in a series of crises in which each point, rather than being the root itself, represents the moment when a situation of constant near-crisis reaches a breaking point and exposes the fragility of the equilibrium that had existed beforehand. The coup was one such moment; when the president was removed from power, the extent to which the rule of law was a selectively enforced and performative fallacy was laid bare. A decade earlier, in 1998, when Hurricane Mitch devastated Honduras's social and material infrastructure, it led to the first wave of massive out-migration and also the consolidation of disparate street gangs into what would eventually become the infamous MS-13 and Barrio 18 gangs.[4] Mitch did not cause these phenomena. Rather, in shattering what fragile infrastructure existed, the hurricane exacerbated and exposed the extent to which people were already unprotected in Honduras and left to their own devices to survive.[5] A tenuous stability existed before Mitch, as it existed before the coup, and these inflection points showed how precarious that equilibrium had always been; they broke the delicate balance that people had found to make life work and illuminated its frailty. The inflection points—Mitch, the coup, and other events[6]—did not create the crisis; they revealed the ongoing emergency that is ever present in daily life. And this condition of constant emergency informs growing Honduran out-migration.

For a long time, Honduras did not share migration patterns with its neighbors. El Salvador and Guatemala each saw enormous migrations toward the United States during their decades of civil war and genocide, but Honduras did not have full-scale armed conflict and migration remained moderate throughout the '80s and '90s.[7] While the banana industry generated a long-standing migratory connection between the country's northern coast and the United States (New Orleans in particular), and Mitch precipitated the first era of mass migration, over the past two decades Honduras has seen steadily growing out-migration—sometimes dubbed an exodus[8]—with the vast majority of Hondurans hoping to resettle in the United States. In the year 2000, there were about 200,000 Honduran nationals living in the United States; the 2020 census counts over one million.[9]

Accompanying growing out-migration has been a corresponding steady rise in deportations back to Honduras. Over the course of a decade, from 2014 to 2024, Honduras counted over 600,000 deportations, almost entirely from Mexico and the United States. In a country with a population of about 9.5 million, these data alone suggest that deportation has become an important social phenomenon. The dynamics in that circle in La Libertad were emblematic; all but one of the gathered young men had experienced deportation.

Numbers, however, rarely tell the whole story. First, knowing how many people have been detained and deported cannot tell us much about those who make it to their destinations without being detected. We can see shifts over time, from year to year, but those who successfully circumvent interdiction, whether at the border or before it, defy statistics. In addition, while certain trends are clear, these numbers do not represent *individuals* deported but rather deportation events. While a level of growing ordinariness could be interpreted from the numbers alone, ethnographic research can tell us something more about the meanings and experience that lie behind them. My research suggests that many of the people who are deported back to Honduras do not stay there, despite many mechanisms designed to make them do so. Many of the people who make up these numbers, like Manuel, are sent back only to turn around and leave again a few days later.

By focusing on this kind of deportation experience, this book advances the deportation studies literature that has centered on an experience of removal as akin to exile. While this prior experience of deportation is also ongoing, in Honduras we see an additional pattern emerging. This study is situated in a moment when the effects of border externalization and border hardening are expanding the contours of what deportation means regionally and globally. As the deportation regime has evolved, it has endeavored to capture, immobilize, and return people before they have the possibility of settling into a life elsewhere, before they can build a new community, before "home" can become decoupled from the place where one holds citizenship. For these deportees, home is not yet located elsewhere, but their country of citizenship may never have felt much like home to begin with.

This shift is a consequence of the twinned processes of ever-tightening enforcement at the US-Mexico border and the externalization of the US border regime, where border controls are steadily decoupled from the physical boundary they are meant to enforce. Since the mid-1990s, the United States has increasingly enlisted its neighbors to the south to carry out its immigration enforcement agenda, by detaining and deporting more people—especially Central Americans—before they can make it to the border, much less settle into lives within US territory. One clear indicator of this is that since 2015 far more Hondurans have been deported from Mexico than from the United States.[10]

The violence of this kind of deportation is often hidden from view, at least from the vantage point of a US audience. This book aims to render visible the long-reaching violence of a deportation regime that does not only look like workplace raids and sobbing children being ripped from their parents' arms. While the second Trump administration revels in the spectacle of scenes like these, this is only the most visible piece of a long-standing and expanding policy of deportation whose cruelty and the people subjected to it are kept far from US territory and mostly out of sight.

"The Murder Capital of the World"

Long before focusing on Honduras, I was immersed in the world of transit migration in Mexico, as some combination of a volunteer at migrant shelters, a migrants' rights activist, and a budding researcher. I also accompanied migrant caravans beginning in 2011, long before they made headlines (and made Donald Trump so very angry). This history and familiarity with migration in Mexico heavily informs the content of this book. I first considered studying dynamics in Honduras when, while volunteering at a shelter in southern Mexico, I noticed two shifts taking place. In 2010, when I first began, a roughly even number of Salvadorans, Hondurans, and Guatemalans would regularly come through the shelter. By 2012, this had changed, and it was evident that Hondurans were far outnumbering their Central American neighbors. This is not to say that people from El Salvador and Guatemala had stopped migrating. Instead, the numbers of people leaving Honduras seemed to be exploding.

In addition to this demographic shift, something else was changing. In 2010, people generally reported economic reasons—lack of work, poverty—for deciding to migrate. Often, in conversations, people would discuss violence and insecurity as a secondary factor, but the economic motivations were the first thing people would bring up. By 2012, this had shifted, especially among Hondurans. When asked why they were migrating, the answer was often immediate—and urgent. Now people talked about being targeted for murder, about fearing for their lives *first*. Poverty and scarcity and hunger often emerged as secondary, connected reasons, but insecurity was top of mind.

I wanted to understand what was going on in Honduras. Like many people from the United States, I had much more familiarity with the histories and politics of El Salvador and Guatemala but knew relatively little about Honduras. I knew there had been a coup d'etat a few years earlier. And I knew that headlines everywhere were screaming about Honduras, dubbing San Pedro Sula in particular the "Murder Capital of the World."

After a devastating spike of 86.5 murders per 100,000 people in 2011, Honduras has, fortunately, seen a steady decline.[11] In 2023, Honduras's homicide rate was at the lowest in a decade; yet at 31.1 murders per 100,000 people, it continues to be the sixth highest level in the world.[12] Any rate in double digits is considered an epidemic level of homicide by the World Health Organization. For comparison, the United States registered a murder rate of 6.9 per 100,000 people in 2021; Canada had a rate of 1.9 per 100,000 people in 2020.[13]

Homicide is not the only kind of violence that matters, of course. Honduras also has alarmingly high rates of other, interconnected forms of structural and physical violence—including gender-based violence, political violence, and environmental violence—and accounts of disappearances have increased even as the murder rate has gone down.[14] The homicide statistics are also likely partial; in interviews I conducted with Honduran officials, they repeatedly indicated that they are likely only able to recover the bodies of and therefore register the homicides of at best seven in every ten victims (and in many parts of the country it is probably more like three in ten.)[15] Still, the homicide data—albeit partial and limited—is so thoroughly alarming in scale and continuity as to be both a reflection of a general condition of insecurity and an index for the wider mosaic of violence.[16]

There are many reasons that Honduras has such high rates of violence, but frequently blame for the country's troubles is placed on the street gangs that came to be known outside of Central America as the *maras*. In Honduras, the term "mara" is generally used to refer to the Mara Salvatrucha, also known as MS-13. *Pandilla* can mean Barrio 18 or any of the other smaller gangs operating in Honduras. The frequently used compound term in Honduras, *maras y pandillas* — which would be translated as "gangs and gangs"—covers all street gangs. Whether mara or pandilla or gang, the term refers to essentially the same thing: groups of young people, mostly men, who exercise control internally, within their own neighborhoods, through lethal violence and strict enforcement of their rules. They impose order on their neighborhoods and understand themselves as protectors of the residents under their control, engaged in an eternal, existential war with rival groups who would take over their territory and their people.[17]

Throughout this book, I sometimes refer to Barrio 18 or MS-13 directly, but I often avoid identifying the specific gang that controls a specific neighborhood.[18] In addition to using pseudonyms for people and neighborhoods, I refrain from identifying people, neighborhoods, and gangs as they relate to each other. I obscure names and neighborhoods and gangs in constellation because it is precisely the relationality among them that could lead to identification. A *New York Times* article appeared in 2019, for example, that included a map of Rivera Hernández with neighborhoods labeled and the gang that controlled each neighborhood identified. Some of my interlocutors pointed this map out as particularly problematic, putting the lives of people in those neighborhoods at risk—especially community leaders—as that kind of relational identification might be used to prosecute certain people, justly or unjustly.[19] While I do not want to conceal the relationships of power and mobility control at play, it is not necessary for the analysis offered here to identify which groups control which neighborhoods. To the contrary, I want to draw attention to the patterned dynamics that hold beyond the specific actors in specific spaces. With this in mind, while I sometimes name MS-13 and Barrio 18, especially in reference to their rivalry, I will often be vague about which gang is in question, simply referring to "the gang" or "the pandilla."

While I did not go to Honduras intending to study the maras and pandillas directly, I understood that their presence was going to be an important factor for many of the deportees I intended to work with. My ethnographic focus on daily life in neighborhoods with a high incidence of migration and deportation, however, offered me a unique window into gangs. Their presence is not tangential to life in Honduras, as an immigration judge once suggested to me during an asylum hearing.[20] Quite the contrary: Life on the urban margins in Honduras has come to be shaped by the gangs, just as the gangs are shaped by all the features of life in Honduras that contribute to migration. The gangs sometimes cause people to flee and are also, at the same time, a consequence of the underlying structures that make so many people unable to stay.

An Ethnography of Deportation

The interventions of this book derive primarily from ethnographic fieldwork I conducted in and around the Sula Valley, in Honduras's northern coast, from 2017 to 2019. My fieldwork here included interviewing deportees and their families and friends and conducting participant observation in their neighborhoods. I crisscrossed the Sula

Valley, visiting people in their homes and participating in the rhythms of daily life in their *colonias* (neighborhoods). This included watching soccer matches played under the searing sun; attending backyard church services; kneading dough to make *baleadas*, the freshly made, slightly spongy, large flour tortillas that are a Honduran staple; and a lot of sitting around in plastic chairs, collectively complaining about the heat, drinking too much soda, chatting about what was going in our families and in the neighborhood and the world, running through lists of who among their neighbors had left for the United States recently, who had just been sent back, and who was making plans to leave. Sometimes this conversation was directed by me, but often it was not; talk of migration—and deportation—was everywhere.

I also returned to Mexico a number of times during my work in Honduras, weaving together spaces of migration and interaction with aspiring migrants while en route with the stories of deportation experiences I was learning in the Sula Valley. When people gathered at the San Pedro Sula bus station to form a migrant caravan in the fall of 2018, I did not, at first, think to join them. Caravans had been a relatively regular occurrence during my years in Mexico, and I thought I ought to stay in Honduras and continue my research as planned. As the caravan grew to a larger size than anything we had ever seen—in no small part due to the wall-to-wall news coverage after Trump directed his attention, and the media, to this mass migration movement—I realized it had become much more than a replica of past mobility-related protests of which I had been a part. This caravan was an expression of the brewing Honduran exodus. I joined them in Arriaga, in southern Mexico, and incorporated the 2018 caravan and its reverberations into my understandings of Hondurans' experiences of deportation in an era of hardening and expanding migration controls and narrowing paths to protection for those fleeing violence.

Anthropologists have developed a multitude of interpretations in our understandings of what ethnography means. I have come to think of ethnography as the attempt that we make to approximate, as much as possible, the rhythms of daily life of the people, community, country, business, organization, or neighborhood with which we have chosen to work. We recognize, collectively as a discipline, at this point that for those of us who are engaged in research in communities of which we are not already a part, we can never fully be *of* that community, neighborhood, or organization, but the task at hand is to get as close as possible to everyday life there and, in so doing, learn the patterns and processes, the unspoken, taken-for-granted things, how life, society, and the world unfolds. I think of doing ethnography as cultivating serendipity, being present with enough consistency and depth to be there when simple but meaningful things occur, when the accumulation of everyday life teaches you something and the patterns take shape.

Deportation itself can be hard to conceptualize, both because of how complicated it actually is and how deceptively simple it might be thought to be. It involves sending people away, back, somewhere, beyond the realm of the here, of the present, of the visible. Deportation's core function is to put people outside, out of sight, which makes an ethnographic approach all the more important. Ethnography can help us get insight into the many moving parts of the multifaceted experience of deportation. The challenge for me, though, was how to go about conducting ethnography of a process like deportation that rests on displacing and removing from view those subjected to it.

Nathalie Peutz, in her article calling for an "anthropology of removal," notes the particular methodological challenges of this endeavor: Deportees may be difficult to locate, any identity as a group is tenuous and fleeting, and access to the "deportation grid" may be difficult to attain.[21] In San Pedro Sula, like many parts of Honduras, people who have been deported are everywhere. Everyone I meet seems to have a family member or a neighbor or a friend who has been deported. This ubiquity means that having been deported is not a defining characteristic for many. It is neither something people broadcast nor something people try to hide. This was not always the case in Honduras, nor is it the case everywhere. Frequently deportees do face extreme stigma and hardship because of their category "deportee."[22] In Honduras's urban margins, however, deportation is so common that the fact of it does not carry much weight for a person's social standing. On the one hand, this ordinariness means that deportation is not a topic about which people were reticent to speak. On the other hand, if anyone anywhere might have been deported, if deportees are not marked or separated out from the rest of society in any meaningful way, figuring out ways to communicate with those who had been deported presented a particular methodological challenge.

With this in mind, my initial research plan involved affiliating with a Honduran nongovernmental organization (NGO), which I am calling Faith in Action (Fe en Acción, or FeAc), which offers programming for deported youth and young adults in the Sula Valley. From 2014 to the summer of 2017, their Return and Rebuild Program (Programa de Retornar y Reconstruir, or Pro-R) had a presence in each of the three deportee processing centers in Honduras. Adults deported by airplane are processed at the Centro de Atención al Migrante Retornado (CAMR-Lima), housed in an old military airport adjacent to the Ramón Villeda International Airport in La Lima, Cortés, just outside of San Pedro Sula. Adults deported overland by bus are processed at a center in Omoa, Cortés (CAMR-Omoa), on the coast near the border with Guatemala. Minors and their families, whether deported by air or by land, are processed at Centro Belén, in San Pedro Sula.

In the summer of 2017, the Honduran government suspended access of all Honduran NGOs to the deportee processing centers. The official rationale was that the whole procedure had developed haphazardly, and the government wanted to review everything, streamline it, and make sure that the privacy of the deportees was fully protected. The decision was made, however, after an NGO that specialized in offering services to deported minors kept issuing reports that contradicted the government's official discourse regarding migration and security.[23] This was also a moment when the sitting president, Juan Orlando Hernández Alvarado (often referred to as JOH), was ramping up an unconstitutional reelection campaign and there was a general retreat from transparency. While Honduran NGOs like FeAc were expelled, the operations of the three processing centers were still run by *international* NGOs, the Scalabriniana order of nuns, the International Organization for Migration (IOM), and the International Committee of the Red Cross (ICRC), respectively.[24] This decision meant that Pro-R had an increasingly difficult time locating enough deportees to fill the slots it had available in its programs. It also meant that I would not have regular access to the deportee processing centers as I had planned. Through colleagues with the international NGOs, I was able to be present in one of the centers on a few select occasions throughout my fieldwork, but my attempts to secure permission to have regular access through the Honduran government never went anywhere.

Despite this complication, I maintained my affiliation with Pro-R. Through them, I was able to meet an initial group of deportees, conduct a first round of interviews, and begin to build relationships with Pro-R participants outside the organization's programming. During preliminary fieldwork in 2016, I met Pamela during one of the Pro-R workshops. She was friendly, bubbly, and sharp-witted and eager to talk about her experience. I suggested we keep talking and told her I would like to interview her, and she enthusiastically agreed. When I offered to visit her in her home, though, she looked at me, confused and surprised.

"You know I live in Chamelecón," she reminded me.

"Yep!" I said. "It's not a problem for me if it's not a problem for you."

"Oh no," she laughed, "it's fine with me! It's just, you know, some people won't go there."

A few days later, Pamela met me in the center of San Pedro Sula, and I rode the bus with her into her neighborhood, at the far end of Chamelecón. After that first visit, I returned to visit her and her family many times and got to know many of her neighbors and my way around their corner of San Pedro Sula. Later, a friend from Mexico came to Honduras as part of his ongoing project to help reconnect families from Central America with loved ones who had migrated but lost contact. When I learned that one of the people he was hoping to track down happened to live in this same part of Chamelecón, I called Pamela, and she took us door to door until we found the family.

I would replicate this method throughout the course of my research, trusting residents to know the rules of their respective colonias and invite me in—or not—depending on what having visitors entailed. A few times a person would be willing, even eager to talk to me but would then indicate that their neighborhood was too tense, too *complicado*, and it would be better for us to meet elsewhere. In cases like that, I never pushed and always agreed to meet wherever the person felt would be the best option. But if someone invited me into their neighborhood, I went.

Having Pro-R as an initial institutional affiliation during my stay in Honduras was useful methodologically, but it also proved to be an important choice because of the outsized role that NGOs play in the country. Over time, I came to understand that analyzing the state and institutions requires engaging with NGOs. The Honduran president at the time of my fieldwork, Juan Orlando Hernández Alvarado, spoke with pride about the *tercerización*—the "third-partyization," or outsourcing—of government functions. I initially thought this was just another example of the general neoliberal bent of Honduras, the idea that everything is done better, more efficiently and with less corruption, through the private sector. The roots of this, however, are not just in current initiatives like the public-private partnerships to build highways but also stem, as anthropologist Daniel Reichman shows, from the post–Cold War turn in Honduras toward the NGO-ization of governance, particularly in the realm of social welfare.[25] Even the government, Reichman suggests, gave up on government in Honduras, and NGOs and foreign aid increasingly replace what would have been functions of the state. Consequently, throughout this book, the language and programming of NGOs figure prominently in my analysis. Migration, among many other aspects of life in Honduras, is almost entirely "managed" by NGOs. This coheres with the neoliberal governmentality of the global deportation regime, where NGOs, development agencies, private enterprise, and governments work together to detain, control, return, and "reintegrate" migrants.[26]

When it became clear that I was never going to be able to secure regular access to the processing centers, I had to rethink my methods. This led to two shifts. First, I incorporated trips to Mexico, where I had a long history of conducting migration-related research and where I had a deep network of colleagues and contacts. Second, I returned to the basics of ethnography, doing sustained participant observation in neighborhoods across the Sula Valley, chief among them Rivera Hernández in San Pedro Sula and Choloma's López Arellano. Eventually, my presence and familiarity in these neighborhoods had enough depth that when a resident was deported, their neighbors would notify me, and I would refer them to the Pro-R program (if they wanted me to do so).

· • ·

I turn off my audio recorder and we start picking up the stray napkins and collecting the plastic cups to return our trays to the counter. Before we stand up from the table, Suyapa takes a deep breath, lifts her head, and a smile breaks across her face.

"What are you," she says to me, with a confused but pleased chuckle, "a psychologist or a witch? I feel so much better now!" With that, she stands up and we make our way out of the restaurant, returning to my car and exchanging light banter and gentle humor.

I was relieved; the interview had taken a turn that I had not expected. I had come to know Suyapa through a women's organization in the López Arellano sector of Choloma and knew the general outline of her and her adult daughter's entanglements with migration. Suyapa was always friendly and warm with me, and I had expected the interview to be intense but centered on migration. Instead, I found myself listening to her talk about her own experience of childhood neglect, abuse, and trauma. My questions—and deep familiarity with migration matters—seemed ill suited to the stories that she wanted to tell. I followed her lead and let her tell me about her life in the way she wanted to, gently encouraging and focusing mostly on showing her empathy. Her assessment at the end, that speaking with me had been a positive experience for her, was a welcome surprise. For both of us, I think.

My approach to interviewing leans heavily on the "semistructured" part. Although I have a general sense of the kinds of questions I intend to ask, I also tend to allow the person I'm speaking with to take the interview in another direction if there are other things that they wish to discuss or topics that they would prefer not to speak about. As I frequently ask people to talk about difficult experiences, I try to avoid retraumatization as much as possible by giving people the space to speak about what they wish, as they wish.

Over the course of my long-term participant observation, I conducted 135 semistructured interviews with migrants, their families, their neighbors, pastors, police officers, prisoners, prosecutors, community leaders, government officials, and current and former gang members. Just over half of these interviews were recorded using a small voice recorder or a cell phone. Most of these interviews happened in people's homes, but frequently the person being interviewed preferred to leave their colonia, and I would offer to treat them to a coffee or a meal while we spoke. Quite a few interviews were conducted in Pizza Huts and Denny's, the venue chosen by the interviewee in part because it was a bit of a treat and in part because they thought I would feel most comfortable in the air-conditioned US chain restaurants.

Whether or not I was able to record a given interview, I took notes afterward, often in the form of voice notes to myself on my cell phone. While I sometimes also produced written field notes, frequently, rather than wait until I returned to my apartment, I would record my reflections of an interview or an interaction as soon as I got in my car and could roll my windows up. These audio field notes are punctuated by reggaetón on the radio, the *ding ding ding* of the car telling me to put my seatbelt on, and short interactions with windshield washers at intersections.[27] Throughout this book I mix a narration of the stories that people shared with me and experiences that I shared with them with vignettes taken from my field notes, like the opening scene in La Libertad. I draw directly from the field notes to offer a glimpse into how I was narrating the world around me to myself in the moment.

As I returned to my notes and turned audio from interviews and my own recordings into code-able text, I would often stop and try to determine where the person was in the moment of writing, whether we were still in contact, and how I might contact them again if we had lost touch. This constant process of revisiting and reconnecting has sometimes resulted in finding out that people have won an asylum case or reconnected with family. Sometimes it has made me aware of a death, an imprisonment, or a disappearance. Sadly, while writing, I learned that several deported young men with whom I interacted as part of this research have since been killed. And while I am in contact with people from Honduras nearly daily, whether or not I am writing, the process of pausing writing to reach out reminds me, always, of the urgency of the stories that people shared with me. And the responsibility I have to try my best to tell them well.

Research in a "Violent" Field

Field Notes

Today the police stop me on my way into Rivera Hernández. They ask for my license and the *revisión del carro* and they're very confused about who I am and what I'm doing here. The older police officer says, "Do you know where you're going?"

"Yeah," I say.

"Have they told you what this place is, what Rivera Hernández is like?"

"Yeah," I say again, "I come here a lot."

"Aren't you afraid? Aren't you scared to go in there?"

"No," I say, wanting this conversation to end.

"You're *really* not afraid?"

The officer continues, warning me that the *mareros* might try to use me, take advantage of me. Then he asks if I happen to have any heart medication with me that I might give them because they work so long, so many hours, they only get two hours of sleep.

I try to be friendly. "Right? It's a hard job," I say. "I just came from the caravan, and there are police officers who are part of it who just couldn't take it anymore."

Now the younger officer pipes up for the first time "SI OMBE!" he concurs, in the *caliche* of Honduran youth.

Ah, the police. Asking me if I'm afraid to go into Rivera Hernández. And then asking me for stuff.

. • .

In many ways, I embarked on this project because when people tell me that a given place is *really violent*, my initial, gut reaction is to want to go directly to that place and speak with the people who actually live there. This instinct comes in large part from my experience growing up in Reading Pennsylvania, in the 1990s—a small city that had a local reputation for being a *really violent* place. Reading, Pennsylvania's fourth largest city, has made the news twice in recent years. First, it earned the dubious distinction of being the country's poorest city (with more than 65,000 residents) in the 2010 census.[28] Second, in the lead-up to the 2024 election, it received ample attention for being Pennsylvania's most Latino (68.9 percent)—particularly Puerto Rican—city.[29] Long before, though, as I was growing up, there was already a clear demarcation between my city—with high rates of poverty and a racially and linguistically diverse population—and the surrounding, mostly white, and much more affluent suburbs of Berks County. Just the idea of "going into the city" sparked fear for certain suburbanites. Above the entrance to one of the primary bridges connecting Reading to its suburban twin, West Reading, the words "LOCK YOUR DOORS" were scrawled in graffiti. I always imagined it was a fellow city-dweller who had written the warning, using urban sarcasm to stoke and play with the fears of those who clutched their pearls and their purses close and dared not enter.

As a young white girl from the inner city, people from the suburbs with whom I came into contact during countywide events like junior orchestras and community theater would frequently ask me some variation of the question, "But aren't you scared to go to school every day?" I knew that the rates of violence in my city were higher than the surrounding areas, and I had classmates who were involved in gangs from an early age. Many of us, however, lived violence-free lives. I also knew that we were surveilled and policed in accordance with the reputation we had. In high school, after a small fight broke out in the cafeteria, nineteen uniformed police officers were marched into the lunchroom to dismiss us in an orderly fashion. When the local paper sported headlines claiming the students were rioting, my classmates and I looked at each other and smirked, "Did you know that we were rioting?" My suburban counterparts also saw fights in the lunchroom, but they were never met with a heavy police presence, and they did not make the news.

In this way, I learned early on that white, affluent communities tended to *say* danger when what they *saw* was poverty, people who looked different from themselves, and structural disadvantage. Because of this experience growing up, I understand intrinsically that places that are poor and marginalized for a host of other reasons can get labeled as violent by those who do not live there. I know that *really violent* places are also places where people live full, complicated, beautiful lives, and my intention in Honduras was to get past the police checkpoints and stigma and get to know the neighborhoods that, like those of Rivera Hernández and López Arellano, had a reputation for violence.

At the same time, I learned to take the particulars of the context of violence there seriously, and I developed a number of measures to try to ensure my safety and that of my interlocutors. I was always hyper-aware of the fact that while I could leave the country relatively quickly and safely if it was necessary, the people who chose to talk to me could not, for the most part, just get on a plane and fly away. I began this project with substantial experience and a solid network of connections in Honduras, and I had a general familiarity with the situation of the neighborhoods where I expected to conduct research. That said, no matter how much we might believe ourselves prepared to undertake research in contexts of violence, there are always unexpected elements, and we cannot fully protect ourselves or those who choose to speak with us.[30] Even the most well-planned research methods courses frequently fail to prepare us for the violence we might encounter in the field, especially as women,[31] and methods we may think will assist in cultivating safety may not actually prove to be effective.

One example of this, for me, is that I collaborated with two research assistants, Javier and Sandra, for short periods on specific projects. Javier was on staff with Pro-R, and his job and my research agenda dovetailed perfectly. He helped me set up some of my initial interviews and learn the geography of the Sula Valley. Sandra, a sociologist, is a friend and colleague who had long ties to the women's organization in La López. She was instrumental in beginning the process of developing familiarity in La López. However, while I had expected having local research assistants would facilitate access, I quickly learned that my status as outsider was actually helpful rather than a hindrance. As a particular kind of outsider (white, female, in my thirties, with a US passport), I did not, nor could I, figure into the gang-related landscape of domination and control in the same way that a Honduran person would, which made my presence less suspicious. The privilege to be able to leave, to access safety by going elsewhere, contributed to my relative safety as I moved around in Honduras. At the same time, as an outsider, I was less likely to be somehow connected to the government or political parties, which made people more willing to trust that I did not have some ulterior motive for wanting to speak with them. While some, like the police officers, would assume that I came with charity to distribute, I was not read as a threat.

My clear and unabashed outsiderness became a protective posture. Rather than striving to blend in, I maintained and cultivated my not-being-from-there-ness and not-belonging-to-any-neighborhood-ness. The neighborhood-by-neighborhood geography of gang control in San Pedro Sula creates a particular kind of risk for those who are in a neighborhood where they do not belong. Being obviously and openly *not* from *any* neighborhood, not belonging to any specific space within that landscape of control, was crucial. The impossibility that I might fall under their domain was heightened by my total openness about what I was doing, my willingness to speak with anyone at all, and the fact that I did not come with any protective buffer, whether police officers or pastors.

After the first few months in Honduras, I purchased a used car, a two-door hatchback with nearly 200,000 miles on it, that was a bright, distinct shade of orange-red. Getting into and out of neighborhoods in my own vehicle was safer than relying on taxis, hiring a driver, or using public transportation. As an outsider, I could move in and out of neighborhoods controlled by different groups and better resist efforts by police to solicit bribes. My car became a known entity in many of the neighborhoods, and this hypervisibility was one essential factor in conducting research as safely as possible. I knew from previous trips that upon entering a neighborhood, you must roll down your windows and put your flashers on (*bajar los vidrios y hacer cambio de luces*) as a signal to those in charge that you are not hiding anything or anyone in your vehicle and you present no threat to their authority. And I took that as a general guide for how to approach the work. This disposition, of being distinctly *not* of the neighborhood, working alone, and being visible and open, proved to be the key to cultivating as much security as possible.[32]

"We Tell Our Sons to Leave"

I spend hours visiting Doña Licha's in Vista del Cielo. With a house on a corner lot, she seems to know everyone in the neighborhood and everyone in the neighborhood knows her. People come in and out, to say hello, ask a question, drop something off, or pick something up, all day long. We pop over to a pulpería one of her daughters runs, just around the corner, to buy the ingredients to make baleadas. Doña Licha is determined to teach me how to make them. Even after years of trying, I have never mastered the technique to *palmearlas* well.

People tell me it's because my palms are too hot. Or too cold. Everyone has a theory, but my baleadas—which should go from risen ball of dough to uniform, large circles—always come out oblong. As I fight with the masa I notice: It's all women. All day long. It's all women. Doña Licha, her older daughter, her granddaughter, her son's pregnant girlfriend, and her teenage daughter (who rarely looks up from her phone). Two neighbors come by to visit for a while, women with their own daughters in tow. It's all women. Doña Licha's husband had just left for the United States a few months earlier.

I mention this to Doña Licha, how it's all women around, and she says to me what so many have said: It's so hard for the boys. It's just so hard for the boys. Her nineteen-year-old son, he's *really* the one in trouble. That's who she worries about. The older ones, they're OK. The girls in general are safer than the boys. It's the nineteen-year-old boy, that's the one she worries about. He's a *busero* (bus driver), working on one of the private bus lines, and he's maybe just a bit too friendly with the *muchachos*—a euphemism frequently used to refer to gang members. They respect Doña Licha, everyone knows her, and although her son is not involved with the gang directly, he's maybe skating the line of what is OK, maybe getting too close. She's worried about him. She's also worried about the police, that they are going to detain him, arrest him, take him away at some point. Because young guys from Vista del Cielo get picked up by the police. That's just a thing that happens to them. She's thinking about sending him to the United States to join his father. He doesn't want to go. His pregnant girlfriend does not want him to go. But all the women around him are thinking that he might not have a choice.

.   .   .

Two colonias of Rivera Hernández figure prominently in this book, places I call Vista del Cielo and La Libertad. I want to emphasize here the unexceptional nature of the dynamics that I discuss in these neighborhoods. These are the places that I came to know the best, but I know enough about many other gang-controlled neighborhoods to know how the patterns of in/security I detail here are replicated across Honduras. While gang control is violent and can be ruthless, it is also navigable and survivable for many residents. This varies depending on the character of the gang leaders, the relationship between the individual members of the gang and their civilian neighbors, and whether or not the colonia is being fought over, among other factors. The point I want to emphasize here, however, is that the neighborhoods I discuss with the most depth, and the people who inhabit them, are not outliers in the relationships they demonstrate among police, gangs, and residents. Many people can and do live full lives in tandem with the overlapping powers of organized crime and state forces around them.

As Doña Licha explains to me, the danger, however, is patterned, not exclusively a question of chance. It is young men who are most at risk of death, both from the violence of the gangs and from that of the state, in these neighborhoods. Older men have mostly aged out of the category of people seen as intrinsically risky, as long as they abide by the general rules of life in the colonias. Women, even young women, are not targeted the same way as young men for murder, though they are subjected to other kinds of violence, especially sexual and intimate partner violence, at much higher rates while also living with a brutal kind of daily, grinding, gender-based structural violence that is especially not well reflected in statistics. All the women in Doña Licha's home that day deal with violence on a daily basis; many of them are also considering migration. For them, however, it is not as much an urgent matter of survival as it is for the nineteen-year-old bus driver. And they are not personally as afraid of being targeted by police. When Doña Licha's eldest daughter does leave for the United States a few months later, it is a reflection of a hope for a better future—including one with less violence—for her and her children more than it is fear for her continued survival in Vista del Cielo. In the years since this scene in Doña Licha's house, the few young men who would gather there—her son, his few friends—are all gone. Some have migrated, some are in jail. Some are just gone. But Doña Licha, her son's now ex-girlfriend, and her youngest daughter remain. This is not to say that all women are always safe from the kinds of pressures and dangers that the gangs represent for the men; they can also be determined to have crossed the gang in some way. And when women are the ones who have crossed—or perceived to have crossed—that line, the consequences can be especially brutal.

While I interviewed both men and women during my fieldwork, this book primarily focuses on the experience of poor, urban young men like those sitting around in La Libertad that day. This was not my primary intention when I planned this project, but it responds to both the conditions in Honduras as I came to understand them and the gendered dynamics of immigration enforcement in the United States. Both sociologists and historians have found the same pattern: The constructed "immigrant threat" in the United States was once gendered as female, taking advantage of social services, having too many babies, possibly engaging in prostitution, but that shifted in the late twentieth century.[33] Since then, economic changes in the labor market and the fallout of the "war on terror" combined to frame immigrant men as the particular target of both anti-immigrant rhetoric and heightened immigration enforcement.[34] We hear this echoed in the right-wing mediasphere's hysterics about "military-age men" from all over the world coming to seek asylum in the United States. It is worth remembering that there was a time in recent US history when these same young, able-bodied men were constructed as the ideal migrant (worker).

In the case of Honduras, while women are migrating with more frequency than in previous generations, the vast majority of those being deported continue to be men.[35] Young Central American men are frequently cast as exceedingly, inherently, violent and criminal. This informs policing practices in Honduras, shapes the contours of young men's lives, and is replicated in regimes of international protection. Honduran men make up a higher percentage of those who are deported in general, but they are less likely to win asylum cases, even though it is their lives that are most in danger upon return.[36] As Central American women and children are more likely to be cast as sympathetic victims in need of protection—or saving[37]—the unspoken perpetrator is always Central American men. While I do not minimize the profound problem of gender-based violence in Honduras,[38] the brutality to which unsympathetic young men are often subjected is also a product of patriarchy's insidious violence.

I consider this a study focused on men from a feminist epistemological perspective in its approach to power, subordination, and agency,[39] as well as in its attention to the everyday experience of marginalized, gendered people.[40] This draws on critical feminist scholarship of men and masculinities that insists on understanding and interrogating the multiplicity of masculinities in existence (and their shaping through colonial-inflected processes of power.)[41] Matthew Gutmann, a leading anthropologist of gender and masculinity in Latin America, has noted that despite the growing field of anthropological scholarship on men and masculinities,[42] and a robust history in Latin America in particular of feminist scholars studying masculinity, "remarkably few ethnographies have been devoted to the study of men, masculinities, and migration."[43] While this project is not a study of masculinity itself, in that it is not asking how entanglement with migration and deportation produces or precludes a particular experience or performance of manhood, my ethnographic observations encourage us to consider what it means when a certain kind of maleness and youth together are a vector of risk at home, and, when trying to flee those conditions, these same young men are cast as inherently dangerous abroad precisely because of their gender, age, and social location.

The experience of the young men discussed in these pages, however, is emphatically *not* meant to be taken as a universal exploration of the experience of migrants. The men whose stories are depicted here are understood to be *marked* in their maleness, their urbanness, and their experience of mobility control. Women who migrate face a variety of different challenges and threats and kinds of violence; they also sometimes have distinct opportunities and strategies available to them.[44] The same is true for members of the LGBTQ communities who migrate; they suffer particular violences, exclusions, and discriminations and have developed a particular array of survival mechanisms and support networks. The migration experience of the coastal Afro-Indigenous Garifuna population is also distinct and layered; they are frequently targeted even more directly in Mexico and face the unique intersection of anti-Black racism and anti-immigrant policing in the United States. Their experience is also not the one chronicled here. I am not interested in constructing a hierarchy of suffering among migrants and deportees; this is simply to say that this study is particular in its highlighting of the experience of young, urban, male deportees. Their expulsion from the neighborhood, expulsion from Honduras, and expulsion from Mexico and the United States link structures of gendered and racialized criminalization transnationally.

Furthermore, the dynamics at play in this book suggest an additional, gendered dynamic of the social reproduction of migration.[45] In the context of migration studies, there has been much attention paid to the "international division of reproductive work,"[46] where the feminization of migration in the context of neoliberalism and globalization emerges from the twinned processes of responding to the social reproduction needs of their own families in the global south and the vacuum of care as women enter the workforce (and the state retreats) in the global north.⁴⁷ Much of this work illuminates international chains of care, women migrants doing care work and the care that women provide for their transnational kin networks. In parallel, Gabriella Sánchez has focused on how the work of women in facilitation operations is essential to the functioning of clandestine migration and the profits made from smuggling. Though often invisibilized, the nature of the work that women frequently take on, the public-facing labor of collecting money transfers and the client-facing labor of caring for people being smuggled, disproportionately exposes them to criminal charges.⁴⁸

In the account here, however, we see the gendered social reproduction of migration from a different angle, as those who get caught up in the circulations of multiple displacements, migrations, and deportations are facilitated and cared for by those who stay—most often their mothers, aunts, sisters, wives, and girlfriends. The labors of women—eking out a modest living by selling prepared food or washing clothes, maintaining a house where those deported return to, collecting proof and paperwork, caring for the injured, delivering clothes and supplies, and even challenging authorities—are a continuous subtext in this story, making the circulations and continued migrations after deportation, as precarious as they may be, possible. This turns some historical migration dynamics on their head, where migrating men maintained households (and families and a gendered division of labor) back in their country of origin precisely through their absence, access to work, and the sending of remittances. In the story told here, the young men who migrate do not often reach a place or a status where they are able to contribute economically to a household they have left behind. The women are often, then, responsible for sustaining everyone, including those who migrate.

This dynamic is replicated throughout this book: women intervening on behalf of their male loved ones, women holding families and homes together, mothers preferring to have their sons far away from them where they imagine they will be safer rather than close to them and at risk. Deportation brings boys home, but it also, often, brings home danger.

Doris, a mother of two young adult sons in another Rivera Hernández neighborhood tells me how her sons were almost killed by police the night before we meet. Though they survived, she connects this to stories of others from the neighborhood who have not been so lucky. She recounts how police routinely target young men, disappear them or kill them, then blame their deaths on other young men. They "get rid of two of our kids at the same time this way" she adds.

"Por eso a veces les decimos a nuestros hijos que se vayan, para que se salven," she explains. (This is why, sometimes, we tell our sons to leave, so that they might save themselves.)

"Salga Si Puede"

One of the first Pro-R participants I got to know was a tall, thoughtful young man who had been deported four times—always from Mexico—by the time I met him. From a neighborhood on the outskirts of the outskirts, on the far side of La Lima, Lenín was eager to take advantage of the opportunities offered by Pro-R, hoping to start a micro-enterprise, maybe cell phone repair, with Pro-R's support. A sharp analyst of the world around him, Lenín liked the idea of becoming a journalist, but this dream was tempered by knowing that being a real journalist in Honduras would make his already risk-filled world even more dangerous. When I interview him, Lenín stirs sugar into his black coffee and waxes on for nearly three hours about politics and philosophy and life in his country. Mostly he talks in metaphors rather than details. But when he talks about how limited life is, how circumscribed choices are for youth like him, he gets specific.

"Here there are neighborhoods, where, you know what they say? *Entre si quiere, salga si puede*. And the neighborhood where I live, they have this rule. Enter if you *want*. Leave if you *can*."

I would hear this phrase, or some close variation of it, frequently in Honduras.[49] It is a shorthand that people use to describe the dynamics of a certain neighborhood. "You know," they would say, "it's one of those 'entra quien quiere, y sale quien puede' kind of neighborhoods." Anyone who wants to can enter, but only those who are able to, who can fight their way out, can leave. Enter if you want, get out if you can. These neighborhoods, controlled by one kind of organized crime group or another, are easy to get into. Anyone who wants to can walk down the streets. There are no gates or guards or clearly marked entrances; if you didn't already know you were crossing into the neighborhood, nothing would necessarily alert you to having done so. But once you're there, the complex nature of life under gang control, the eternal possibility of being read as a threat or a spy, being a person walking down a street in a neighborhood in which you do not belong—especially if you are a young man—means that you may have to fight your way out. Leave *if* you can.

And navigating these dynamics is at the heart of life in Honduras's Sula Valley. Knowing who controls which neighborhoods and who is allied with whom is crucial for survival. Especially for the young, especially for the boys. People employ a range of strategies to manage these dangers, but, frequently, the only choice, the best choice, the last choice that people feel they have is to migrate. If you can get out, if there's a chance of doing so, you do. *Leave* if you can.

1 *Fronteras Internas*

A Social Geography of Violence

Pastor Luis takes me to meet Ramón at the *cancha* in La Libertad. I've known Luis for a while at this point, and we've developed a friendly rapport and a good base of trust. I pick him up at his house, in one neighborhood in Rivera Hernández, and we drive toward La Libertad, a different colonia set back, but not too far, from the central neighborhood where Luis lives. We go maybe ten blocks, or so, and although I am driving slowly down the dirt road, my little hatchback has trouble with a particularly steep speed bump that seems to come out of nowhere. As we bounce ungraciously over the bump, Luis looks at me and grins: "We've just crossed the border."

After a few more blocks, Luis directs me to park in front of a small church. He asks the person tending the grounds if Ramón is around. "Ya viene." (He's coming.) Ramón should be expecting us. A handful of solar-powered streetlights fill the back of my little car. Luis is delivering them to Ramón, part of one of his many neighborhood improvement projects. A second-generation pastor, Luis has deep roots in Rivera Hernández and a vocation to work with the poor, the downtrodden, the social outcasts. He's involved in a number of social projects, and while evangelical in his theology, his approach to this work is remarkably, consistently a-ideological. He will work with the US Agency for International Development, (USAID, despised by many of the social movement, grassroots organizations because of its dirty history with the CIA in Central America) and the police (who are widely viewed with suspicion in Rivera Hernández), as well as political parties of all stripes, Christian missions of all denominations, brigades of doctors from Cuba or the United States, and the gangs themselves. Anything and anyone, he says, as long as it is in service of the youth of the sector. He is warm and friendly and has a well-earned reputation for being a reliable, honest, and devout pastor. It is his well-known, perceived-to-be-authentic religiosity (along with his age) that allows him to go from neighborhood to neighborhood, crossing borders like the one we had unceremoniously bounced over to get to La Libertad to find Ramón.

Luis and I stand outside the church and chat for a bit when a short man, a little older than Luis, I'd guess, appears. I don't realize at first that he's the man we have come looking for. Trailing Ramón is a handful of skinny teenage boys. They seem to surround him and buffer him all at once. With a few head nods and pointing fingers from Ramón, the boys grab the lights and move them into the empty space next to the church. We trail behind them, walking around the corner into an empty lot that they are in the process of turning into a bona fide soccer field. The promised cancha.

The boys spread out, squatting, leaning, standing watch. They've got the two exits from the field covered, and although they've backed away from us, their attention doesn't drift. Luis, Ramón, and I talk. Luis introduces me. This is my chance to make the right impression to be able to come back here, to continue speaking with Ramón, and to have safe passage in this neighborhood.

Luis had prepped me beforehand. Ramón isn't a pandillero exactly. But he is an ex-pandillero from before the gang lines had hardened and the battles had moved from knives and dances to guns and massacres. He also has a certain kind of leadership in the neighborhood; the muchachos look up to him. He helps them, gets them involved in positive activities like rehabbing a soccer field, finds ways for them to make an honest living. His brother had been the *jefe de la pandilla*, the boss of the gang at the neighborhood level, but he was murdered a few years earlier. Ramón's closeness to the gang is vague, a murky relationship that is not uncommon. What is clear to me, though, as we gather to chat that day, is that the neighborhood pandilleros are both protective of and deferential to this middle-aged man. They follow his lead and take direction from him; and they are also very careful to never leave him alone with me, a stranger, always keeping a watchful eye. Luis also told me that Ramón, unlike some other neighborhood leaders and people who have a relationship to the gang without being *in* the gang, does not seek the spotlight. He is uninterested in giving interviews or talking to the media. Luis thinks he might talk to me—he's seen how I work and thinks it's different enough—but an introduction was all Luis could offer me.

At first, we discuss basic things: how the lighting will work; how the progress on the cancha has come along; what their plans are for the parts that are still overgrown; how hard it is to play soccer in the mud; what teams (and neighborhoods) they can include in a tournament he's organizing. I'm trying to think how to explain who I am, what it is that I'm doing there, why I want to talk to him. I'm always concerned people will place me in one of the few categories of gringo that are familiar here, as a way to make sense of my otherwise unusual presence. I'm worried he's going to think I come from an NGO or a missionary group and that I can offer them material support in a sustained way. I'm also worried he's going to think I'm one more journalist writing about la Rivera, eager to report back that I talked to real live gang members.

Then I see his hat. Ramón has a US Border Patrol baseball cap on. So we're talking, circling around issues, and there's an opportunity. I say, "Mire, yo puedo aceptar cualquier cosa, Ud., menos apoyar a la patrulla fronteriza." (Look, I can accept just about anything, Sir, except supporting the Border Patrol.) And I gesture toward his hat. He cracks up.

Now we start talking about the story of the hat. He takes it off his head and shows me the thickness of the brim, the reinforced stitching. It's a real Border Patrol hat, not a random baseball cap with the Border Patrol logo on it. He tells me about the times he's been caught by Border Patrol, how he convinced one agent to give him his hat. I offer my credentials, both academic and otherwise—being in the desert, riding the train, the years in Mexico—and I settle on what had become my standard explanation for my presence in Honduras: I'm here to document how life really is, to write a book about what people don't see. He likes the idea. And we agree to meet, without Luis, to keep talking.

Afterward, as we drive back across the speed bump/border, Luis is triumphant. "Now, you can go into La Libertad whenever you want," he says, grinning, "now they all know you, and your car. That's what I was hoping for!"

Ramón messages me that night. He says how nice it was to meet me. How he is happy to talk to me. And he mentions, casually, carefully but insistently, how much he values loyalty.

Ramón would become one of my most trusted interlocutors, explaining how the world works, sending those who had been deported to talk to me. After a long day of interviews, I came to look forward to showing up in Ramón's neighborhood and drinking a beer with him on a rickety wooden bench across from a pulpería at twilight. Neither of us was a big drinker, but one crisp Imperial for me and a Coors for him would break the unrelenting heat and the heaviness of the day in just the right way. Because Ramón approved of my presence, La Libertad would become one of a handful of neighborhoods where I was probably the safest in San Pedro Sula, even as I came to learn that the small neighborhood is also, simultaneously, always potentially a place of danger.

In urban Honduras, the neighborhood where you are from is one of the most important points of reference and social location in young people's lives. The colonia shapes your experience of the world and, to a large extent, determines where you can and cannot go, especially as neighborhood identity intersects with age and gender. People are identified with their colonia, and this has ramifications for mobility, education, and access to jobs but also shapes relationships and people's imagined possibilities. The colonia is home, where you are known and rooted, where you are understood to belong, and that belonging *feels* like safety. The colonia can be this space of protection, of safety, of *home*, yet it can turn, quickly, into a source of vulnerability, danger, and violence.

La Libertad is on the edge of the Rivera Hernández sector of San Pedro Sula. Like many of Honduras's urban zones, Rivera Hernández comprises a sprawling geography of small neighborhoods, or colonias. A colonia usually consists of several square blocks, but the size can vary. There is rarely signage indicating where one colonia ends and another begins, though perhaps a shop like the neighborhood corner store might be called Pulpería La Libertad, giving an outwardly legible indication of the neighborhood's identity. There might be an exaggerated speed bump in the dirt road, a *frontera interna* or *frontera invisible*, an internal border or invisible border. Mostly, though, this geography is just known by the people who live there.

Juan, a teacher who lives at the edge of La Libertad, at the border of the next neighborhood, explains the seriousness of these internal borders:

Tenemos a los jóvenes presos en las cuatro cuadras o en las diez cuadras, que es su territorio. Hay muros en medio de las calles que son más altos que los de concreto, porque son muros que nos representan peligro, muerte. Porque estamos hablando de fronteras de violencia, fronteras de muerte.

We have young people imprisoned in the four blocks or in the ten blocks that is their territory. There are walls in the middle of the roads that are higher than those made of concrete, because they are walls that for us represent danger, death. Because we are talking about borders of violence, borders of death.

Profe Juan recognizes the risk associated with the way young people are identified with their colonia: They live as though imprisoned, unable to cross the invisible borders without risking death.[1] He emphasizes the way this circumscribes mobility, especially for youth, but he also—well into his thirties himself, with a young child—continues to be mindful of the power of these neighborhood divisions. Though he is no longer considered a "youth," he understands that he would not be immune to the consequences of consistent transgressive mobility.

Por ejemplo, a mí me iban a nombrar en una escuela de aquí del sector. Yo no quise que me nombraran en esa escuela, aunque me quedaba muy cerca de mi casa, porque yo iba a estar pasando y cruzando una de las fronteras de esas para llegar a la escuela . . . Entonces, evitando esa situación, mejor preferí que me nombraran allá, un poco largo, pero con la seguridad de que nadie me va a decir, "Vos sos de aquí, vos sos de allá."

For example, they were going to place me in one of the schools, here in the sector. I didn't want them to place me in this school, even though it's really close to my house, because I would have been passing and crossing one of these borders to get to the school . . . So, avoiding this situation, I preferred that they place me there, somewhat far away, but with the security that nobody would be saying to me "Oh, you're from here, you're from over there."

FIGURE 1. A neighborhood in the Sula Valley, Honduras, 2019. Photo by author.

Profe Juan has to navigate the potential dangers associated with crossing gang boundaries within his sector, because doing so frequently would arouse suspicion by the gangs who control both neighborhoods. Living safely within the colonia is predicated on refraining from engaging too much or too deeply in places, particularly other similar neighborhoods, beyond the colonia. Navigating this fraught geography is at the top of mind for many young people in Honduras. Frequently, migration is one response when the safety of being in one's own neighborhood is lost, when one has crossed those borders of violence, either intentionally or accidentally, or is perceived to have done so.

The people fleeing Honduras are simultaneously displaced and emplaced. They are not always excluded from all places, even as they are frequently structurally marginalized. When people make the choice to leave Honduras, they are also leaving something, some *place*, behind. Without the colonia as a space of home but still bound by the socio-spatial identification they carry with them, Honduran youth often have nowhere to go, no option but to try to leave their country altogether.

Maras y Pandillas

Field Notes

I drive Marlon home. Marlon lives in El Trébol, on the outskirts of San Pedro, in a neighborhood at the far end of a long, single road. As we're driving, and driving, and driving, he starts to talk about how all of this is MS-13, everything here is the MS. See how *tranquilo* it is? It's all MS. And he starts to point out, "Look, up here you'll see, we're being reported. This car is being reported. Since we turned off the highway onto the *pavimentada*, the car is being reported, *reportado, reportado.*" "Look," he says, "we're going to pass a *llantera* [tire shop]. There will be someone there with a cell phone reporting, and then up farther, there'll be someone." I ask at some point if I should roll down my windows. He says not yet.

Once we get to a certain point, he says, "OK, now. *Bájelos si quiere.*"

Marlon isn't currently active in MS-13. But he was. And he's still loyal to them. He kind of regrets leaving, because then, he says, he was respected. But he had a daughter and wanted to make different choices. He's not sure, though, if leaving was the right decision. He's had a hard time getting a job. He's nineteen and has already been deported twice.

For a while he worked for a big hardware store chain, and he had to deliver stuff to different neighborhoods. Twice they sent him to Barrio 18 neighborhoods, and he got beaten up. I say, "How did you survive it?" He says, "Well, the police came, but that's because the police are working with the big hardware store to protect their merchandise." "After the third time," he says, "I'm not going to chance it." He would just refuse to go. Like one time they came to pick him up for a job, and on the way, they told him it was La Newton, a Barrio 18 stronghold.

"Heh! La Newton," he says. "*O no, me baje, me baje, me baje, y de regreso* [moving his hands to indicate, I'm out of here!]. That is a place I will not go in." He quit the job.

I say, "But, like if you go into a Barrio 18 neighborhood, how do they know you're from an MS-13 neighborhood?"

"They come up to you, and they say, 'Where are you from,' and if I say, say I lie and I say, 'I'm from Rivera Hernández,' and they say, 'What colonia?,' and I say one, they say, 'OK, who are the *locos ahí?*'[2] And I say, maybe because I know somebody there, I know a name, I say a name, they take my photo to send it to those people, they say, 'Is this guy from you?,' and heh! if they find out I lied? Well, they'll kill me. So it's better to just say the truth, cause if I just say the truth and say I'm from an MS-13 neighborhood, maybe they'll kill me too, but if I lie and say I'm from another neighborhood, they'll also kill me."

And, well, I ask, can you go into other MS-13 neighborhoods? And he says yeah, he can go into any MS neighborhood anywhere because even if they do the same thing, they'll report back to the MS-13 here, and he's on really good terms with them. He says he left, he says they let him leave, *le dieron pase*, he just went and asked and said he wanted to make some more money, he wanted to have other opportunities in life. He joined when he was fifteen, and then three years later he just wanted to try something else, and they le dieron pase.

He said if he had *saltado*, passed to a higher level, having killed someone, then there's no leaving. But he wasn't at that level yet. He started out as one of those *banderas*, reporting. Twenty-four hours a day there are people on this pavimentada reporting back who's coming in and who's coming out.

He adds, "And if the police come in, from the moment they turn off the pavimentada, we know."

I say, "Man, so you know every colonia, *colonia por colonia*, neighborhood by neighborhood, who controls what?" "Yeah," he says, "You kind of have to know."

. . .

Marlon lays out clearly the geographic knowledge that is essential for survival for young men like him in the Sula Valley. He also notes, as many people do, that the uncontested control of the whole area by a single group, by the Mara Salvatrucha in this case, can make a place *tranquilo*, calm. He knows what most youth know, that being in the wrong neighborhood means putting your life at risk. Life, however, doesn't always allow for a person to stick closely to these geographic rules, and people continue to push at these boundaries, sometimes for work, sometimes by choice, and sometimes because boundaries just start to chafe.

Over the past thirty years or so, colonias in places like Rivera Hernández, El Trébol, and López Arellano have developed an association with one organized crime group or another. At first these were local, homegrown pandillas, with a variety of colorful names. These street gangs, made up of local youth, would fight with rocks and sticks, over girls and turf, often outside community dances. The description sounds too much like *West Side Story*, but this is the origin story told by many of the now-older men who had been involved in these fledgling gangs in the '80s and '90s. This, before they consolidated into the maras y pandillas, into Barrio 18 and the Mara Salvatrucha, before they traded rocks for guns. Over the years, many of the local street gangs became absorbed into, entered into an affiliation with, or were annihilated by the famous gangs. Some of the small gangs held on, becoming more violent, "crazier" (*somos pocos pero locos*, say the Vatos Locos, for example), to maintain their neighborhood identity against the expanding rule of Barrio 18 and MS-13.

There may not be a single, uniform history of the emergence of the gangs in Honduras. Anthropologist Jon Horne Carter's *Gothic Sovereignty* chronicles much of their rise and evolution in the Tegucigalpa area in particular and Salvadoran anthropologist and journalist Juan Martínez d'Aubuisson's *El que tenga miedo a morir que no nazca* narrates this history in San Pedro Sula.[3] The rough strokes outlined above, however, form the basis of a now hardened and deadly gangland geography that is the foundational backdrop that shapes people's sense of identity, safety, possibility, and mobility.

In Honduras, the term "pandilla" is used to refer to Barrio 18 and the smaller street gangs that operate in a similar fashion, like the Vatos Locos.[4] The "mara," in Honduras, is used mostly to mean the Mara Salvatrucha. A member of Barrio 18 or Vatos Locos will call himself a pandillero; only a member of MS-13 will call himself a marero in Honduras. This nomenclature is unique to Honduras; it is also not a hard and fast rule. Barrio 18 will also often be called just "el barrio"— a shorthand that can be confusing when certain neighborhoods are also *barrios* (in San Pedro Sula, the older neighborhoods within the city's central ring, for example, are barrios and not colonias). To cover all the gang-like organizations and actors in the country, laws, edicts, and initiatives often refer to "maras y pandillas." Gangs and gangs.

The maras and pandillas are not the only important actors in the geography of violence, but they loom large, frequently becoming the stand-in for all forms of violence and insecurity that exist in Honduras. As Carter notes, the maras must be understood as "a kind of synecdoche pointing to the intersection of state and criminal worlds of which street gangs are just the most visible appendage."[5] Their visibility, while being part of what allows them to be construed as the primary problem in the country, is also part of how they maintain their intimate geography of control.

While I recognize the heterogeneity of organized crime in Honduras,[6] in this book I focus on gangs and the police, as it is their presence that is felt most acutely in daily life in the urban neighborhoods of the Sula Valley. One of the primary narratives about how the gangs came to have such a presence in Central America focuses on people being deported back there from the United States in the mid-1990s and bringing Los Angeles gangs and gang culture with them. While this has been well documented in neighboring El Salvador, a closer analysis of the situation in Honduras reveals that while it is part of the story, it is not a sufficient explanation on its own.[7]

In addition to the presence of deportees in Honduran society, a handful of other factors were also at play in the 1990s: a recent transition to civilian rule, the end of the Cold War and a corresponding decrease in military funding from the United States, the end of mandatory military service, neoliberal economic policies and structural adjustment programs, and Hurricane Mitch in 1998. The end of the Cold War and the decrease in military spending had major ramifications for Honduras, which had long relied on substantial US assistance as the staging ground for the US counterinsurgency agenda in the region. These cuts were coupled with the global turn to the Washington Consensus prescriptions for economic growth—liberalization, stabilization, privatization—where Honduras was encouraged to dismantle (and was rewarded for dismantling) the few existing yet precarious social welfare programs it had in place.[8] There is also an argument to be made that Honduras was essentially a neoliberal state long before the Washington Consensus and the rise of neoliberalism. Historian Dario Euraque's excellent book, *Reinterpreting the Banana Republic*, details this history before the 1980s.[9] The "retreat of the state" exacerbated already high levels of poverty and inequality,[10] and the era's focus on export agriculture and *maquila* manufacturing contributed to other major demographic shifts, as people from throughout the country's rural territory moved into the infrastructurally ill-equipped urban zones—chief among them the Sula Valley—in search of jobs.[11]

The worsening economic situation combined with changing trends in the region's drug trade. As the US-led drug war ramped up, Colombian cartels looked for different routes to get cocaine to the United States. Honduras, strategically located between South and North America, has substantial territory largely unsurveilled by the central government.[12] In addition, as the Colombian cartels were disrupted by US-led interdiction efforts, the Mexican cartels begin to fill the void and establish operations through Honduras.[13] It was a Honduran narco-broker, Juan Matta Ballesteros, who was instrumental in connecting the Colombian cocaine providers with the Mexican traffickers.[14]

While the shifting contours of the drug trade in the 1990s throughout the Americas is an important factor, I want to be careful not to conflate the major drug trafficking operations with maras and pandillas. The gangs are at times used by drug cartels as instruments, cannon fodder, or scapegoats,[15] and some of the gangs are evolving into organizations that more resemble drug cartels. However, the wealthy, well-organized, and influential transnational organized crime groups are not the same as the poor, teenage, unruly mareros and pandilleros. There is some convergence in Honduras, especially between MS-13 and the cartels, but their operations and neighborhood-level street presence are still substantially distinct. Their ends are different: Cartels are businesses, focused on making a profit, whereas gangs are focused on control, power, and what they believe to be protection of their territories. Money, though welcome, is not ultimately what organizes them (nor is amassing wealth the primary operating logic behind their use of violence).

Another crucial factor that contributed, perhaps above all else, to the consolidation of gangs in Honduras was Hurricane Mitch in 1998, which devastated the country, hitting the poor, urban slums that had sprung up over the previous decade especially hard. Thousands died, and many more were displaced. In this context, youth turned to gangs for survival.[16] Carter points to Mitch as a pivotal factor in the formation of Honduran gangs, discussing the youth made homeless or orphaned in its wake, gathering in the ruined structures around Tegucigalpa's riverfront, defending themselves from paramilitaries and vigilantes.[17] He writes, "The *maras* emerged as an international league of marginalized individuals, stranded between law, borders, conflict, and natural and economic disasters."[18] In Carter's assessment, while neighborhood street gangs and mara groups existed here and there before 1998, it was the devastation of Mitch and the lack of response to it that enabled the ranks of the gangs to swell.

Ostensibly in response to gang violence, Honduras, along with most of Central America, adopted "mano dura," or iron fist, policing.[19] Modeled after US-based law enforcement strategies, Honduran President Ricardo Maduro (2002–6) was an early adopter of mano dura tactics in Central America.[20] In Honduras, this suite of laws allowed for the prosecution of youths for membership in a gang, the crime of "illicit association," regardless of whether they had committed any other crime.[21] Markers of urban youth culture are criminalized, as having tattoos, dressing in a certain way, having a certain kind of haircut, and simply associating with gang members is made sufficient for detention. "Associating" with mareros and pandilleros, however, is an unavoidable feature of life in neighborhoods they control.

While all of that is codified as legal, extrajudicial "enforcement" and "social cleansing" aimed at young, poor, urban men also arose,[22] including the return of unmarked cars that would drive through neighborhoods and murder youth.[23] I say "return" because these unmarked cars were familiar in the dirty war era of death squads in Honduras, as in much of Latin America. Mano dura produces and legalizes the widespread criminalization of poor, male, urban youth, turning their social and spatial location into a category of potential delinquency and grounds for arrest and imprisonment. Anthropologist Adrienne Pine notes the curious turn of many of her interlocutors during the early days of mano dura in Honduras when the people whose children are or would likely be targeted applauded the heavy-handed tactics and even called for greater militarization of policing.[24]

In this context, young people—especially young men—are rendered suspect and even criminal if they are too public, too mobile, too active outside their homes. Staying safely tucked indoors might convey innocence, to both gangs and police, while being perceived of engaging in transgressive mobility heightens the risk of being criminalized, targeted, or banished.

Antony: "I Just Inhabit Here"

Antony meets us where the paved road ends. Hopping into the pickup that Javier, my friend, colleague, and sometimes research assistant, is driving, he directs us up the maze of steep dirt roads, winding away from the older, more established colonias in Choloma. Antony is buoyant, chatty, friendly with Javier, and at ease in part because of Javier's presence and in part because that is this young man's nature, gregarious and relentlessly positive. We get as far as we can go in a vehicle, park, and walk farther up to Antony's current home. He rents a single room in a little complex, a *cuartería*, a collection of *cuartos*, rooms. An initial entrance leads into an outdoor hallway with rooms opening off from there. There's a small courtyard, a common *pila*, a concrete basin, to hand wash dishes and clothes, a bathroom.

Antony is very thin and at first I think he looks so much younger than twenty. As we talk, however, I get the opposite impression, that this young man is actually aged well beyond his years. He says the neighbors are kind to him, and while he tries to keep a positive outlook, he has an overwhelming air of loneliness. We sit down on his bed—the only furniture he has in the room he rents—and he tells me his story.

Antony lived most of his young life surrounded by family in a neighborhood all the way on the other side of the Sula Valley, in Co-fradía. His eyes well up when he touches on the topic of not being able to be near his family any longer. He has no one to talk to when he comes home from work now, no one to tell how his day went.

He recounts getting beaten up, almost being kidnapped, being sure that his death was imminent without his words catching. But when he mentions the loneliness, the feeling of not being around his family, that's when he falters. That's when he fights back the tears.

It all started three years earlier. Antony found himself out of place. He came from a neighborhood controlled by one gang, MS-13; he found himself, accidentally, in rival territory, a nearby neighbor-hood controlled by Barrio 18. He was on a trip with a youth organiza-tion. He was young, it was daytime, and he trusted the organization wouldn't put him in harm's way. The local gang, however, recognized him and got suspicious. He was abducted, interrogated, and eventu-ally released. The gang that controlled his home neighborhood, how-ever, heard about his interrogation, and now *they* had him in their sights. The fact that Barrio 18 let him go left Antony marked with an enduring aura of suspicion. He gets abducted by MS-13 this time, his "home" gang, and is nearly killed but manages to escape. This leads to his first displacement; he goes to live in another municipality in the Sula Valley for six months. It would have been a bus ride of about an hour, but it might as well have been on the other side of the globe, that's how far away his family felt to him. Eventually, his family thinks that the threats against him must have faded. They talk to the gang and make a deal to let him return. Back home, he's OK for a while, though he hardly leaves his mother's house. Power shifts within the gang, however; the leadership changes, and the new per-son in charge is less willing to give Antony the benefit of the doubt.

He gets a warning from a sympathetic gang member who had been charged with keeping tabs on him: "Lo mejor sería que te fueras. O no salgás de tu casa o te vas." (The best thing would be if you left. Either you don't leave your house, or you get out.)

This time he leaves for good. He moves from place to place, all across the country, from Tegucigalpa to a rural coffee-growing region to Amapala, a tourist island in the south, to La Lima.

"Y siempre andaba con miedo de encontrarme con este tipo de personas, pero igual yo trataba de evitarlo, no saliendo. Llegaba a un lugar, estar ahí el máximo tiempo posible, y no salir, ni a la pulpería, siempre con un miedo." (And I always went around with the fear of encountering those kinds of people, but at the same time, I was trying to avoid it, by not going outside. I would arrive in a place, and be there the maximum time possible, not going outside, not even to the corner store, always very afraid.)

He ends up alone in this room in Choloma. Everywhere, he says, he felt suffocated, *encerrado*, enclosed, locked in, scared. He couldn't leave; he wouldn't go outside. He always felt like people might be watching him. He says he doesn't feel at home here either; he's not sure he ever will.

La verdad que aquí siento que habito y si lo ves, no compro muchas cosas porque nunca se sabe si me tocará moverme de un lugar a otro nuevamente. Entonces trato de no tener mucho que cargar, pues, entonces por cualquier cosa, porque después de todo lo que me ha pasado me doy cuenta de que todo puede pasar a un segundo.

The truth is, I feel like here I just inhabit, and if you notice, I don't buy many things because I never know if I'm going to have to move from one place to another again. So I try to not have much to carry, so just in case, because after everything that's happened to me, I realize that anything can happen in just a second.

This tension that Antony experiences between heightened mobility—being made to move around, being unable to stay—coupled with heightened *im*mobility—living locked in within a single room, enclosed, encaved, imprisoned—is connected to the later experience of migration, detention, and deportation that he and other young people like him experience. When he does eventually leave his country of citizenship, which he will do a few years after I meet him in his room in Choloma, Antony is long familiar with life in circulation. Antony was effectively exiled by the gang that controlled his colonia. His mobility, like that of so many Hondurans who migrate, is delimited first not by ICE agents and border walls but by the microdynamics of power and belonging that shape the social landscape on the urban margins in Honduras.

A Social Geography of Everyday Violence

Spatial relations of varying scales combine with social location to shape the experience of navigating, surviving, fleeing, and at times employing violence for Hondurans. Understanding the unmarked, internal geography of the Sula Valley is essential for staying alive. Antony accidentally appeared in the wrong neighborhood. That small lapse in judgment made him forever marked as out of place, as suspicious, and led to his ongoing displacement and eventual migration. Still, he recognizes—as do those around him—that his personal tragedy started by pushing the geographic and social boundaries that a young man like himself knew to abide by. He learned this lesson and even in exile sought safety and security in minimizing his movement as much as possible.

This condition of enclosure as the only possible, yet always limited, means of staying safe was a theme that recurred among many of the young people in their navigations of violence. As part of my affiliation with Pro-R, I ran a focus group with youth who had been displaced because of violence in the Sula Valley. Pro-R had a pilot project with the UN High Commissioner for Refugees (UNHCR) in Honduras to offer support and programs for youth like this.

During the focus group session, I ask them about their perceptions of violence and insecurity. I ask, "How do you navigate all of this, deal with all the potential for violence around you? What kinds of things do you do to stay safe?"

Everyone starts talking at once, describing different methods of hiding money or your wallet on your body when you're on the *rapidito*, the bus. The participants debate animatedly about whether it's better to stick to yourself or make friends with your neighbors. Then philosophical, analytical Lenín's voice cuts through the chatter: "Estar encuevado." Be encaved. Stay inside. And everyone agrees: Staying inside, locking yourself in your home, in your room, gives you the best chance of avoiding danger.

One of the important aspects of the socio-spatial nature of how violence is understood in Honduras is that it makes it *appear* knowable and predictable, offering the tenuous illusion that violence is manageable as long as one stays within the geography as defined. If he had just not gone into that other neighborhood, Antony reasons, the tragedy of being taken away from his family would never have happened. Knowing where neighborhoods start and end, knowing which neighborhoods are controlled by allied or rival crime groups, and knowing where your social location allows you to go (and where it does not) is crucial. There are, however, a multiplicity of ways that people violate the bounds and become out of place and are then, predictably, subjected to violence. Job opportunities, school, romantic relationships can all entice someone to think they might not be risking that much by going *there*. But being out of place, being in the wrong place, means risking your life. Simply being perceived to be out of place often becomes the final factor, the one additional thing, that pushes people into migrating.

A social geography of violence gestures toward how violence is deeply embedded in the social. Other scholars have masterfully theorized violence in its many forms, but this book attempts to deal with violence by replicating the way violence exists for the communities I worked with in Honduras. Violence is not extraordinary, even as it is something that people are always trying to manage. It is there, lurking in the background, always. It pops up, it interrupts, and it scares, but its presence does not surprise. Antony is terrified when he gets abducted, but he is not shocked that such a thing could happen. In another example, Chico, a teenager from López Arellano, was shot three times. Once he was released from the hospital and sent home, his cousin, Magui, remarked to me, "Pobre chico, tan joven para ya saber qué es una bala." (Poor Chico, so young to already know what a bullet is [like].) Magui was sad, but she expressed her lament in a way that suggests that the violence that hit her cousin in his leg and back was something that he would inevitably, eventually, encounter.

Chico's older brother had been killed a few years earlier. They were growing up in another neighborhood with an earned reputation for being *complicado*, "complicated," the frequently used euphemism to refer to places that have high rates of violence (and, in particular, violent death). Choloma's Sector López Arellano was once controlled by pandillas. Those gangs were effectively liquidated, however, by a drug cartel known as Los de La Rumba, which established strict order in the area. Curfews on the streets at night. No tattooed young men allowed, ever. Then, in 2016, the powerful leadership trio of La Rumba was jailed, killed, and fled, respectively, and the power vacuum led to multiple groups—some count as many as ten—fighting over the territory.[25] As is often the case, when control is firmly established, when gang rule is deeply entrenched and undisputed, violence goes down. When the borders are contested, homicides increase. Here, however, not everyone is equally as likely to be the victim of violence. Chico's shooting was predictable not only because of his geographic location but also because of his social location. Chico was young, male, and poor, about fifteen years old, and hadn't stayed in school past sixth grade. He spent most of his time hanging out in the narrow streets near his grandmother's modest house. All this made Chico the kind of person who—in the areas dominated by organized crime, especially during periods of warring over territory—is most likely to be seen as a threat, a problem, a potential rival, a potentially disloyal subject, an unruly body.

Not everyone in López Arellano equally expects to learn what a bullet feels like. While Honduras does have alarmingly high rates of femicide,[26] young women do not figure into this landscape of violence in quite the same way as young men. Magui hasn't been shot; Magui doesn't expect to know what a bullet feels like herself in the same way that she does for her cousin. Chico's sister has not been shot either and does not expect to be a target of the same people who targeted their brother. Boys who survive adolescence and young adulthood may eventually age out of being at such high risk as well. Men like Luis and Ramón, for example, who might have tangled with violence in their youth, breathe a bit easier upon entering their late thirties and forties, understanding that if they follow the geographic rules, their social location may no longer be quite as dangerous.[27] They worry now instead, like many Hondurans, about their own teenage sons. And with good reason. In the years for which data are reported, around 90 percent of homicide victims in Honduras have been male; nearly half were between the ages of fifteen and twenty-nine. In 2021, the country's National Violence Observatory noted a jarring piece of data: When a boy turns fifteen in Honduras, he is 1,043 percent more likely to be murdered.[28] This is not to say that older adults or women of all ages are immune to violence, only that their demographic traits combined with geographic location do not put them necessarily at the same heightened risk for murder. The risk of homicide for girls, for example, upon turning fifteen, increases by

272 percent, devastating in its own right but paling in comparison to the increased risk for boys.[29]

Like many scholars, I am concerned with how violence is represented in the writing of it. Anthropologists have rightly identified the violence done when people are essentialized as somehow uniquely, inherently violent,[30] especially in service of perpetuating the myth of a less violent "us" in contrast to a highly violent "them."[31] These are perennial questions, unresolved tensions that continue to trouble us regarding how to responsibly and honestly write violence without either dehumanizing those who experience it or sensationalizing it,[32] while finding a way to sensitively depict those who do "inhuman things" and at once "do justice" to their victims.[33] The ever-present risk of giving in to the sensorial excess of violence and turning it into "a sensational object of interest, pleasure, or profit"—of engaging in the pornography of violence—must be avoided, while we must also be careful not to sanitize such violence or "flatten it down into theory."[34] Allan Feldman suggests that a "crucial ethnographic stance salvages the particularity of the victim while systematizing the violence arrayed against the subject."[35] Philippe Bourgois puts a similar direction another way, to "clarify the chains of causality that link structural, political, and symbolic violence in the production of an everyday violence that buttresses unequal power relations and distorts efforts at resistance."[36] Ted Swedenberg, in grappling with how to communicate to those in the United States the violence in occupied Palestine, writes that "perhaps the hardest thing is how impossible it is to convey the everyday normality of the violence."[37]

With the work and advice of these scholars and others in mind, I approach writing about violence in Honduras by taking direction from the people whose stories appear in these pages. As such, my approach is to reference violence directly, unflinchingly, but without sensationalizing it or lingering on it. I do not try to minimize, sanitize, or flatten the violence with which my interlocutors contend, but neither do I offer gratuitous details or use language intended to shock. As much as possible, I strive to recount stories of violence in the same tone as the storyteller. When Chico is shot his sister, Estefani, sends me a text message to let me know, so I can meet them at the hospital: "Esq balearon a mi hermano Chico le pegaron dos disparos :(." (It's that they shot my brother Chico / two bullets hit him / sad face emoji.)

The concept of everyday violence recognizes the toll that structural violence takes on the intimate lives of the marginalized.[38] This is not necessarily direct physical violence, though it frequently results in illness and death, but it is more about the pressures of precarity that seep into people's bodies and shape their chances at life. In the scholarship that expands this core idea, the "violence of everyday life" and "everyday violence" are essentially interchangeable. In approaching the life of youth in López Arellano or Rivera Hernández, however, there is a useful distinction to be made: The former we can use to identify the ways in which structural violence produces quotidian suffering; the latter, to suggest the situation where direct, physical violence has become an ordinary occurrence and forms the backdrop of everyday life. The two meanings fold into and reinforce each other, of course, but there is a subtle difference.[39] In the case of Honduras, the violence of everyday life is seen in the grinding poverty in which people live, the stark inequality, the lack of access to resources, opportunities, and mobility. In the hospital, there is no blood for a transfusion, so Chico is left to wait until his body recovers its blood supply on its own. There are also not enough beds in the children's ward of the only public hospital, so as soon as he can more or less stand on his own, he is shoved out of the hospital into the blinding heat, no wheelchair, no shade, no waiting room for him. The violence of everyday life.

Everyday violence, on the other hand, could be used to describe life where young people recount seeing men hacked to death by a machete, rattle off the names of loved ones and friends who have been murdered, and anticipate that your cousin will eventually know what it feels like to have a bullet pierce his body. It is not solely structural violence that shapes life and possibilities, but it is also this familiarity with brutal violence and violent death. Chico's younger brother, about ten years old at the time, tells me about the first time he saw someone murdered in front of him. Then the second, then the third time. Horrible stories, horrible deaths, things he wishes he hadn't ever seen. I tell him, gently, "You know what? I've never seen anyone killed." His eyes widen; his young brain has trouble accepting this truth, that someone could really get to be my age without having witnessed that kind of violence.

Later I accompany Chico's mother as she prepares her family to leave the country. With one son dead and another lucky to still be alive, she cannot take it any longer. She collects medical reports and police reports. Even though Chico declined to identify the person who shot him, his mother tries, unsuccessfully, to get some official document from the police indicating that he had been shot. I go with her to multiple police stations where she pleads with them to give her some documentation, but she is at best given the runaround (try some other office) and at worst dismissed condescendingly or with contempt. The police officials all seem to determine that since no police report was filed, it's likely that her son *andaba en malos pasos*, that he was walking in bad footsteps, gang-involved himself. Thwarted, she instead gathers report cards, letters from her pastor, anything to show that she and her children, including her son, are good people. As soon as Chico can walk without wincing, the whole family leaves for Mexico, hoping to make it to the United States.

Migration is frequently categorized as being either due to economic reasons or violence, or both ("mixed migration" has come to be used), but those categories are not actually discrete experiences. In a country where most government functions—except for repression—

have been privatized, safety and security become the responsibility of individuals to procure for themselves. In this sense, everyday violence intertwines with the violence of everyday life to produce migration; poverty and insecurity are inextricable. Chico had already been deported twice before he was shot; his mother had been deported once. Deportation, then, has also become a feature of the violence of everyday life.

This is not to say that the ordinariness of violence means that it is accepted as normal or goes unnoticed. Scholars of everyday violence have been careful to emphasize that living under these conditions, even getting used to them, does not imply that people are unaware that they should not have to do so. People have to *learn* how to live with violence; it is not natural or automatic.[40] Anthropologist Henrik Vigh cautions that we should not confuse normalization and routinization with indifference. "People see hardship and suffering as a fact of social life," he writes, "yet they are equally aware that life is lived differently and better elsewhere."[41] As Lenín explains:

Cómo me gustaría que, como adolescente, fuera a una discoteca de acá. Yo pudiera parecer relajado con amigos, mis amigas, mis amigos, lo que sea, en una discoteca . . . no puede, no se puede. Ud. tiene que saber a dónde va. Ud. no puede decir simplemente vamos a entrar a una discoteca porque se mira bonita, no. Se tiene que saber si hay alguien, fulano de tal, mengano, fulano, Pedro, Pablo, o sí ahí todavía no está prohibido por alguien. Tiene que saber todo eso y si no lo sabe, lo va a aprender. Bajo la mala, porque aquí no hay buenas.

How I would like to be able to, like a normal teenager, just go to a club or a bar here. That I could just seem relaxed, with friends, in a club . . . but you can't. You can't. You need to know exactly where you're going, you can't simply say: Let's go to that club, it looks nice. No, you have to know who is there, if so and so is there, or if perhaps it's forbidden by someone for you to go there. You need to know all of this, and if you don't know, you're going to learn. The hard way, because here, there is no easy way.

Lenín emphasizes the situatedness of these dynamics. It's not simply that this is the way life is, he emphasizes, that's the way it is *here*. He recognizes that there is a different way to live your adolescence, and he wishes that he and his friends could have that kind of existence. But here, as he says, there are all these layers of knowledge that you must have in order to move around. The socio-spatiality of safety and danger shapes what is possible in the Sula Valley. Young men especially must navigate these overlapping, violent regimes of mobility control.

Leaving La Libertad

As a teenager, after his father died, Kevin, a young man who grew up in La Libertad—Ramón's neighborhood—started working in a market in an area controlled by MS-13. The gang in La Libertad started to suspect that Kevin could be a spy, was maybe an MS sympathizer or—even worse—a member, so they beat him up and told him to get out. He fled the country and headed for the United States. He was detained in Arizona, and after about six months he was deported back to Honduras. He thinks he started an asylum claim, but he's not totally sure what exactly happened.

Within days of being back at home, the pandilleros of La Libertad abduct him. They smash his hands with a hammer, cut him, tell him they're going to kill him. "These were the same guys I went to elementary school with," he tells me. His mother manages to get the police to intervene, and Kevin is rescued. He's alive, but now neither he nor the rest of his family can safely live in La Libertad. Speaking to the police is high treason—everyone in Rivera Hernández knows that. On top of that, his rescue by the police only confirms his imagined links to MS-13 for the pandilleros. Everyone also knows that the police favor MS-13.

Kevin waits just long enough for his hand to heal a bit—so he can grab onto the metal ladders of the freight train cars that he will climb while in Mexico—then he sets out again for the United States. His mother moves with Kevin's siblings to another area of San Pedro Sula, and she never sets foot in La Libertad again. It's causing trouble for her younger children. In order to register them for school she needs a certificate of home birth to prove their personhood, but the midwife who would issue it lives in La Libertad—she was their neighbor—and Gloria, Kevin's mom, cannot go back there to get it.

When Kevin is deported the second time, he stays a little while longer, a couple of weeks, but soon the pandilla learns that he is back. They send a cousin to tell him they know he's in Honduras, they know where he is. The threats start again. Now they swear they will kill him both for being an MS spy and for being a *sapo*, a snitch. I listen to the threatening voice notes sent via Facebook messenger, taunting him, warning him to be vigilant because they are after him. "Ponéte buzo, te vamos a quebrar. Ponéte buzo, te vamos a pelar. Por sapo." (Be alert, we're going to break you. Be alert, we're going to peel you. For being a snitch.) "Break" and "peel" are well-known euphemisms for murder. Kevin leaves again.

Gangs are often discussed as though they were an external presence, imposed from the outside, but, as Kevin says, he knew the guys leaving him these threatening messages from elementary school. The young men who abducted Kevin are his neighbors. Gloria had watched them all grow up, grow into the young men who rule their neighborhood. When she intervened, they tried to dissuade her, saying, respectfully, "No tenemos ningún problema con Ud., madre. Pero ya sabe." (We have no problem with you, Mother. But you know.)

The surveillance the gang exercises over Kevin's mobility, both within and outside the neighborhood, is a constant feature of life in the Sula Valley. He gets in "trouble" with the gang at first because he pushes the boundaries of acceptable mobility by moving in and out of his neighborhood and into a space controlled by MS-13. The first consequence of this transgression is banishment—by the pandilla that rules his colonia—and as long as he remains in exile, immobile elsewhere, his family is fine. When he returns, when he is deported back to Honduras, the problems resurface, involving his whole family, and then their movements, along with his, are watched. They all flee the neighborhood, but as long as Kevin remains in Honduras, they are all uneasy. When he's deported the third time, he barely leaves the two rooms his mother has rented in a different part of the city, but still they find him.

Kevin leaves again. This time he spends years wandering across Mexico, the country that lies between his home, where he cannot live safely, and the United States, where he cannot get refuge. As many times as Kevin is deported, he will keep leaving Honduras, as long as he is able. Because Kevin knows exactly what is waiting for him there. If he stays in Honduras, eventually they will kill him. The danger Kevin faces in La Libertad is real. The boys who control that neighborhood will always be after him, as his perceived transgression is understood to be an existential threat to them and their neighborhood.

But Kevin's story is not that of all youth in La Libertad or elsewhere. Eric, for example, has spent his whole life in the same neighborhood, grew up alongside Kevin. When Eric reaches high school age he stops going to school entirely—in part because of the costs and in part because the local public high school is located in an MS-13 neighborhood, even though it is only a few blocks away. He loved to play soccer and was a very talented player, but he only played in the informal, neighborhood league organized by Ramón. He knew all the games would be played exclusively among people from their own neighborhood and other neighborhoods controlled by the same or allied gangs. No danger there. Eric is on good terms with the pandilla, though he is emphatically and decisively not involved. As long as he maintains this friendly allegiance and refrains from arousing their suspicion of any kind of disloyalty by, among other things, not challenging the boundaries of his mobility that the gang has set, he trusts he will never have to leave La Libertad. Migration beckons, as it does for so many, but he does not make plans to go. On the contrary, he settles down with a young woman from La Libertad and throws himself into being a father to his infant daughter, his entire young family both of the neighborhood and loyal to it.

For Eric, and many young men like him, the colonia is the space where he is known, where he is safe. For him, venturing beyond the neighborhood is where danger lies, because he carries the identity of being from a neighborhood controlled by a particular gang with him everywhere. The police frequently harass and belittle him and the other young men in La Libertad, whether or not they have any actual gang affiliation. The gang, however, has never threatened him. His life is limited, small, but tranquilo.

This same geography of everyday violence shapes how youth understand the opportunities before them. It contributes to why so many feel compelled to migrate while also preparing them with the familiarity of not being allowed to cross imaginary lines on the earth. It shapes how gang members understand their own place and power in society; it provides the backdrop for the criminalization of urban youth that is wide and deep in Honduras. And it is precisely this control of territory and the intentional or unintentional transgressive mobility of young men, in particular, that is not fully legible in asylum courts, extending the exclusion they face at home through the mechanisms of humanitarian care and the system of international protection.

Ultimately, the tension between multiple immobilities, being stuck between internal borders and forced movement across international borders, is a fundamental component of the continuity between life in Honduras and life as a migrant and deportee. Where one can and cannot go is circumscribed first not by national boundaries but by a landscape of domination, exclusion, and persecution. The shrunk down world of life in Honduras, limited to the inside of your home and, perhaps, the invisible but very real borders of your colonia, is juxtaposed strikingly with the expansiveness of migration. Being out of place in Honduras pushes people into an international placelessness, where those who leave are made to move, again and again, through ongoing cycles of unwanted movement.

. . .

Field Notes

I'm leaving La Libertad, it's 9:30 at night. This is probably the latest I've ever been in Rivera Hernández. I spent the evening with Ramón. People are asking him to take them north. So tomorrow he's actually leaving to take a family to Villahermosa. Then he'll come back.

We just hung out and drank some beers in front of a *pulpería* in La Libertad. He took me to see the *cancha*, which is now *alumbrada*, lit up, and there were kids playing football, and we talk about how he thinks more people are leaving now than before. He thinks more people are preparing to go, he thinks life here is getting harder, things are getting worse.

At night the air is kind of smoky. People are burning trash or wood but mostly trash, I think. The air is kind of filled with that smoky smell, not bad smelling but not quite the delicious smell of a bonfire. And it's so humid and the air is so heavy that the air is kind of filled with dust. Ash, I guess it's ash. It makes the evenings hazy.

At one point we heard gunshots in the distance, but Ramón didn't flinch, and I didn't flinch. Nobody said anything about it. But it wasn't the backfiring sounds of a car. It sounded more like *tiros* in the distance but *tiros*.

I asked him tonight if he's ever shot anyone. And he said yes. He told me about a time that narcos came and tried to get the *muchachos* to sell drugs for them. And he said, "Look here we don't sell drugs. Marijuana sure. But we don't sell cocaine, and we don't sell meth . . . we don't sell that here." That makes people crazy, we don't do that. And they threatened him, and he threatened back, and it was all like *quién sos vos, quién sos vos . . . yo no soy nadie pero yo sé qué onda acá,*[42] and they came a couple of times, and they shot up his house and he shot back, and that's one of the reasons he says that people in the neighborhood have so much respect for him.

He takes me to see a pickup truck that he has at his house that's full of corn, and the idea is for the *muchachos* to go sell the corn. He said people like to say that he's the *jefe de pandilla*, but he's like, "Man, I just want to give them a chance."

His brother was, he was the *jefe de pandilla*, and they only killed him a year ago. He's like, "Look, Amelia, if I were the *jefe de pandilla*, do you think I wouldn't have taken revenge? *No te creas, duele, duele cuando te matan a un hermano. Duele. Si yo fuera jefe,*[43] wouldn't I have gotten revenge for my brother's death?" He says he tried to talk his brother out of that life, but his brother wanted to be the *jefe*, wanted to be the most powerful, and Ramón is like, "And what did it get him? Now he's dead."

There is something about the way the *muchachos* have kept La Libertad out of the hands of the *sicarios* or the narcos or even MS-13 or Barrio 18 that is beautiful even as they are violent. I think about Kevin and his mother, and I believe them that Kevin is not a *marero*, but I also understand for the first time tonight why they are so hyper-vigilant about anybody who might have links to the mara. They are keeping the neighborhood safe in their own way, in their violent, feudal, in-the-absence-of-the-state way. That's what they feel they have to do to keep their neighborhood and their neighbors safe. They're constantly worried about MS-13 coming in. They're constantly worried about being taken over by them. So if someone from the neighborhood might possibly be working with them, I guess I get why that means banishment.

. . .

Ramón tells me that he's starting to get worried. The police are stopping people from the neighborhood more frequently, accusing them of *cobrando renta*, collecting extortion payments on behalf of a gang, even if they only have 300 lempiras on them. He's worried about carrying any cash on himself at all, anything to give the police the excuse to detain him. People are talking about this elsewhere—the charge of cobrando renta being used against anyone the police want to target— but I'm surprised to hear that Ramón is concerned for himself. He's not the typical target, I think. But here Ramón's closeness to and visible defense of the muchachos not just from the police, but from MS-13 explains his personal fear. They are one and the same from their perspective. And if MS-13 can't get him through intimidation and gunfire, he suspects that they might try to get him through the police.

I tentatively ask Ramón at some point about Kevin. He waves me off, he was MS-13, he says, and changes the subject. By this point, he makes clear, I should understand enough to know that this allegation is sufficient on its own to explain everything. From his vantage point, the possibility that one of their own had betrayed not just the gang, but the whole neighborhood by getting involved with their rivals, with those who would take them over and endeavor to rule them, warranted expulsion and perhaps even death. Ramón isn't in charge, he couldn't simply direct the muchachos on how to handle this or any other situation, but he understands their reasoning. And, without ever condoning their actions, I realize that I do as well.

2 Mañana Me Mandan, Mañana Me Vengo

Rerouting Deportation Through Circulation

An almost mischievous smile spreads across Yadira's face as she shakes her head defiantly and says, "Mañana me mandan, mañana me vengo."

We are sitting on the bed tucked into the corner of the cement-block room. The mattress has that musty sour smell of humidity and sweaty bodies, but, compared to the pieces of cardboard that most migrants sleep on, it is the prized spot. Yadira is the current occupant, a status earned because of her lengthy time at this shelter and the ordeal she has been through. She is the star witness in a case against Mexican police officers who took her children away from her and accused her of being a *coyote*, a smuggler. Yadira is dark-skinned with tight, curly hair. She suspects that the police thought they had an easy case because her children are *cheles*, fair-skinned, with fewer apparent markers of their family's Afro-Honduran roots. But the police did not imagine that she was, in fact, their mother; nor did they count on her being the kind of person willing to put her own journey on hold for months to fight them for violating both Mexican law and her (and her children's) rights. When they threatened to deport her, in an effort to cow her into submission, she scoffed. "Mañana me mandan, mañana me vengo," she tells me. (They send me back tomorrow, tomorrow I'll come back.)

Yadira was one of the first Central Americans in transit I interviewed, nearly fifteen years before writing this book. Many of the details of her story have faded from my memory in the intervening decade, but these broad strokes and the phrase, "Mañana me mandan, mañana me vengo," have reverberated in my mind as my engagement with Honduras and migration has deepened and expanded over the intervening years. Before I met her, Yadira had already been deported multiple times from the United States and from Mexico, yet here she was, again, on her way north. Deportation was hardly the end of her journey. It was a frustrating setback, to be sure, but she would turn right around and start out again. And again.

After living in Texas for a few years, Yadira had been deported back to her native Honduras. At first, she tried to stay. Her family there welcomed her; she had children in Honduras who she had left behind when she first migrated. Things changed, however, when Yadira witnessed a massacre. Then she was sure that she had to leave again. The last time she had been deported from Mexico her sister met her at the airport in San Pedro Sula and gave her some money and a change of clothes, and she left the country again right away. She didn't even go home to see her parents.

At the time, that was the remarkable part of Yadira's story: her resolution to keep trying, the casualness with which she took the threats of deportation. After working with many more Honduran deportees, those in transit and those in Honduras, I read another layer from Yadira's story. The mistreatment, racism, and threats from the police didn't dissuade her, nor did being jailed and separated from her children or the poverty and deprivation of life in transit. Rather, each facet of her story involved experiences already familiar from daily life in Honduras.

Her words, that she would come back, frame what has become an increasingly common experience of deportation: continued movement, circulating through spaces of containment and migration.

On the map:

Tijuana
Nogales
UNITED STATES
Ciudad Juarez
Saltillo
Reynosa
Tenosique
MÉXICO
Coatzacoalcos
México City
Ixtepec
Arriaga
Tapachula
GUATEMALA
HONDURAS
EL SALVADOR

* approx. 425 miles from San Pedro Sula to Tapachula
* approx. 2665 miles from San Pedro Sula to Tijuana

✦ Valle de Sula

MAP 2. Migration corridors in Central America, Mexico, and the United States. Designed by Catherine Calderón of *Contra Corriente*. ©Author

Deportation, as a consequence of a changing landscape of immigration control, I argue here, is becoming less an experience of exceptional rupture and more one of familiar, everyday, ongoing violence. As people move through these circuits, so too do the exclusions that generate the move to migrate as well as ideas of ways to be more successful on the next attempt. Yadira's story is a bridge, in a sense, from an experience of deportation that was something like exile—where people who had lived in the United States were uprooted from their homes and sent to distant countries of citizenship—to one that looks more like circulation—where people are detained and deported before having a chance to build that life. Trying to get back to a life she had before in the United States, Yadira is also trying to get away from a life she knows all too well in Honduras.

What her experience and that of the others whose stories fill these pages tell us is how the shifting, expanding, and hardening practices of US-led immigration control in the region have contributed to an emerging experience of deportation that is qualitatively different from that of a previous generation. As this coincides with micro regimes of mobility control, criminalization of the urban poor, and the ever-present possibility of physical and structural violence within their home country, many Hondurans today experience deportation as a kind of circulation as they keep trying to escape from and are pushed back to a home that is inhospitable. This approach to deportation attends to the constancy of the experience and the violence embedded therein rather than focusing on its exceptionality.

Locked in, in Honduras

When Ulises is deported the second time it takes him longer to recover. He is depressed, broken-hearted at the prospect of being back in Honduras and traumatized by the three months he had been held in detention in the United States. He laughs, without mirth, when he compares this experience with his first attempt to migrate. That first time, a few years earlier, he had been kidnapped by a drug cartel in northern Mexico and held in a warehouse for three months, unsure each morning whether he would be killed or allowed to live another day.

Despite the horror of being kidnapped, he felt mostly unchanged when he was deported back to Honduras the first time. He was undeterred, immediately ready to try again. This second time, though, he finds himself unable to sleep or sometimes sleeping too much. He loses a lot of weight. He wanders between his mother's house in the rural region of Santa Bárbara—where he cannot find work—and San Pedro Sula, the city he'd grown up in—where he fears for his life.

Ulises and I had first met during the 2018 migrant caravan months earlier, sharing french fries and stories at a Carl's Junior in Tijuana. Shortly after I returned to Honduras, Ulises turned himself in to border agents and began the process of seeking asylum in the United States. After months in detention without any prospects of getting released, he decided to give it up and sign a voluntary deportation order.

Ulises started on this path of migration for a confluence of reasons. He was in his mid-twenties, with a specialized high school degree in computers, but he could never find a job in his field. He found work for a while with a company that would send him out to different sites to fix machinery. One day he was sent to the Rivera Hernández sector, to fix something at the local branch of a low-cost chain grocery store. Taking a short lunch break, he drove the company vehicle around, trying to find tortillas. All of a sudden, he was stopped. A young man put a gun to his chest and demanded to know what he was doing there. Unbeknownst to Ulises, he had crossed gang lines, inadvertently leaving the relative safety of the neutral main road and moving from the territory of one gang into another. All in the course of a few blocks. Just trying to buy tortillas. He swore he was just a worker, promised to never return, and got out of the neighborhood and the sector. The company told him to change his shirt and tried to send him right back to finish the job. He quit that same day.

Then Ulises tried to work as a taxi driver for a while, but he never felt safe, knowing that if the company he worked for didn't pay the extortion payments demanded, he was a potential target for any organized crime group that wasn't getting paid. After an uncle, who was also a taxi driver, was killed, Ulises and his family moved to a different neighborhood in San Pedro Sula, then left for the village in Santa Bárbara. Sometimes he picks up a shift working construction, but the pay is low, and the shifts are few and far between. While he would be a good candidate to pass the entrance exam to get into the public university, he no longer sees the point of trying to get a college degree. When he was younger, Ulises had dreamed of being a lawyer. "But why bother now?" he asks. "I know lawyers who can't find a job."

Despite feeling broken by his last attempt to migrate, Ulises says, without enthusiasm, that he will try again to reach the United States, as soon as he starts to feel better. Moving between bad options, Ulises is adrift both within his country and outside it.

Ulises's story is not remarkable or exceptional. He is one of hundreds of thousands of young Hondurans who have left their homes multiple times and been forced back.

"Aquí estamos como encerrados, no hay ni un país donde podemos ir," he tells me. (It's like we're locked in here; there's not even one country where we can go.)

Ulises feels trapped, contained within his country where he sees little chance at a future for himself. His language is revelatory, his use of the term *encierro*, of being enclosed, locked in. In this case, Ulises describes a condition of encierro at the international scale: He is locked into his country of citizenship, unable to migrate to another place. His language both reflects and scales up the way that many young people described their existence in Honduras as well.

Joel, an almost eighteen-year-old resident of La Libertad, explains his life in Honduras in similar terms. He had tried to go to Mexico once but had to give up and come back. When I speak with him in 2018, he is considering leaving again because, he says:

It's just here, there's no way to live here. You're not free here, you're not free, I'm not free. *Solo paso encerrado.* I just pass the time enclosed, locked in. The police, they've stopped me so many times.

One time they pulled out a bag of marijuana and tried to say it was mine. And then everybody says that if you're from Rivera Hernández you're a *marero* . . . and I can't go to other places. I don't even tell some people that this is where I'm from.

Joel experiences encierro first at the level of his house, then at the level of the colonia. His unsuccessful attempt to migrate, to leave Honduras, suggests that he's experiencing the encierro at the country level as well. This turns the safety that being *encuevado* (encaved) is intended to cultivate into a kind of imposed carceral existence. The embodied identity that Joel carries with him—young man from a gang-controlled neighborhood—which makes him a target of the police, suspicious to Honduran society at large, also reverberates in the kind of reception he can expect beyond Honduras.

Whether in Mexico or in the United States, having their mobility constrained is an existentially familiar experience to these young men. When they return to Honduras, nothing has improved for them, but the conditions they find are not unfamiliar or incomprehensible. They know them all too well.

Deportation-as-Exile

For Yadira, Ulises, Joel, and others, the violence of deportation is not rooted primarily in disconnect and rupture, in being sent back to an unfamiliar place. Their deportation experience, however, was not the predominant one in the late twentieth and early twenty-first centuries. Consequently, this is also not the kind of experience that is the foundation of deportation studies as it emerges as its own field of study at the intersection of security studies and migration studies.[1] In addition to explorations of the governmentality of deportation and its infrastructures, the ethnographic contribution primarily centered on illuminating the experience of those sent back to largely unfamiliar countries of first citizenship after having grown up and lived full lives elsewhere.[2]

Scholars of deportation studies have conceptualized deportees in this condition as "the new American Diaspora," as "reverse refugees," or as people "exiled home" or "banished from the kingdom."[3] These diverse configurations that span disciplines and geographies collectively identify a common thread of experience for deportees: It involves ripping people out of the worlds they know and sending them back to a country that does not feel like home. They are exiled *to* the place that is supposed to be their homeland.

While this broad literature includes the experience of people across the globe,[4] much of it emerges in the context of deportation from the United States to Central America and the Caribbean. Here the focus has been on the experience of deportees who either lost legal status, sometimes after a criminal conviction, or lived as "unauthorized permanent residents,"[5] those whose life experience parallels that of legal permanent residents, except for the official designation. In this context, scholars have examined what happens to those who grew up in the United States and are sent back to places that are legally their homelands but are not felt to be so, focusing on the difficulties of reintegrating into an unfamiliar society and the longing those who are deported feel for the lives and communities they knew in the United States.[6] Collectively, this scholarship reveals the violence of deportation and the dangers that deportees face when sent back to countries with which they are unfamiliar, where they are unequipped to deal with daily life. What might be otherwise uncomfortable and depressing turns especially dangerous in countries that are already grappling with insecurity; not knowing the language and social norms can become deadly in that context.[7]

El Salvador, Honduras's neighbor, is one of the primary sites where these studies have emerged. In part, El Salvador takes prominence because of the relationship between the deportation of gang-involved youth from Los Angeles and the emergence of those same gangs in El Salvador.[8] Elana Zilberg, in one of the earliest studies that focuses specifically on exiled deportees, notes how the young men she works with speak frequently about being Salvadoran but being *from* Los Angeles, locating themselves in terms of neighborhoods in Los Angeles even while being physically present in San Salvador. Their "street smarts," formed in the urban United States, did not map onto the worlds waiting for them in El Salvador.[9] Deportation in these cases does not sever ties between the deported person and the United States. Those ties, though strained and frayed, still tether that person to the United States and the life they had there.[10] The experience of those "exiled home" to El Salvador may be the most well-studied kind of deportation experience and, at least in the Americas, sets the kind of baseline assumption of what deportation means.[11]

Parallel to the literature that focuses on this disorienting dislocation and profound sense of loss for those who have been deported, there is a related effort to study the collateral consequences for those who are left behind, struggling to remake their worlds after someone has been torn away.[12] These twinned bodies of scholarship constitute a crucial project that pushes against a long-dominant legal fiction that deportation is, at its core, a simple matter of returning people to where they belong.[13] Adam Goodman, in his history of the "deportation machine," details how US law came to rest on this idea that deportation was an administrative fix, not a punitive measure.[14] As anthropologist Shahram Khosravi notes, the etymological origins of the word *deportation* reveal something about its conception within the law, coming from the French *deportment* and indicating how one carries oneself, how one behaves.[15] Rather than a process of punishment for criminal acts, then, deportation is imagined as a corrective measure for the bad behavior of being out of one's place.

Although deportation has in practice never been a benign process,[16] legal scholar Daniel Kanstroom locates a new era of deportation that results from changes to criminal and immigration law in 1996.[17] The Illegal Immigration Reform and Immigrant Responsibility Act (IIRIRA) made more crimes deportable offenses, meaning that those with permanent residency and other noncitizenship legal statuses were now made deportable for a wide array of criminal convictions—including retroactively. Lawful permanent residents who had previously been convicted and already served their sentences, for example, were now subject to losing their status and being deported under IIRIRA. The act also expands a new category of crime, "aggravated felony," a category uniquely relevant to immigration proceedings, which aggregates what might otherwise be misdemeanors into a felony and thus renders the "offender" deportable.[18] IIRIRA makes the underlying punishing function of deportation clear, even while maintaining the legal fiction that deportation is simply administrative.[19]

This research also figures into larger questions about the international order of nation-states, the rights and privileges of citizenship, and the very nature of what it means to belong. For example, while there is a robust scholarly and humanitarian community focused on "forced migration," philosopher Matthew Gibney rightly points out that "deportation" is rarely discussed as a form of forced migration. He argues that those who are focused on forced migration have resisted characterizing deportation as such precisely because it is implicitly understood to be a *legitimate* form of forced migration. It does not violate the key principles of a liberal-state world order in that "coercion is used to send people to a country where they belong and out of a country where they do not."[20] Deportation, in other words, moves people *along* the grain of the international order. It is unauthorized migration that causes friction, that disrupts; deportation, in going *with* the flow, masks the coercion involved. The literature that shows the violence of being sent back to where one "belongs" has played an important part in unmasking that coercion.[21]

Ricardo: "He Cannot Be Here"

Twenty-nine-year-old Ricardo has been migrating since he was a teenager. When I meet him at the deportee processing center, CAMR-Lima, he had already been deported a handful of times. He is mostly unbothered, almost delighted, to be sent back to Honduras this time. He is so used to the whole process that he didn't even tell his family ahead of time; he wanted to show up and surprise them. He told his friends in the United States that he was just going for a short visit, as though it were a vacation. Four years had passed since his last deportation, since the last time Ricardo had seen his mother. He was eager to visit her, but he knew he would not be staying.

Ricardo took a taxi from the deportee processing center directly to his aunt's house in a *residencial*, a low-income but nominally gated community, on the outskirts of the city. Before he could knock on her door, however, a group of boys pulled him into a *mototaxi* and drove him to the edge of the neighborhood, where the residential area gave way to the woods. They roughed him up a bit and interrogated him, demanding to know who he was, why he was there. They made him strip down, completely, so they could examine his body for tattoos. Ricardo has a few—his mother's name, a marijuana leaf—but he was able to convince the boys that they were harmless, unrelated to any gang affiliation. It was enough to buy him a few days at his aunt's house, but when they dropped him off at her door, they waited to make sure she recognized him. And they made it clear that he shouldn't get too comfortable, he shouldn't plan on staying. *Cuidadito*. Watch yourself.

Two days later, I'm sitting in Ricardo's aunt's little living room. Ricardo sits, perched, on the armrest of the chair where his mother is seated, one arm gently draped around her shoulders. His cousins run in and out, and he tells me, proudly, how he made breakfast for all of them this morning. The house is small, compact. Like so much of the architecture on the city's outskirts, it feels like a shrunken version of a suburban home in the United States. The tightly packed single-family homes of the residencial project an aspiring upper-middle classness, but the promise of safety that developments like these might once have offered never materializes. Ricardo chose to come here rather than visit where his mother lives, in Choloma, precisely because he thought in a place like this his presence would stir up less trouble. As we chat, he's happy, at ease, almost giggly, like a young boy might be when getting lavished with attention by his mom and aunt. Both middle-aged women are visibly pleased to have him back. They can't stop hugging him, patting his hand, his shoulder. Proud of the man he has become. Still, after he recounts the "welcome" he received in the neighborhood, his aunt says, placing her hand on her chest, "Él no puede estar aquí. Me duele decirlo, pero acá no se puede estar." (He can't be here. It hurts me to say so, but he cannot be here.)

His mother agrees with his aunt: Ricardo has to go. Here, they tell me, he cannot go outside, he cannot get a job, he cannot study. It's like he's in prison. They won't even let him go to the pulpería by himself. But, referencing the fact that being caught again in the United States after deportation could lead to a prison sentence, his aunt adds that it would be better to be in jail *there* than in this kind of prison here, echoing the language of encierro and the feeling of carceral existence that Ulises and Joel express as well.

Ricardo leaves Honduras shortly after my visit; he stayed in his country of citizenship this time for just four days. While in Mexico, he gets shot by a criminal group that controls the train lines—he doesn't tell me why; he might not even know himself—and he's hospitalized in Tenosique, Tabasco. He convalesces there for a while, and ultimately the doctors decide not to remove the bullet that's lodged in his leg. He continues northward, and just two months after being deported to Honduras, he lets me know that he's made it back to the United States. He knows he'll be picked up and deported again sooner or later, but in the meantime, he is happy to be able to send money back to his mom.

The Border Widens: A New Era of Deportation

The stories of men like Ricardo show this emerging shift in deportation becoming one segment in ongoing, ever-extending circuits of migrations and displacements. Ricardo, and others like him, is not sent back to a wholly unfamiliar world, and deportation does not put an end to his life of migration. Deportation disrupts his life, of course, but it does not represent the "confounding rupture" experienced by an earlier generation of deportees.[22] His return to Honduras *does* bring him back home. Home, however, is at once familiar and inhospitable.

Ricardo's experience of deportation is shaped by a confluence of factors, including the distinct history of Honduran migration over time and the changing logics and landscape of immigration control. Mass Honduran migration really began in the late 1990s and early 2000s, as people struggled with the consequences of the structural adjustments of the post–Cold War era and, importantly, after Hurricane Mitch devastated the country in 1998. In contrast, Salvadorans, Guatemalans, and Nicaraguans had been migrating in greater numbers toward the United States since the early 1980s, as civil wars, brutal repression, and economic crises forced hundreds of thousands of people to flee.[23] This timeline means that the population of Hondurans already in the United States was comparatively small when multiple reforms were issued in the 1980s and 1990s that permitted other Central Americans to adjust their statuses and become lawful residents.[24] Consequently, fewer Hondurans were able to benefit from these reforms and secure legal status, and fewer Hondurans were able to confer that status on subsequent generations. This also meant that when reforms stripped people of their permanent residency and deported them in the wake of IIRIRA in 1996, relatively fewer Hondurans were affected.[25] Since IIRIRA is, in many ways, a generative cause of the rise of the "criminal" deportee and the "American diaspora" being sent to Central America, it is an important distinction to highlight in the case of Honduras. Although some Hondurans were deported due to the changes in the law in 1996, this crucial turning point that underpins much of the deportation-as-exile literature does not shape the history or general experience of deportation in Honduras to the same extent as in other places.

At the same time, expanding beyond the specificities of Honduras, much has changed in Mexico since the last time Ricardo had made his way across the country; and the last time was also a lot different from the time before that. Over the past two decades, US immigration enforcement has evolved in a multitude of ways, including the systematic expansion of border policing ever farther from the physical, territorial boundary. The collateral consequences of this border externalization in Mexico have resulted in migrants like Ricardo having to dodge immigration enforcement at more points throughout the country, which makes them ever more exposed to assault and exploitation from actors—both criminal and government affiliated—who would prey on their vulnerability.

The process of border externalization from the United States outward involves a series of agreements between the United States and Mexico (and, later, Guatemala and Honduras, and beyond) that effectively deploy Mexican immigration enforcement to stop migrants, primarily Central Americans, from reaching the US border. This collaboration is not wholly new,[26] but the pressure exercised by the United States, and the corresponding intensity and violence of Mexico's migration enforcement activities, has increased substantially during the past twenty years. This period of border practices moving ever farther south also coincides with moments of greater—and more visible—migration from Central America in general and Honduras in particular.

Though there is a longer history of patchwork immigration enforcement collaboration, systematic externalization of the US-dominated immigration agenda in the Americas can be located as notably intensifying in the wake of the North American Free Trade Agreement (NAFTA), when, in 2001, Mexico enacted "Plan Sur," or the Southern Plan,[27] aimed explicitly at keeping migrants, primarily Central Americans, from reaching the border with the United States. This was further entrenched when Mexico and the United States entered into the "Security and Prosperity Partnership" in 2005. Laura Carlsen calls this plan "Armoring NAFTA," explaining that as the economic disruptions of the free trade agreement would dislodge people, the United States wanted to ensure a broader effort to immobilize would-be migrants.[28] Not coincidentally, the launching of NAFTA also fundamentally shaped the United States's own border security plan and the logic by which all border projects would be governed, Prevention Through Deterrence (PTD). The initial implementation of PTD in 1994 involved fencing off and guarding the heavily populated and historically used crossing points at the US-Mexico border, thus funneling people into the more remote parts of the borderlands where the terrain is inhospitable. The logic here is that if enforcement pushes border crossing into paths that are so difficult, even deadly, the increased risk will serve as a deterrent to those who might be considering migrating clandestinely.[29] Then, in 2008, the Mérida Initiative, framed around security cooperation in the context of the drug war, brought Mexico further into the effort to detain and deport non-Mexicans on behalf of the United States, with the latter providing training, equipment, technology, and direction to Mexico's immigration enforcement agency.[30] The initiative has four pillars, one of which is "creating a 21st century border," though the details on how that was to be done or what that means in practice remained thin.[31]

The trajectory of externalization again intensified steeply in 2014, in response to the so-called crisis of unaccompanied minors.

This time, "Plan Frontera Sur," or the Southern Border Plan, launched by then-President Enrique Peña Nieto (2012–18), heavily concentrated and further militarized immigration enforcement in Mexico's southernmost states.[32] Frontera Sur marked an important turning point: For the first time, Mexico began to consistently deport more Central Americans, year over year, than the United States.[33]

The accumulation over time of externalization policies has resulted in people identifying all of Mexico as a "vertical border" or an "arterial border,"[34] noting the geographic dislocation of the border regime and its violent consequences from the physical boundary between the United States and Mexico. Amarela Varela Huerta notes, however, that Mexico moved from being a vertical border to a *país tapón*, or stopper country, in particular in the aftermath of the 2018 migrant caravans.[35] The notoriety of the caravans in 2018 sparked a backlash in the form of a new level of externalization plans. First, the United States launched a new program—the absurdly named "Migrant Protection Protocols," which expelled Central Americans seeking asylum in the United States back to Mexico and made them wait outside the country for hearings in US immigration courts.[36] The first Trump administration then entered into Asylum Cooperative Agreements with Honduras and Guatemala, essentially mandating that asylum seekers seek protection in one of those countries first and making those who passed through but failed to have done so ineligible to seek asylum in the United States.[37] These policies did not much outlast the first Trump administration (2017–21), but the subsequent Biden administration (2021–25) continued these policies in spirit, making most people who sought asylum at the US border ineligible if they had passed through another country beforehand and failed to seek protection there, under their Circumvention of Lawful Pathways Rule (CLP). Upon taking office in 2025, the second Trump administration almost immediately suspended the mechanisms the Biden administration had put in place to register asylum seekers before en-

tering the country and effectively shut down access to asylum altogether for anyone not already inside the United States, unconcerned
about the legality of such a measure.

In analyzing this trajectory, I think we can identify a move from
deterrence to containment in the strategy of externalization pro-
moted by the United States. Varela's país tapón is emblematic of this,
as migrants are increasingly made to wait in the southern Mexican
city of Tapachula, not necessarily deported but unable to advance
into central or northern Mexico due to the militarized enforcement,
led by the *guardia nacional*, a militarized police force, on the highways leading out of the city and to the next state, Oaxaca.[38] This can
also be seen in the clumsily enacted Asylum Cooperative Agreements
or in the fundamental reshaping of the regional immigration regime
enacted by the Biden administration, not solely in the CLP rule, but,
also in the conditions placed on its humanitarian parole program,
where people were only eligible for sponsorship to be paroled into the
United States if they applied *before* the Darién Gap,[39] for example, or
the plan to establish regional processing centers in Colombia and
Guatemala, containing people in "their" zones and making it less
likely and less possible that they would make it to the US border. Even
the introduction of the short-lived CBP One App, which allowed non-
Mexican nationals to be contingently legally present in Mexico while
waiting for an appointment to start an asylum application in the
United States, amounted to a strategy of containment. At first, people
had to be located in a certain part of northern Mexico to make an appointment; then they had to be located in the southernmost part of
Mexico. In both iterations, they were kept waiting, confined in a temporary geography, and only selectively allowed to present themselves
at the border and start the process of seeking asylum after meeting
certain criteria and being granted an appointment.

Part of this shift to containment is in response to the increasing
number of people who had initiated asylum claims at the US border.

The collateral consequences of the PTD strategy included a costlier and more dangerous border crossing, encouraging people to invent alternate pathways to realize migration, including asking for asylum. Maribel, a young woman from Choloma, hired a coyote to get to the United States after she accidentally witnessed gang members disposing of a body when she was making the rounds to her Avon clients. Her husband, who had a steady job in one of the maquilas in the area, and her son stayed behind. The family pooled their resources in order to get Maribel to the United States and to safety; the plan was that once she was established, she would send for her family. She did not know when she left Honduras that there was such a thing as asylum.

Maribel was detained while crossing the US-Mexico border. While in detention, as part of her deportation processing, she was asked the question that all people put into removal proceedings are supposed to be asked: Are you afraid of returning to your country? "Yes!" she answered, honestly, desperately. The gang members she had seen had been showing up outside her neighborhood, and she was sure they were looking for her, making sure she wasn't there, making sure she would not talk. This answer started her on the process of seeking asylum, though her claim was ultimately denied, and she was deported back to Honduras.

Maribel's experience was increasingly common in the 2010s: detained Central Americans asked by US border agents if they were afraid in Honduras, learning in the course of being detained that there was a legal process that might potentially allow them to stay in the United States. In 2010, very few people moving through the shelters in southern Mexico were talking about seeking asylum; in 2014, we heard the language used more often, more strategically; by 2018, many people were talking about how to prepare "their case"—even before leaving Honduras. This is not to say that asylum is a "loophole," as some would paint it. Rather, the idea of entering into a legal process where your experience of insecurity in your home country might enable you to have legal status in the United States was circulating along with the people who were detained and deported (as well as those who were able to stay in the United States and await a court date). While the nuances of asylum law in the United States were not always well communicated or understood, the fact that there was a legal pathway for people who had suffered some kind of violence became increasingly common knowledge in Honduras. And this as many Hondurans were experiencing terrifying violence.

The move to containment, then, responds in part to this increasing attempt to access the legal process for seeking protection in the United States. The logic behind these efforts is that once a person has physically entered US territory, they are guaranteed certain rights[40]—perhaps not many but certain rights, nonetheless. While those who do show up and ask for asylum are not necessarily likely to get it,[41] containment keeps more people from enjoying even these limited rights, from even being able to *ask* for asylum. At the same time, this turn to containment is a reflection of the fact that deportation, on its own, is simply not working according to its purported aims. Deportation produces more movement, not less. People who are deported leave again and again; deportation often becomes circulation.

To be clear, these policies have not been enacted explicitly to target Hondurans. Rather, the increasing focus on pushing US border controls farther from the physical border—the process of externalization—has been intended to keep all people stuck elsewhere, in their country of citizenship or otherwise, what David FitzGerald has called the remote control of borders.[42] Broadly, the evolving contours of the migration enforcement regime in the Americas has created a situation where deterrence blends with containment, detention, and removal, and where people are increasingly unable to reach let alone build full lives in the United States.

Ezra: "We Can No Longer Be Here"

Ezra messages me two quick lines on Facebook: "We're going in the caravan. We can no longer be here." This was January 2021, when Honduras was still in the throes of the COVID-19 pandemic and the Sula Valley, Ezra's home, was reeling from back-to-back hurricanes, Eta and Iota. Like thousands of other Hondurans, Ezra was ready to set out on foot, with his family beside him, in hopes of making it to the United States. As rumblings of this new caravan forming made news, both Mexico and Guatemala had already promised to stop it, but Ezra was not dissuaded.

This would not be Ezra's first attempt to make it to the United States. It would be at least his fourth but maybe fifth or sixth; his multiple attempts in his teenage years blend together in his memory. He has never achieved even the short periods of life in the United States that Ricardo has. Yet Ezra's determination to leave Honduras in this new caravan does mark a shift in this young man. The last time I had seen him, in person, was almost two years earlier, in the spring of 2019, when he told me—with equal conviction—that he would never again try to get to the United States. He was disgusted, angry, and wholly disillusioned. Ezra was part of one of the many families who had been separated under the first Trump administration's "zero tolerance" policy that led to parents being detained and deported without their children. Ezra and Amanda, his eight-year-old daughter, were separated in January 2018. He spent four months in different detention centers before being sent back to Honduras, alone. It would be nearly another four months before Amanda, now nine, would join him in San Pedro Sula. I accompanied Ezra to pick up Amanda when she was finally sent back to him. As we drove away from the processing center for deported minors that day, father and daughter recited the alphabet and counted in English in the backseat of my car. She showed off her new language skills—proud to know more numbers than her father—and Ezra let himself smile for the first time since I had met him.

Ezra said that immigration agents had told him that they were doing this to them, taking his child away, so that he would never think about trying to come to the United States again. When he recounted those words to me, he steeled his gaze and said, "You know what? It worked. Ya no quiero saber nada de Estados Unidos." (I don't want to know anything about the United States.)

This wasn't his first time trying to migrate, but he swore it would be his last. His fear of losing his daughter mixed with a newfound contempt for the United States. He threw himself into making sure that Amanda did well in school. A devoted single father, he moved them out of his mother's house, where his brothers and cousins all lived crammed together into a few rooms, and rented a single room, not far away, for just the two of them to share. I connected him to FeAc's Programa de Retornar y Reconstruir, and he eagerly studied a trade and accepted their help when they offered to cover the start-up costs for a business raising pigs. For a while, Ezra was literally the poster child for the NGO, appearing in their promotional videos, grateful for the help they had offered him and his daughter. Ezra met a young woman from the program, and they got married, blending their families and their dreams.

Then, about a year and a half later, he tells me they are once again thinking of leaving. His trade certification hadn't helped him find a decent job. Things were getting more dangerous in their neighborhood, as a new gang was trying to take over. He wasn't eager to leave Honduras again, but he was starting to feel the pressure to get out. I ask him if he would take Amanda with him this time. "Where I go, she goes," he answers.

Before he has time to think it through, the COVID-19 pandemic hits Honduras. Fears of gang violence give way to concerns about having enough food to eat. Then, in November 2020, the northern coast of Honduras is devastated by back-to-back hurricanes, Eta and Iota. Ezra's neighborhood becomes a lake. He and his whole family flee, taking refuge under a highway bridge for days. Like hundreds of others in the northern coast region of Honduras, their homes are wiped out. Even after the waters subside, there is nothing for them to go back to. And the gang problems that had been troubling Ezra only intensify in the wake of the disaster. Uprooted communities are all jumbled together. The gangs would take a while—and a toll—to reestablish the careful choreography of territorial control across the Sula Valley.

When Ezra decides to join the caravan in early 2021—a caravan that, from the start, was very likely to fail to even reach Mexico—it is an act of frustration less than one of hope. He knows, as well as anybody, the dangers of migrating. He had ridden the infamous freight train through Mexico a handful of times, once with his daughter in tow. He nearly lost his leg from an untreated wound while in detention. They took his child from him. The idealized version of the United States that he once had as a teenager had crumbled into a stubborn, defiant realism.

Deportation alone never deterred Ezra from trying to migrate again. Having his child taken from him almost convinced him to give up trying to migrate, but, in the end, the conditions in Honduras outweighed his rage and his fear of losing her. So he and his wife and Amanda join a caravan of people trying to get out.

They make it to Chiquimula, not far across the border Honduras shares with Guatemala. They are blocked by the full force of the Guatemalan military. Stores have been ordered to close. Residents have been told not to give food or water or aid to the *caravaneros*. Ezra messages me: "They won't even let us buy water. Our kids are hungry. We need food and water. And masks." This was months before vaccines would become available in Central America.

The regional migration regime, dominated by the United States but carried out by the Guatemalan military in this case, endeavors to force people like Ezra to stay put. This is done through physical removal, psychological torment, and military force. The full security apparatus of the region is aimed at making him immobile, pinning him in his country of citizenship. Yet, in Honduras, Ezra is also unmoored, abandoned, already living like a refugee. Deportation sends him back to the familiarity of exclusion, displacement, and insecurity, leading to ongoing, unwanted circulation.

Circulation: Deportability Begins at Home

Elana Zilberg, in her groundbreaking study of deported gang members in El Salvador, offers one kind of ethnography of circulation.[43] She focuses on the circulation of gangs and policing models, identifying a transnational "securityscape" through which circulate both the methods and the logics of policing that target youth by criminalizing everyday behavior and limiting movement and the forms of social organizing and control that street gangs develop. The gang member/deportee is multiply excluded, moved and made immobile, removed from his community, jailed, detained, deported, and, often, unable to engage in free public life once in El Salvador, as the policing models that targeted him in Los Angeles have him in their crosshairs in Central America too.

Circulation is important for Zilberg's analysis, though in her account it is not the young men who are described as circulating (even as they sometimes try to remigrate). They mostly experience restriction of their mobility, a kind of carceral existence in and out of detention,[44] where their movement is restrained within nation-states. Though some of the deportees she worked with do attempt to remigrate, they were headed *back*, to a home they had been removed from. Life, in the fullest sense of the word, was waiting for them on the other side of a border, beyond the rupture of deportation and the risks of remigration. In the years since Zilberg's study, the circulation that she identifies, of policing tactics, gang control, and authorities, has contributed to a parallel and ongoing circulation of Central American youth. New generations are repeatedly compelled to migrate, without the clear directionality of return that animated the Salvadoran deportee-exiles. Whereas those early deportees knew a life beyond migrating and hoped to get back to that life, the deportees whose experience forms the basis of this book come to inhabit circulation. They are not trying to get back but to get out.

An important aspect of circulation as an analytic in anthropology is the relationality embedded in the concept.[45] Circulation knits together people; it makes and maintains communities and societies. At the same time, circulation draws attention to both that which is circulated and how that circulation is shaped, channeled—the relationship between the circulating object and the structure that produces its movement (or is perhaps produced because of the movement). If we think about migration and deportation as circulation, we are pointed toward the relationality of the experience: Ricardo's circulation knits together his aunt in her residencial and his daughter in Los Angeles, what has been described as transnationalism,[46] but, at the same time, it also highlights how his inability to stay in Honduras—the threats to get out, the prison-like life he would be required to lead—is related to the precarity of life for him in the United States and the nearly inevitable expulsion he'll again face. Circulation ties together Ricardo's movement, his circular migration, with the forces that make him keep moving and unable to really *stay* anywhere.

Thinking about deportation in terms of circulation connects the deportability experienced by immigrant communities living in the United States with the criminalization of poor youth who have not yet left Honduras but who are likely to do so one day. It connects the expansiveness of mobility that migration entails and the constraints on mobility felt by poor, young Honduran men wherever they are, including Honduras. Legal anthropologist Susan Bibler Coutin, in describing the circumscribed existence of the undocumented in the United States, writes, "Even migrants who are not apprehended experience exclusionary tactics such as being denied access to employment, housing, higher education, social services, healthcare, and public benefits. Such exclusionary practices situate migrants ambiguously as outside of national territory even when, physically, they are within."[47] Coutin notes the carceral quality produced by living with deportability for those in the United States. This description could also be extended to include the kind of life that young urban Honduran men also already lead in Honduras. They do not have access to employment, housing, higher education (or primary education in many cases), health care, or public benefits. They are, essentially, already familiar with exclusionary practices that render them outside before they physically leave the boundaries of their country of citizenship. Circulation shifts the relationality between "home" and "destination," further unsettling the idea that "citizenship" means safety and freedom or the potential to flourish.

The deportation regime produces immobility among those confined within territories: those undocumented or underdocumented who cannot leave for fear of being unable to return, those deported and unable to once again access the lives they had been made to leave behind. Coutin writes, "The fact that national territories in some ways resemble detention centers—both of these confine, both restrict movement—challenges liberal notions of nation-states as entities through which individuals can realize their capacities."[48] This carceral quality of nation-states—and the corresponding challenge to the liberal notion that Coutin identifies—also applies to life before migration and both the lack of opportunity to "realize their capacities" in the first place and the mechanisms increasingly put in place to keep Hondurans, as others, from being able to leave and move across space.

Ricardo's story contains some of the features of circulation that I want to highlight: his multiple deportations, his (dis)comfort in

Honduras, the effective expulsion he experiences by both the United States and Honduras. While he has made a life, if temporary, in the United States, the experience of circulation continues. Ricardo, like many immigrants, moves around within the United States, from California to Louisiana to Tennessee, depending on where there is work, where word has spread that immigration enforcement is lax. His circulation is punctuated by periods of stillness, though that stillness is never permanent.

For many Hondurans like Ezra, however, even those moments of stasis remain elusive. Ezra's circulation is channeled by a hyperneoliberal and deeply corrupt state in Honduras that has essentially abandoned its citizens to deal with insecurity, a pandemic, and back-to-back hurricanes on their own. It is channeled through a regional migration regime that has increasingly militarized borders ever farther south, making the kind of individual migration of Ezra's youth toward the United States even more dangerous and impractical. It is channeled also by a history of mass migration movements growing in Mexico and Central America that make this idea of collective mobility, the caravan, something that seems like a viable alternative to people like Ezra. His circulations are a product of this evolving deportation regime that pushes people into continued movement to keep them from reaching the border they hope to cross, from arriving at the place where they imagine another kind of life might be possible. In doing so, the United States pushes the violence that people are made to suffer further from public view. It keeps Ezra and others out of frame, an arrangement that caravans disrupt.

Ezra can now add deportation from Guatemala to his list of countries that have sent him back to a Honduras where, although it is the only place he has ever lived and the place where, in the international order, he "belongs,"[49] multiple forces converge to expel him as well, over and over again. Ezra was displaced from his home, untethered, unhoused, shuffled and channeled by gangs, natural disasters, and a negligent, abandoning state. This experience of prior displacement is also connected, through the idea of circulation, to the multiple displacements of migration and deportation.

Ezra, Ricardo, Ulises, and Yadira all point us toward a different engagement with deportation than the experience of exile that has been so well documented and theorized. The violence of deportation, for them, is not primarily borne of rupture. It is, rather, a segment in a process of ongoing disruptions and dislocations. Deportation is a frustrating yet familiar experience. Echoes of being pushed around, and out, and back contribute to the violence of this kind of deportation, this embodied experience of circulation.

What does this rerouting of deportation studies through an idea of circulation do for us? On the one hand, I think it contributes to the call for scholars to look at displacement, migration, detention, and deportation together rather than as discrete experiences or distinct phases.[50] Rather than focusing on life in transit, or life after deportation, or life as undocumented immigrants, operating from a foundation of circulation encourages us to look at how the precarity of those who are in transit connects to the threat of deportation for the undocumented or liminally documented and also to a prior condition of exclusion, one that spills over into migration. Looking at deportation through the lens of circulation further shuffles the chronology, extends the geography, and de-segments the experience of migration. It also offers a stance in line with resisting the methodological nationalism that continues to run through much deportation and migration studies, which tends to analyze everything from the experience of the United States outward.[51] Thinking about deportation in terms of circulation allows us to start from life in Honduras or elsewhere, move outward from there, and back again. Circulation also encourages us to consider how migrant caravans emerge in response to an increasingly militarized approach to migration moving ever further south, so that migration is channeled into collective, public action, which further shapes the response and public sentiment. At the same time, if we look at migration from the vantage point of circulation, it directs us toward the circuit, the connections, the coherences across time and space. This book focuses on those who live this circulation, but as they move through displacement, migration, and deportation so, too, does the structural violence of exclusion and criminalization.

3 ¡Bienvenido a Tu Tierra!

Problems of Return, Reintegration, and Remigration

The first time I visited the Centro de Atención al Migrante Retornado, the center where adult deportees who are sent back to Honduras by airplane are processed, it was still a rather makeshift operation, a labor of love and vocation run by Scalabrinian nuns, a Catholic order dedicated to accompanying migrants. CAMR was housed in an old military airport, next to the country's busiest commercial airport, Ramón Villeda International Airport in La Lima, Cortés, just outside of San Pedro Sula. Soon after this visit, after Central American migration would start to receive more media and political attention from the United States and deportations to Honduras would accelerate (along with international aid and scrutiny), CAMR would become more institutionalized and better resourced. But in 2013, CAMR was doing the best it could for recently deported individuals with the intermittent governmental attention and limited resources it could piece together. On the wall, brightly colored, shiny letters—like the kind you might get at a party store to celebrate a child's birthday—were strung up. They read: ¡Bienvenido a tu tierra! Welcome to your land.

By 2017, the infrastructure dedicated to receiving, processing, and reintegrating deportees in Honduras had become much more developed: CAMR-Lima, for adults deported by air; CAMR-Omoa, for adults deported overland; and Centro Belén, in the center of San Pedro Sula, designed specifically for the processing of minors and their families. The Scalabrinians continue to run CAMR-Lima, while the International Committee of the Red Cross (ICRC) runs CAMR-Omoa, and Centro Belén is run by the International Organization for Migration (IOM), the UN-adjacent international organization dedicated to promoting "safe" and "orderly" migration. While the daily operations are managed by an international NGO, the centers are all under the infrastructure and supervision of the Honduran government. Each center now includes social workers, psychologists, a first aid team, and cell phone charging stations (with the IOM logo), along with police officers and government workers equipped to provide temporary identification for those who arrive without any official Honduran ID. There is also a small army of trained volunteers who do meticulous intake interviews. When a person fits a certain profile, these volunteers can refer them to the low-profile representatives from the UNHCR and the Norwegian Refugee Council (NRC), who are there to gauge the possibility of assisting people whose lives are in danger. The support they can offer is not exhaustive, and most people do not get referred to them, but in extreme cases they can sometimes intervene.

Above the door of Centro Belén a professionally made sign in cheerful lettering announces: *¡Bienvenido a tu tierra!* Welcome to your land.

The growth of the infrastructure designed to welcome, process, tabulate, and reintegrate Hondurans upon deportation reflects the heightened attention those who are deported have started to receive in recent years. In addition to the government and international organizations, a variety of NGOs have pivoted their own programming toward deportee reception in Honduras, both noticing a rising need and responding to the funding priorities of international donors. Broadly, these organizations aim to fulfill the words on the wall and on the sign, welcoming people back to their land by assisting them in reintegrating into Honduran society. But what does it mean to be welcomed back to a land that also made you leave?

In this chapter, I look at two primary areas of deportee-specific programming in Honduras, those aimed at education and those aimed at entrepreneurship, as each cluster represents a suite of interventions that the Honduran government, foreign aid, and NGOs promote as the antidote to remigration. The underlying logic motivating the design of these programs rests on the idea that deportees have needs, challenges, and limitations that derive explicitly from the condition of having been deported. In Honduras today, given the nature of the experience of deportation in the context of border hardening and externalization, people's post-deportation frustrations are often not particular or uniquely tied to having been made to return. Much of the programming designed for them, however, starts from the premise that what they need is *re*integration, into the educational system and into the economy.

Echoing the larger argument of the book, I highlight the *continuity* of experience before and after deportation in the realms of education and labor. Non-integration, a prior *lack* of integration, in the form of structural exclusion, marginalization, and criminalization, shapes daily life for many well before they try to leave, and this is the same condition that awaits them upon return. Consequently, adopting interventions designed to "reintegrate" those who have been away for a long period of time, to scare people out of trying to migrate, or to combat social stigma or structural discrimination based on deportee status fail in their aim of reducing migration. More importantly, exploring the flawed logic and limited success of these programs both demonstrates the changing nature of the deportation experience and illuminates the underlying existential frustrations that animate migration.

Education as a Site of (Re)integration

Profe Juan, a teacher from Rivera Hernández who works in a public school in another sector of the Sula Valley, is participating in a pilot program run by the Secretaría de Educación, or Ministry of Education, in conjunction with UNHCR and IOM. This pilot program is designed to educate students about the risks of migration and deter them from trying to leave Honduras again. Like many reintegration programs, the underlying goal is deterrence, preventing recidivism in migration. The program is being introduced first at a handful of schools in the Sula Valley; the Secretaría specifically chose the schools with the highest rates of students rematriculating after deportation. Juan's school is among them. I meet Juan at the initial training for the teachers who were chosen from each of these schools, and I ask him if I might shadow him on the day that he would teach the program lesson plan with IOM representatives.

A few weeks later, I sit in the back of Juan's classroom in a school on the outskirts of San Pedro Sula. Far from Rivera Hernández, this school sits in a hilly neighborhood at the far end of the long, paved road entering El Trébol. In Juan's classroom, we turn out the lights and start the video. A family on the screen recounts how the coyote they hired to take them to the United States stole their money and left them stranded. The movie ends with close-up shots of pained faces, fighting back tears, as each person says some variation of "If I would have known what could happen, I never would have left." It's meant to end with impact. The lights come up. The students are unimpressed.

The second activity is designed to combat stigma: The observing IOM employees assist Juan by sticking literal construction paper labels on the students' foreheads with masking tape. Words like "lazy" and "criminal" and "stupid" and "flirt" are written across the brightly colored sheets of paper. I watch as the students then walk around, interacting with each other, unaware of what their "label" is. They laugh at the words on their classmates' foreheads, snickering in the way that teenagers do at the more vulgar and suggestive descriptions. They are then directed to remove their cardboard labels and stick them on the blackboard at the front of the classroom. The IOM representatives try to lead a conversation, to get the students to talk about how they felt to be labeled in such a way, driving home the idea that labels are not *who people are*. The point of the exercise is to train young people not to see deportees differently, to see past those "labels." Once again, the students are politely aloof, disengaged without being disruptive.

This "lesson" is a battle for another context, from another time. Whereas in El Salvador, Mexico, and elsewhere deportees have dealt with the stigma of being seen as criminals,[1] this is not the situation at present in Honduras, especially not on the urban margins. Rather, most deportees are greeted with a mix of pity and outrage and worry *for them*. Rarely are they faulted for not having made it to their destination. People feel a collective sense of sorrow, but in a Honduras where deportation has become an increasingly common experience, it is not a defining or even particularly interesting feature for a young person. It certainly does not come with a stigmatized label.

Juan and I speak at length before and after these activities. Before we get to the school that day, he tells me:

> Voy a dar esta charla ahí, de que no se vayan los niños. Pero es una charla hipócrita, yo me siento hipócrita . . . Que venga el Gobierno y me diga, da una charla para que el niño no migre. ¿Pero qué oportunidad le da el Estado a este niño? No hay oportunidad. Yo me siento hipócrita . . . Vos le podés decir a la gente que la van a bajar los Zetas. Le vas a decir a la gente que se va a caer del tren, y se le va a caer una pierna. Le vas a decir a la gente que en Estados Unidos va a estar

presa en una cárcel . . . pero dice la gente yo prefiero eso a quedarme acá . . . me voy porque en Honduras descuartizan a la gente, la ponen a la orilla de la carretera en sacos . . . ¿Cómo yo le digo a un joven que no emigre, con qué autoridad moral?

I'm going to give this talk there, telling the youth not to go. But this is a hypocritical talk, I feel like a hypocrite . . . The government comes and says to me, give this talk so the children don't migrate. But what opportunity does the state give to this child? There is no opportunity. I feel like a hypocrite . . . You can tell the people that they are going to get taken by the Zetas. You tell them that they'll fall from the train, that they'll lose a leg. You tell them that in the United States they are going to be in prison . . . but the people say I prefer that to staying here . . . I go because in Honduras they chop people up, they leave them in sacks along the side of the road . . . How am I going to tell a young person not to migrate, with what moral authority?

He continues: "Si a mí, un niño me dice, 'Profe, yo me voy,' yo lo que puedo hacer es tomar su mano, si tengo dinero, dárselo, decirle que le vaya bien, que espero que Dios lo cuide, lo guarde en ese camino, y que llegue." (If a child comes to me and says, "Profe, I'm leaving," all I can do is take their hand, if I have money, give it to them, wish them well, and say that I hope that God protects them and takes care of them on this journey and that they make it.)

After the students file out of the classroom, and the IOM reps pack up their materials, get Juan's signature, and leave for the day, Juan reiterates his frustration and anger with this whole approach. Most of his students have family members who have left, have left themselves, or are in the process of planning to leave, he tells me. He's considered it seriously from time to time himself. They all know the risks; a video about bad coyotes or the dangers of migrating does not surprise, shock, or educate. These stories are already well known. Juan subtly points out a number of students who have already tried to migrate and have been deported. They are just waiting for the right time to try again, he adds.

Juan works at two schools, a private high school in the mornings and this public school in the afternoons. Like many private schools in Central America, Juan's morning school is subsidized by a religious charity and is aimed at serving a low-income population; even so, many of the families cannot afford the low monthly payments. Teachers and staff often go without their full salary; the buildings are in desperate need of repairs and updates. In Juan's classroom, the dropped ceiling is stained and breaking from unaddressed leaks. Still, the private school's situation is unquestionably better than the public school's, where teachers like Juan sometimes wait months to get paid. The buildings don't always have electricity; the bathrooms don't always work. Juan will often share his lunch with his students because they haven't had a full meal in days. He warns me before we get to the school that many of the children appear blond. It's not because they're actually blond, he says, it's a symptom of malnutrition.

Quality education is already inaccessible to many Hondurans, whether or not they have attempted migration. An average of 30 percent of the students who finish primary school do not transition to secondary school;[2] as of 2021, the illiteracy rate was 12 percent among adults over the age of 15.[3] Even public school, which is supposed to be free, can be prohibitively expensive for families with limited means. Students are responsible for buying their own uniforms, books, notebooks, and other school supplies. Frequently, their families must also pool resources to provide things like toilet paper and cleaning supplies to their children's classrooms. On top of this, teachers are often underpaid or irregularly paid and sometimes resort to charging their students for materials, raffles, trips, and other things that they invent to supplement their own salaries. Most of the deportees I know did not finish high school. A significant number of them only made it to sixth grade. Many of them cannot really read or write very well.

In nearly all cases, the reason for not continuing with school was because they and their parents simply could not afford it. This is reflected in statistics showing that matriculation rates drop from 93 to 52 percent between 11 and 12 years old, then down to 31 percent at 15 years old.[4] Forty-two percent of students between the ages of 6 and 14 who are not studying report "lack of resources" as their primary reason for dropping out.[5]

Programs designed to "reintegrate" deportees into the educational system after return do not address these issues. Rather, insufficient access to public education contributes to the decision to leave the country in the first place. Their status as deportees *does not make it harder* for them to get an education; access to education for poor youth was already elusive due to a combination of economic reasons, security reasons, and a lack of infrastructural commitment to and investment in educating all Hondurans. In 2018, I happened to be present, for example, when the two-room public elementary school of one neighborhood in Sector Rivera Hernández got electricity for the first time. The community had come together—pooling resources, materials, and technical knowledge—to install it; they got tired of waiting for the government to electrify their school.

Juan was skeptical of the IOM program from the start, but, like the other teachers who were part of the pilot program, he was not given a choice in the matter. The Secretaría de Educación signed on to the program, eager to take the funds from IOM and USAID that came along with it. This is also just one of the many areas where the Honduran government under Hernández proved to be willing to go along with the anti-migration agenda of the first Trump administration.[6] For Profe Juan and the other teachers selected for the pilot program, it meant a day of training and then choosing among five options of activities to replicate with their students. Juan chose the two activities that seemed the least objectionable to him, that would take the least time. It also meant IOM would provide him and his students with snacks on the day they came to his class. As with any organization bringing resources to his students, Juan saw real utility in that.

Juan, like all public school teachers, is employed by the state. But Juan, like most public school teachers (and principals), does not see himself as an agent or a representative of the state. Teachers frequently place themselves in opposition to the Honduran government, even as they are obligated to conform to dictates from the Secretaría de Educación. There is a long history of public school teachers being thought of as a "radical" element in society in Central America, and in Honduras, many of the principals I met, a generation older than Juan and his peers, were once Marxist-inspired student activists who then channeled those aspirations for a better world into education. Parents—including many of the community-minded ones I had come to know—would sometimes grumble that all teachers do is teach kids to protest.

In moments of social unrest, it is frequently the unionized public school teachers who form the backbone of protest movements. In 2019, for example, the Honduran government proposed "reforms" to education and health care that essentially would have fully privatized these public institutions. Notably, a powerful NGO, the Association for a More Just Society (ASJ) had recommended this "restructuring" project to the Honduran government.[7] ASJ receives substantial funding from USAID and had a particularly close relationship to the Hernández government. In response, teachers and health care workers—along with many others—mounted a month-long national strike that brought much of the nation to a standstill.[8] Eventually, the pressure succeeded in pushing the government to roll back the proposed reforms. Juan, like most of his cohort, sees himself as on the side of, as part of, the community—in opposition to a state whose presence is felt primarily if not exclusively as a corrupt, repressive force in their lives. They see the government as an entity in opposition to their role as teachers; the state wants to disinvest in education, with little interest manifested in making sure that poor Hondurans learn. Some teachers discussed this explicitly, almost conspiratorially with me, suggesting that the government would prefer for the poor youth of the country to remain ignorant.

Profe Juan turns to talking about his sector, Rivera Hernández, where he declined to take a position in the public high school because it would have meant crossing from his neighborhood into another neighborhood controlled by a different gang. But the larger problem with the local high school goes beyond the geography of gang control. Juan adds, "There's only one public high school in the whole sector, so there isn't sufficient teaching capacity to serve all the students, but with the aggravating factor that many of the young people cannot go to this school because it's in a specific zone," referring to the gangland neighborhood geography that shapes mobility in Rivera Hernández and elsewhere. Because of this, many families choose not to send their children to school at all once they reach high school age. Juan faults the state both for not genuinely working to ensure his safety and that of his neighbors and their children and for not building enough schools to adequately serve the population. It is not solely that the gang lines prevent some young people from attending high school in Rivera Hernández; it is also that, like elsewhere in Honduras, there wouldn't be enough space in the classroom for all of them even if they *could* get to school safely.

Field Notes

I show up at Jayson's house in Potrerillos to pick up the disposable film camera he has from a photography workshop.[9] His mother comes to the door and gives me the camera, but she tells me Jayson is just waking up. I make a good-natured joke about teenagers sleeping in—it's well into the afternoon—but she corrects me quickly, not wanting me to think ill of her son. "No, *viera*, it's because he was up

all night waiting to be able to register for high school this morning."
I'm confused, and she explains that this happens every year. He had
to stay in line all night in order to get a spot in the public high school
in Potrerillos. Registration started in the morning, but the *fila* (line)
began forming the day before. The teens camped out on the side-
walk. Like queuing up for concert tickets.

If he didn't get a spot—*si no hubiera cupo*—he would be out of luck.
He would have to wait until next year to enroll.

.　•　.

While I was surprised in the moment—and a bit embarrassed to have
made light of this young man making such an effort to enroll in
school—I would come to learn that the yearly battle to register for
school is well known. There are simply not enough public schools for
all the young people in Honduras, especially in the poorer, marginal
neighborhoods. Missing out on a spot means losing a year of schooling, unless the family has the resources to send their child to a private
school instead. This would not have been an option for Jayson's family, like many others. The seventeen-year-old had already been deported once. If he had not secured a place in high school that year, his
backup plan was to try migrating again. A year of idleness would be
too dangerous for a young man like Jayson. The boredom might get
to him, but more than that, that idleness would make him more visible to the gang in charge in his neighborhood. It would also make
him a likelier target for police attention.

I came to know Jayson through Pro-R, a program of Fe en Acción,
the premier organization working with deportees in the Sula Valley
in the post-2015 era. Pro-R based its programming around this idea:
If deportees could learn a skill, if they could be reintegrated into the
educational system and the labor market, they would be more likely

to stay. The Pro-R staff who carried out the day-to-day work of recruiting deportees, enrolling them in training programs, and following their "success" in the program did not wholeheartedly believe in the logic of this approach, but the international donors who funded the materials and their salaries were absolutely sold on the utility of short-term vocational-technical training and ensuring young people could get back into the educational system.

During the same period, a handful of other international NGOs started micro-enterprise and education-based programs in Honduras as well, aimed at helping deportees reenroll in school and catch up with their classmates,[10] or covering the costs of school supplies. In 2018, the Honduran government enacted a law guaranteeing school-age deportees the right to reenroll in the middle of the school year. Public schools were legally prohibited, then, from telling deported students that they would have to wait until the next school year, and teachers and schools would be sanctioned for discriminating against those who had been deported. Through another international donor, FeAc received funds to develop a partner program to Pro-R, focused exclusively on helping minor deportees get caught up in school. This program, however, was short lived as it could not find enough young people who fit their target profile to make use of the budget it had been allotted.

This new law in Honduras that guarantees the rights of deportees to reenroll in school does not help Jayson or his neighbors ensure access to registration. He risks exclusion from school in the first place, not because he was deported, not because the teachers might discriminate against him, but because there just is not enough space in the classroom for everyone in his area. A law designed to facilitate deportee reintegration in Honduras does not address the barriers to education that Jayson and others like him contend with—both before and after deportation.

The Reintegration Paradigm

"Reintegration" is widely used in post-deportation studies and post-deportation management.[11] The IOM holds that reintegration is essential, as it "empowers and protects returnees" and contributes to the "sustainability of return."[12] "Sustainability of return" is an optimistic way of saying that people who are sent back should (be able to) stay put and not (have to) attempt, again, to leave (their place in the international order.)

This commitment to reintegration is replicated broadly by migration-focused NGOs and governments. After 2014, when Central American migration captured the attention of the Obama administration, the US government increased support for "reception and reintegration" in Central America.[13] USAID dedicated millions of dollars to assistance in Honduras, funneled through the IOM, for programs related to reception, reintegration, and prevention through information campaigns.[14] The Honduran government echoed this focus. In an article announcing the support that Honduras would receive from the United Nations for reintegration programming, Ana García, First Lady at the time, who had taken on migration as her personal issue, was quoted as saying, "We are betting deeply on processes of reinsertion and prevention campaigns."[15] The Migration Policy Institute, a Washington-based think tank, has continually issued reports calling for and evaluating reintegration programs, insisting in the early days of the second Trump administration, for example, that support for robust reintegration programs in Central America especially must be maintained.[16]

The predominant language around what to do with deportees borrows heavily from the postconflict setting. Beyond and preceding their ubiquity in deportation discourse, the terms "reinsertion" and "reintegration" are commonly employed in the context of former combatants readapting to civilian life after a period of estrangement, as in the cases of former child soldiers,[17] demilitarized guerrilla fighters,[18] or the armed forces returning home from combat abroad.[19] The common threads that tie together reintegration and reinsertion include a substantial period of separation and an experience of removal from the normalcy of daily life so complete that it requires assistance, skill, and time to once again recover or remember how to live within that normalcy, whatever that may be. This understanding gets translated into the development of programming for deportees, based on a logic that the "problem" for this population is primarily about integrating individuals into a society who have been separated from that society for lengthy periods of time and whose embedded ideas of "normalcy" are consequently mismatched. Whether or not these programs are ultimately successful in that aim is another question, but the point here is that this is how their mission and their goals have been framed: helping deportees who have long been away from their countries of first citizenship to learn (or relearn) how to go about life there.

Scholars of deportation have argued for the need for better programs to assist the reintegration, reinsertion, and reincorporation of those who have been deported to the places where they have been forced to live.[20] Recognizing the historical role the United States plays, Katie Dingeman-Cerda and Susan Bibler Coutin, for example, suggest that the US Department of State ought to fund reintegration efforts in El Salvador to stave off growing violence.[21] Similarly, David Brotherton and Luis Barrios argue that Washington should, at the very least, help pay for the reintegration into the Dominican Republic of the thousands it has deported.[22] This intervention is needed because of the problems that occur when reintegration is not adequately attended to, as scholars have documented in detail the hardships faced by deportees who have grown up elsewhere and are sent back to unfamiliar countries of first citizenship. The challenges vary, but some deportees in this situation do not speak the local language with ease or "native" fluidity; some have the necessary language skills but do not know how to navigate social cues. Others find it particularly difficult to incorporate into the local labor market,[23] as credentials earned elsewhere do not fit into the system at "home," or their being tagged as foreign—whether linguistically, through dress and style, or literally through culturally taboo markers like tattoos—makes potential employers wary.[24] Another issue for some deportees has been one of schooling, getting children back into school or validating degrees earned in the United States or elsewhere to allow access to continued or higher education after deportation.[25]

These are well-intentioned, well-reasoned interventions, responsive to the conditions of deportees in those places at those times and grounded in a recognition of the historical responsibility that the sending country—the United States in most cases—holds for the conditions in which these deportees find themselves struggling. As this book shows, however, there is a substantial and growing population of deportees whose experience does not conform to the patterns that gave rise to these kinds of policy proposals; many deportees are returned to Honduras within months or just weeks of having left. Given this, the idea of reintegration programs—and their related supposed deterrent effect—are inappropriate at best and harmful at worst. Still, this approach predominates.

"Opportunities" for Deportee Entrepreneurs

"Fuiste deportado? ¡Tenemos una oportunidad para vos!" proclaims one of the glossy brochures distributed by Pro-R. (Were you deported? We have an opportunity for you!) One of the primary approaches of Pro-R, and many other deportee-serving NGOs, involves teaching young deportees a trade and helping the most dedicated students start up their own microenterprises. The IOM, for example, offers some direct support for microenterprise start-ups for deportees; the Lutheran Church funds a program in the rural department of Olancho that offers seed money to start small businesses there. The US Committee for Refugees and the International Committee of the Red Cross have each explored starting similar projects in Honduras, and USAID was eager to fund other international NGOs that operate with a similar logic. This reflects the wider neoliberal economic rationalization that, as anthropologist Shahram Khosravi writes, inflects deportation management logics everywhere, "using economic incentives to turn a failed asylum seeker in the host country into a prospective business owner in the country of citizenship."[26]

With Pro-R, deportees could learn how to cut hair, paint nails, fix cell phones, bake bread, repair air-conditioners, and a host of other similar skills. The course offerings would change periodically, but they generally involved a half-day session once a week for about eight weeks. The skills training was accompanied by a series of workshops that focused on building self-esteem, learning some of the basics of "employability," and general life skills. All the students would get to keep the very basic "kit" that they were given to use while learning their chosen trade, but the promise of potentially being offered a full suite of materials to start their own small business was dangled as a carrot for all the people who enrolled in the courses. The best students, those who showed the most commitment, responsibility, drive, and aptitude, were sometimes given this *capital semilla*, which would come in the form of in-kind start-up materials—a salon chair, for example—rather than cash.

While the program offers many other positive experiences to the young people who enroll—they get to go on a handful of field trips, for example, and there is a psychologist on staff to work with the participants who need mental health support—the project is, at heart, an entrepreneurship program. The organizations that fund it are counting on the premise of encouraging young people to see business ownership as a path toward being able to stay in the country. This particular program is not USAID funded. Rather, it is supported by US-based church foundations (the Evangelical Lutheran Church and the Mennonites, chief among them), and the tenets of the gospel of prosperity inflect the shape and goals of the program.

In addition to a broader critique of an operating logic that suggests that getting out of poverty is a question of individual choices, there are particular problems with the idea of organizing an intervention specifically around encouraging deported young people to start their own microenterprises in Honduras. First, echoing the exclusions referred to in the preceding section, the reality is that many of the deportees the program targets have had very little in the way of formal education. Second, the very idea of opening up a business in their own neighborhoods might pose an existential problem: If they open a store, for example, will they be calling too much attention to themselves, will they be made more vulnerable to extortion demands from the gangs that control where they live? Some of the young people in the program simply include *renta*, as the extortion payments are known, as part of the costs of doing business. A young man in a Barrio 18 neighborhood in Choloma, for example, opened up a small restaurant with the help of Pro-R. They took me to visit it, and he showed me the books he kept. Renta was included as a cost, alongside the electric bill and the bushels of plantains. For others, however, entrepreneurship does not address the reasons they had left the country in the first place. It exacerbates them.

Franklin learned how to cut hair when he was incarcerated for immigration violations in the United States. After his first deportation he tried to make it back to the United States but fell ill while in northern Mexico and decided that since he was in no condition to make the border crossing, he would turn himself over to Mexican immigration agents and be sent back to Honduras. He intended to recuperate and try migrating again, but he got involved with Pro-R and decided to try and make a go of it in Honduras. He was delighted to learn that through Pro-R he could get an accredited certificate in *barbería*, turning a skill he had first picked up in detention into a career. The Pro-R staff saw that Franklin was talented and driven and decided to give him the capital semilla, the basic necessary equipment to open up his own barbershop in Los Cerros, his neighborhood in Choloma's Sector López Arellano.

Getting to Franklin's barbershop isn't easy. The roads aren't paved, and there's a steep incline that turns into a mudslide whenever it rains. When I finally make it there, he is bursting with pride to show me around. With the help of his father, he has built a small, corrugated metal room on the edge of a motorcycle mechanic's plot of land. He has to pay the mechanic to rent the space, but the location is good, he tells me, and the men waiting to get their motos fixed are easy clientele. His prices are low, he's open seven days a week, and he is full of hope that his business will be a success. His first investment will be an air-conditioning unit, as the metal room becomes sweltering under the Honduran sun and blowing fans and hair cuttings make for a bad combination. He started seeing a girl who works in a salon, and their dream is to open up a joint barbershop-salon one day somewhere more central, more formal. Maybe in a mall.

A few weeks after I visit him at his barbershop, I receive a panicked text message from Franklin. "Amelia, I'm sorry, I have to go. They're going to kill me." And the next day, he is in Mexico. Via Facebook messages here and there, Franklin tells me the story: The gang that controls Los Cerros had noticed him. His tattoos (from the time he was previously in the States) initially caused suspicion, though he assured them that he had no gang affiliation, and for a while the tension had abated. However, his barbershop was located in a different but adjacent colonia from the one where he lived with his family. Having a small business and crossing neighborhood lines put him further on their radar, and this led to renewed doubts about his allegiances and intentions. The threats resumed and increased.

He decided he had no choice but to flee, leaving behind his beloved barbershop. He was really worried that Pro-R would think that he hadn't been serious about his business, but he was too scared to stay. Once in Mexico, Franklin hears that the same night he left, the gang that had threatened him killed another young man, thinking it was him.

Franklin's story highlights a fundamental disconnect inherent in programming that treats the condition of being deported as specific and distinct from society at large rather than starting from an analysis of the root problems that spur young people like Franklin to see migration as their only option. Franklin had the skills, the infrastructure, and both the familial and NGO support to become a small-scale entrepreneur in Honduras. He certainly had the dream and the drive—in a sense, he was better equipped to be a successful entrepreneur than most. Still, the basic situation of insecurity for a young man in a poor, urban neighborhood made realizing that dream impossible. Going to the authorities was not an option that ever occurred to Franklin; he was regularly harassed by the police who patrolled his sector. He trusted them even less than he trusted the gang that was after him.

Tierra de Nadie: Criminalization and Structural Non-Integration

Field Notes

Late at night, Benjamín and Gladys from Vista del Cielo message me: "Do you know Mariela, Doña Licha's daughter? Her boyfriend, Henry?"

"I don't think so."

"The military police arrested him and beat him up."

"What can I do?"

"Well, it would be good to go to the police station."

I get into my car, pick them up, and they direct me to the station where Henry is being held. It must be after 10pm. Once there, we fight with the officers, bring up the violation of human rights. At first, they say it's too late at night, no visits. Then, well, maybe a phone call. No, no phone call. Then, talk to the *fiscal* or the *abogado*. Then, no, they're in an *audiencia*. Wait, an officer asks, what country are you from? The US. Then back to no visits. Then human rights. Then I know it's not your fault but . . . then . . . all of a sudden, they offer to bring in the father of Henry. He's like—no, not me—I already talked to him. Her. Have her go in.

The officer balks. No no, that's too much. He goes away briefly. When he comes back, he says, "OK, let's go." So I walk through the courtyard toward the cells. He seems to expect me to know where to go. I don't. I giggle nervously. I've never been here before.

"You know there are protocols," he says. "Just like in the US. There are protocols." "Absolutely," I say. "Thank you so so much."

And then he just leaves me to find the prisoner and talk to him.

The cells are dark, the air heavy with the smell of urine. There are no windows and no lights. All I can see are the silhouettes of skinny young men. How many? I don't know. I approach one cell . . . there is just a doorway with bars. I say into the darkness, "I'm Mariela's friend. I'm Doña Licha's friend." No one stirs.

I get to the second cell, the middle cell. Again, I say who I am, and a young man approaches the barred doorway. Henry recognizes me.

Now that I'm here, I'm not sure what I'm supposed to ask. I think I'm here mostly to send a message, so the police know this particular young man is not without friends in the world. I ask to see the bruises on his arms. He extends his wrists through the bars, and even in the meager light I can see the purplish marks on his skin.

I keep talking until the police officer suggests it has been long enough. Henry recedes into the darkness, and I walk back across the concrete courtyard into the San Pedro Sula police station.

. . .

Eighteen-year-old Henry, from Vista del Cielo, had been arrested the day before. The military police took him into custody while he was working at a mototaxi stand in La Newton. They put him in the back of their pickup and drove around for a while, while Henry sweated under the hot sun. Then they picked up another young man, in another neighborhood, while he was working at a barbershop. They took Henry and the barber to police headquarters, where the officers aggressively forced them to take photos with the drugs that the police would later say they had found with the boys. The police were clearly not worried about literally leaving marks on the bodies of these young men, counting on their structural exclusion to render them subjects of little concern in judicial proceedings. Later, in court, the charges would say the police had caught both men, together, in the act of selling drugs. Despite a host of witnesses to refute this assertion, both young men were sent to the adult men's prison for *prisión preventiva*—pretrial detention—to be held while the investigation and trial went on, which could legally be up to two years. Henry, the barber, their family and friends, and even the state-appointed lawyer who was initially responsible for their case doubted their chances of beating the charges, clumsy and fraudulent though they were. The lawyer threw up his hands as I probed. "Surely there must be some way to get the judge to see their innocence," I insisted. His response was to tell me story after story of the grave injustices he had seen carried out; lament how hard they make his job (he's only allowed to present one witness); suggest we file a report with the Human Rights Commission, which might get a response in a few years; and make a not very kind joke about how we could protest—burn tires in the street—but then they might really just kill Henry. While I was surprised and rather offended by the lawyer's glibness, Henry's parents were not. They thought their best chance at protecting their son was making sure the police knew that a foreigner would be paying attention to what happens to him.

The residents of areas like Rivera Hernández are familiar with being treated in this way by the authorities. Henry Giroux argues that the criminalization of poverty is tied to the rise of a neoliberal, "punishing" state, where extreme poverty is rendered a "pathological condition" rather than a consequence of "structural injustice."[27] Adrienne Pine uses the term "neoliberal fascism" to describe the resulting mix—where the state expands in terms of militarized security forces to "punish" the criminal/ized poor while receding in all areas of social welfare, thus leaving the poor ever more vulnerable and ever more suspect.[28]

Henry did maintain a good relationship with the local pandilleros. He did sometimes use his mototaxi in service of favors they asked of him. Had he refused, had he positioned himself as antagonistic to their power and rule, he would have at the very least put his continued residence in his home and his ability to keep working at risk. At worst, he would have put his life in danger. This friendly proximity to gangs is a necessary stance for one's own survival, especially for young men like Henry, but it is also what makes the police certain that all young men in a given neighborhood like La Newton are *really* criminals, whether or not they are guilty of a particular crime in that moment, whether or not they've committed any crime *yet*.

This criminalization of poor youth, however, isn't always as directly or obviously violent as that experienced by Henry. This exclusion, this lack of integration, extends into smaller ways that the authorities interact with young men as well.

Arám is also from Vista del Cielo. He's eighteen years old and is an amateur Christian rapper. Aware of the dangers awaiting a young man like himself, he rarely leaves his mother's house—only to work and go to school. He once started seeing a young woman from the next neighborhood over—both places controlled by the same gang—but it still made his mother too nervous, the idea of her teenage son crossing neighborhood lines, so the relationship ended before it could really get started. His father and younger sister left for the United States a few months earlier, and Arám hopes every day that his father will send for him soon. In the meantime, Arám spends most of his free time in his room, writing song lyrics, sending Whats-App messages back and forth with his friends, who are all tucked away inside their own homes. He likes to spread positive messages about believing in yourself and having faith in God. He says that even if he's feeling lonely, he likes to try to uplift other people.

One day, on his way to school, the police stop him. They interrogate him. They speak to him using the hyper-familiar *vos*, which, he stresses, they would never have done if he were from a different, wealthier neighborhood. "Vos," in Central America, is used in place of "tú" as the second-person, informal pronoun. In Honduras, its usage is classed and regional, where urban, middle-class young people adopt "vos" when speaking among themselves more frequently. Especially among people from lower socioeconomic classes or rural parts of the country, however, "vos" is used exclusively among people who are very close with each other, often not even then. Using the formal *Usted* is common, even within a family. The Pro-R brochures referenced earlier, written using "vos," are aiming to capture the buddy-ness of cool, urban, young people talking to each other. No person in a position of authority would address a civilian for whom they had any respect in this way. The police at the checkpoint in Rivera Hernández and elsewhere never use "vos" with me.

"I'm on my way to school," Arám told the police.

"¿Vos estudiás?" (You study?), they asked him, incredulously.

"And I go to church," he added. "I'm not a criminal."

"¿Vos asistís a una iglesia?" (You go to church?)

"I even sing Christian music," he added.

"Oh yeah? Sing us something."

Arám was livid and embarrassed, "like I needed character references just to walk down the street," he says. The way those officers spoke to him, the humiliating disbelief that *he* could be a student, a person of faith, really stung. The palpable lack of respect the police officers showed him is what hurt the most. Their use of "vos" immediately placed them above him in the social structure, although they were young men not that much older or more accomplished than himself. Police in Honduras are never stationed in the neighborhoods where they come from, and their uniforms, position, and power encourage them to see Arám—and young men like him—as beneath them and always potentially their enemy. Essentially, the way the police view young men from neighborhoods like Rivera Hernández is that they are all potentially and inherently criminal.

Gladys recalls going to the police station to speak up for a different young man a police officer had taken into custody. She was sure it was a mistake. "He's a good kid," she told him, "He's a Christian!" The officer's response stayed with Gladys. "Here there are no Christians," he snapped back. "Aquí todos son diablitos." (Here, everyone is a little devil.)

Profe Juan also notes this broad criminalization of young people in their neighborhoods by the agencies that should, in theory, be there to guarantee public safety. He tells me:

Por ejemplo, este gobierno, estaba la Policía Nacional, montó la Policía Militar, montó la Policía Tigres, montó la Policía ATIC, montó la Policía DPI, y ahora monta la policía anti-maras. Seis policías nuevas, más la policía que ya estaba. ¿Y por qué la situación de riesgo, de violencia y de peligro no cambia en el país? A lo que voy, yo siento más bien que la persecución es contra la juventud de Honduras. Yo siento que hay una persecución contra la juventud de Honduras.

For example, this government, there was already the National Police, [then they] added the military police, added the "Tigres," added the ATIC, added the DPI, and now adds the "anti-mara" police. Six new police units, in addition to the police that already existed. So why doesn't the situation of risk, of violence, of danger change in the country? What I'm getting at is, I feel that actually the persecution is against the youth in Honduras. I feel that there is persecution against the youth of Honduras.

Juan answers his own question, suggesting that the proliferation of policing in Honduras is designed to persecute youth, not protect them. Profe Juan, as he rattles off the new police units formed under then-President Hernández, in fact undercounts the total number of police units in Honduras at the time. By 2019, they totaled seventeen, with the recent addition of a new unit tasked with policing former officers who had been relieved of duty.[29] There are multiple configurations of interagency forces, all aimed, ostensibly, at dealing with the country's organized crime groups and all widely suspected of being involved with those same groups.[30] People in the colonias talk of seeing police officers with gang tattoos on their bodies, of police officers disappearing youth, of police officers spraying over one gang's graffiti with the insignia of a rival gang. César, a bus driver in Choloma, tells me his bus cooperative was being extorted by three different gangs, and when the gangs wanted to raise the extortion amount, the cooperative went to the specialized anti-extortion police force. The officers from this elite police unit told the members of the bus cooperative that they should probably just leave the country, ask for asylum in the United States. When the bus cooperative members said they were not interested in leaving, the officers then acted as middlemen, negotiating down the extortion demands directly with the gangs. César was astounded. The police clearly knew who the extortionists were, they had direct contact with them, yet did nothing to intervene.

In addition to the police, the military has been increasingly involved in policing the civilian population in Honduras, all in the name of combating the maras y pandillas. The military police (Policía Militar del Orden Público, PMOP) are essentially army units stationed in civilian neighborhoods and used to patrol the residents. Barracks housing fatigues-clad soldiers have sprung up in sectors like Rivera Hernández, Chamelecón, and López Arellano. This was a special project started by Hernández when he was president of Congress in 2013, before ascending to the presidency, and the PMOP has since become an entrenched feature of Honduran policing. While their presence is supposedly meant to combat organized crime, when I ask a pastor and community leader from La López if their presence has made things better, he responds emphatically, "No, no no no no no. It makes us feel like we're at war. But who's the war with? Who are we at war with? . . . There's a war, there's a war between drug cartels. There's a war between narcos. But are we at war? . . . With them patrolling the streets, it's like they're at war against us. It's like their war is against us. Is against the *pueblo*." Against the people.

He continues: "Si vivís en tierra de nadie, si venís de tierra de nadie . . . if you live in no-man's-land, if you're from no-man's-land, what are you going to do if you can't count on anything, if you can't count on the institutions?" He adds, "You know there are some people who would prefer to deal with the criminal, the *delincuente*, cause at least you know what you're getting. But with the police, you don't, you don't, you don't."

When the Honduran government and the many NGOs with whom they contract welcome deported people back to "your land" (tu tierra), it is this "tierra de nadie" that actually awaits them. The

FIGURE 2. Military Police stationed in front of a neighborhood in the Sula Valley, Honduras, 2017. Photo by author.

people who grow up there, in this densely populated no-man's-land, are structurally outside of society, outside of its institutions, as the pastor indicates. This exclusion, this inability to be able to count on anything, shapes the extent to which young people are able to feel a sense of belonging, of integration, in the country. Rather than a feeling of coming home, then, many young Hondurans are returning, *reintegrating*, into a place that is, as the pastor describes, no-man's-land.

On the Limits of the Logic of "Reintegration"

Flaco is thin and short, but he carries himself with the energy and posture of a tall, imposing man. He's just twenty-two when we meet, and he has recently become the highest-ranking member of the gang that controls Vista del Cielo.

I meet Flaco through Benjamín, Glady's husband. Benjamín had become one of my closest interlocutors, explaining all manner of things to me, setting up interviews for me before I even asked. Benjamín teaches the local kids basic skills; he gathers them into a soccer team. It's all very low profile, very grassroots, and every activity he engages in is always done with the approval and consent of El Barrio. When he approaches them about a new idea, they sign off, saying yes, "Si es para el bien de la colonia." (If it's for the good of the neighborhood.)

Benjamín won't get involved with any USAID-funded initiatives, precisely because USAID always comes with the police. Like many, Benjamín is deeply distrustful of the police. In addition to that general mistrust, he and Gladys operate very carefully, always with the approval and inclusion of the pandilleros—and their children—in their activities. He can only continue with his projects if the gang is on board, but, more than that, he knows that the gang and the community are intertwined. None of his ideas will ever go very far if he draws a bright line between gang-involved youth and everyone else. In Vista del Cielo, like most gang-controlled neighborhoods, that line is blurry and porous. Benjamín sees his survival, and that of his children and his neighbors, as inextricable, one from the other.

Vista del Cielo has a reputation for being one of the most dangerous colonias in Honduras, and because of this it has become one of the neighborhoods that gets a steady stream of journalists looking for gang graffiti, guns, and tattooed youth. Benjamín decided to help me, he said, because I was the unusual visitor to his neighborhood who came without a police escort or a pastor, who came alone. That showed him something: first, that I wasn't going to share information with the police, which meant I could be trusted, but also, more importantly, that I wasn't scared of him and his children and his neighbors. I was just following my anthropological instincts, searching for spaces, moments of "deep hanging out."[31] I hadn't anticipated how much it would matter, how this would be read as breaking with the quiet indignity of being residents of a neighborhood that gets ample attention from foreigners who, though fascinated, never quite trust the people there enough to interact with them without protection.

When I ask Benjamín if he thinks one of the pandilleros who run things there might speak with me, he offers to ask Flaco. Flaco was newly in charge in the neighborhood, but he had been around for a while, and Benjamín knew him to be a reasonable, smart, and strategic young man. "Ah, ¿la del carrito rojo?" Flaco immediately answers when Benjamín asks whether he might be willing to speak to me. "The girl with the little red car?," referring to the red-orange hatchback I had in Honduras, making it clear to Benjamín, and to me, that the gang knew very well about my comings and goings. So far, my presence had not been a problem for them. My distinctive car and sustained presence without police were both choices I made early on to make sure the gang knew that I was there and that I was not trying to hide anything from them. Flaco agrees to speak with me.

I interview Flaco for the first time while he's *punteando*, standing guard at the entrance to the colonia. He's got an earphone in one ear, and he is constantly interrupted by his cell phone. Benjamín introduces us, then backs away, leaving Flaco and me to speak privately. Every time we see headlights coming, Flaco recedes behind a kind of half fence, enveloping himself in the darkness. I wait and think to myself, "Now I understand why they tell you to do cambio de luces when you drive in these neighborhoods." It never made sense to me in daylight, but at night it serves as a clear indication that you're not police if you're driving around with your flashers on. You're not trying to enter the neighborhood unnoticed. I had always done it, because I had been told to, but it is only here, standing at the edge of the neighborhood where there are no streetlights and seeing headlights appear out of nowhere, unsure if they would be friendly or hostile, that I really understand the importance of those blinking lights at night.

The first interview is short and hasty, but over time Flaco and I develop a friendship. The real war, he explains, is with rival gangs. His gang is not at war with the police, but the police come after them, so they fight back.

"No me voy a dejar de matar de alguien, me entiende, pudiendo defenderme. Y peor de la policía porque la policía lo que hace es matar o golpear, si te agarran." (I'm not going to let someone kill me, you understand, being able to defend myself. And even worse if it's the police, because the police what they do is kill or beat [you], if they get you.)

He goes on to tell me about multiple times the police have picked him up, when they found him sleeping and tied him up and beat him. When the police show up in Vista del Cielo, as they often do, they go after Flaco but not to arrest him on official charges. One time they grabbed him in the middle of the night and left him in a rival neighborhood, counting on the gang there to eliminate him. A major storm hit, and Flaco was able to escape back to the relative safety of his own neighborhood, but a lot of young men—gang members and unaffiliated "civilians" alike—are not so lucky.

He tells me, "La policía dice que nosotros molestamos a la gente, pero la verdad nosotros no molestamos a nadie, sino que nosotros cuidamos." (The police say we bother people, but the truth is we don't bother anyone, on the contrary, we protect.)

Flaco asks me if I have any children. I make a joke about my not-so-young age and tell him that I do not yet have kids, and I ask him, in return, if he does. I mean the question to show him respect, but I'm still a little surprised when he says yes, he has a son, a toddler. But he doesn't have his son with him, he immediately adds, explaining, "Vive aquí cerca y pasa con su mamá. Porque Ud. sabe que los hijos tienen que estar con la mamá . . . y con el papá también. Pero en este caso Ud. sabe que no puedo estar yo con mi hijo porque es un mal ejemplo." (He lives close by and spends his time with his mother.

Because you know that children have to be with their mom . . . with their father too, but in this case you know that I cannot be with my son because it is a bad example.) I ask him, "¿Así lo piensa?" (That's how you see it?) "Sí, o sea, a mí no me gustaría que agarre este camino . . . A nadie se lo deseo." (Yes, well, I mean, I wouldn't want him to take this path . . . I don't wish that for anyone.)

I meet up with Flaco in the daylight a few days later, and we share a coke in the backyard area of a pulpería. A few of his *jomis* walk through as we sit there and talk.[32] They acknowledge him, he acknowledges them. They nod, recognize his rank, give him space to speak with his guest. They are all gaunt, like Flaco, with serious expressions and piercing looks when they acknowledge me. Flaco asks me, fascinated, earnest, "Is it true that in the United States there are pandilleros who live to be thirty, forty years old?" He's already escaped death a handful of times, and the idea that he could live another ten or twenty years seems as extraordinary to him as living another hundred.

Flaco expects to give his life for his gang and, as he sees it, for the defense of the colonia. Flaco emphatically does not want his own child or other kids to join his gang. He tells me when young kids start showing interest in joining, he counsels them against it. And, I gather, kids who do join have to really want it; they have to be all in. He wishes he might have had a different life, but he's proud of the protection they provide, keeping the neighborhood "safe"—as they see it—from outsiders, intruders, thieves, petty criminals, and, most importantly, rival gangs, the gangs that come from different colonias.

Flaco is also a quintessential product of the iron-fisted antigang approach in Honduras. Flaco's "pretrial detention" put a young, low-level gang member in maximum security prison for two years alongside the highest-ranking leaders of his gang. He had been arrested, officially, for stealing cars. He laughed when he told me. "They could have gotten me for so many other things, but stealing cars? Amelia, I don't even know how to drive."

Never able to prove their case, after two years or so, Flaco was released without a criminal conviction. He came out of jail with points, knowledge, and credibility, however, moving him up in the ranks of his gang. There was a need for new leadership in Vista del Cielo. The previous leader had recently been arrested, and things were chaotic. Flaco was tapped to step in. It is a lot of responsibility, and though Flaco is proud of his reputation among the residents, things soon take a turn.

Not long after Flaco and I meet, he learns that he is going to be punished for a series of mistakes he made. His gang's discipline is strict and unforgiving, and he is convinced that they intend to kill him. Flaco had already survived one serious, corrective beating. His only option, he decides, is to flee. He stays with his mother in another municipality for a few days, but his presence puts everyone there at risk so, reluctantly, he makes his way toward Mexico.

If Flaco is deported back to Honduras, what kind of "reintegration" would be available to him, would be appropriate for him? He's a smart young man who joined a gang when he was barely a teenager. It wasn't exactly forced recruitment, but neither was it a choice made free from pressures and coercion. A choiceless decision, perhaps, but a decision, nonetheless.[33] He would rather have stayed in school, he would rather have found well-paying work, but those were not options available to him. He tells me, from somewhere in northern Mexico, that if he's deported, he won't have the chance to flee again. They'll take him straight to prison—and there, his former jomis will kill him. "Ni horas sobrevivo" (I won't survive even a few hours), he tells me with a humorless chuckle.

As far as either of us are able to determine, there are no real programs or assistance of any sort for young people who wish to leave the gang behind, save for evangelical groups that may promise salvation by trading one kind of fanaticism for another. Flaco tells me that if he could have stayed in school, then maybe he would have had a different life. He would have liked to have had a different life. He hopes his young son will have a different life. But by the time I meet Flaco it is too late for him to have a different life in Honduras. His choices have constricted even further. He joined the gang to belong to something, to not be a burden on his mother, to protect his neighborhood, to feel powerful—and for many other unarticulated and perhaps inarticulable reasons. He didn't regret joining; he *loved* his gang. And even though he knows that a different life would have been better, a different life never seemed available to him, and he devoted himself to his gang brothers. The fear he felt when his life was in danger was almost dwarfed by the hurt he felt at the betrayal, that this organization that he had given his life to, that he was willing to give his life for, was now going to end it. Before Flaco leaves Honduras, he sends me a long WhatsApp message, trying to make sense of his story and the conflicting feelings he has regarding his life and his future. He writes about himself in the third person, ending with: "Y ahora no puede ser alguien más porque él ya tenía el destino marcado. Esta es la historia de un pandillero que está a punto de morir." (And now he can't be anyone else because he already had his destiny marked. This is the story of a pandillero who is about to die.)

Imagining More Than Reintegration

Flaco's situation brings the discussion of (re)integration into greater relief. He is not the person that the government or the NGOS are talking about when they tout receiving deportees with open arms, when they welcome them back to their land. He is already excluded, long before he leaves Honduras, and, in fact, he specifically points to lack of access to education and dignified work as the decisive factor that pushed him toward the pandilla as a preteen. An adult now, his chances of being able to settle anywhere are slim. Because of his criminal history in Honduras, he would be ineligible for the most stable form of protection in the United States (asylum), while the stigma he carries with him makes him unlikely to prevail if he sought the other, more tenuous forms of relief from deportation. At least without very good representation—though many lawyers are less interested in taking on the cases of those who might be less sympathetic in the eyes of a US immigration judge. His destiny, as he puts it, is already marked; he can no longer be anyone else. Before leaving his country of citizenship, Flaco is always already deportable, even though deportation means certain death. In this way his story is the extreme, perhaps, but contains the same contours as that of Franklin, Henry, or Juan's students. They are already deportable, already looked at as criminals as though they were Flaco, simply by virtue of growing up alongside him (or people like him), or because they come from a place where young men like themselves could become pandilleros and sometimes do.

Arám and Flaco are opposites in some ways, but they are alike in being stuck within their neighborhoods, marginalized because of where they are from, and limited in the options that lie before them for their future. This is, perhaps, the clearest manifestation of the non-integration that young men living on the urban margins in Honduras experience. They are already viewed as potentially criminal, always already exterior to society. This condition mirrors the way that those exiled deportees of an earlier generation were treated because they were presumed to be both criminal, because of their deportation, and other, because they had grown up elsewhere. Rather than treatment that arises in response to one's status as a deportee, however, it is a condition that exists before migration for urban young men and continues after deportation, largely unaltered because of the added layer of having been deported.

The focus on "reintegration" as the primary need of deportees contributes to masking the inherent violence of deportation. If deportation is framed as returning people to where they belong, then it does not seem to be a matter of uprooting families and banishing them but returning everyone to their proper place.[34] If the sending countries, like the United States, also assist in the "reintegration" of those it forcibly returns, then there is little reason for those who have been deported to not stay "home." Reintegration efforts led by NGOs, both national and international, focus on the individual as the unit to be assisted, instead of taking an approach that recognizes that what is needed, for the most part, is collective and structural.[35] After or before deportation, non-integration is not a problem that can be solved by short-term, individualized, or purely economic interventions.

Furthermore, for many Hondurans, it is precisely this experience of non-integratedness, of already being outside, that fundamentally shapes the move to migrate in the first place. Given a situation of prior exclusion, the fact of deportation does not create a *new* kind of outsiderness for deportees once they are sent back to Honduras. They are returned, rather, to precisely the same situation from which they had tried to flee, life marked by an existential lack of integration. Until that changes, programs and policies aimed at "reintegration" will continue to fail both at easing the pressures of life for deported Honduran youth and at deterring them—or anyone—from migrating.

Indeed, in the communities where I spent most of my time in the Sula Valley, the overwhelming feeling was that most people were one step away from leaving at any given time. One more family member loses a job or falls ill, someone will leave. One more death threat makes its way to their ears, they leave. The neighborhood changes hands from one gang to their rivals, people leave. The new police in the zone are heavier handed then those they replaced, people leave. People are constantly teetering on the brink of leaving, and one additional piece of straw (or drop of water, in the equivalent Spanish expression) tips them over the edge. This is to say that hundreds of thousands of Hondurans are already potential migrants, and the conditions of daily life determine day to day how many of them go that route, at that moment.

When Franklin and the thousands of young men like him are deported back to Honduras, they do not feel out of place or unfamiliar; it is not that they do not know how to survive in their country of birth because their knowledge, skills, and instincts were formed elsewhere or adapted to a different context. It is, rather, that a lack of inclusion and protection—a condition of non-integration—already made life precarious for them, before they ever left. That precarity, that exclusion, is at the heart of why they left. And it is why they will leave again. Not to get back to the life they were torn away from, but to have a chance at imagining another possible life.

Arám, despite his determination to share positive, uplifting messages with those around him, also limits himself for the future he allows himself to imagine. One day he tells me, "Sometimes, I think, man, who am I going to become? Who will I be one day?"

I ask him, "Well, what do you see for yourself?"

"*Es difícil*, Amelia . . . It's hard. I don't know . . . . Because of where I was born, because of the family I have . . . it's hard, Amelia. It's hard to know what future I can even imagine for myself."

This points us to another fundamental flaw in the logic used to design the migration-prevention programming centered on reintegration. Small-scale microenterprise support, basic skills training, or even the support to reenroll in school does not alter the situation where young people understand their position as one that does not offer the possibility of dreaming.

Years ago, the first time I climbed aboard a freight train in Mexico with a group of Central American migrants, I learned an important lesson. As the train barreled across Oaxaca, I was overwhelmed by the beauty of the scenery, the exhilaration of feeling the wind on my face.[36] I leaned over to Carlos, a young man from El Salvador, and said, "I feel kind of bad about this. For me, this is a kind of adventure, while for so many it's a necessity." He gave me a sly smile and said, "No te creas, Amelia, para nosotros también es una aventura." (Don't be so sure, Amelia, for us this is also an adventure.)

Carlos's words resonate back in Honduras, as I see program after program focused on preparing entrepreneurs, offering vocational-technical training, aimed at fitting people back into a life that already felt limited, constraining. For example, the director of FeAc gently rejected a suggestion to help returned young adult migrants who never finished high school get into the equivalent of a GED program. They need jobs, they don't want to study, he explained.

The economic needs of those who migrate are serious, absolutely. I do not dispute this. But I think that this approach misses what migration also offers to poor, marginalized, young people, especially those moving between living encuevado and risking their lives by moving around too much. Migrating is not just a chance to make money, or to simply survive; it is also a chance to see the world, to experience things, to feel independent, to have an adventure, to break out of the circumscribed options available to young men, especially those from neighborhoods like Vista del Cielo and La Libertad, and to allow yourself to imagine an expansive future. Organizations that fund NGOs are unlikely to support projects that describe migration as an adventure or provide programming designed around cultivating big dreams, but an approach to addressing the needs of those who have been deported, of those who are considering migrating, that takes this into account, might be more successful at convincing young Hondurans that it is not only possible to survive if they stay, but that staying could be full of possibility.

4　*Alerta que Camina*

Migrant Caravans and Transgressive Mobility

From the Estadio Benito Juárez the border wall looms large. It's close enough that the late-night lights of the baseball field illuminate the steel slats. The United States is close; it *feels* close, hovering just beyond the bleachers, just beyond the highway, just beyond the canal. You can see the Stars and Stripes, waving in the not-so-distant distance.

When the migrant caravan arrives in Tijuana at the end of 2018, the city first sends them to Estadio Benito Juárez, and the baseball field becomes a makeshift refugee camp. After a few weeks, as the camp spills over onto the streets around the stadium, and in the wake of a chaotic protest march that ended with some caravaneros trying to breach the border and tear gas being launched from the United States into Mexico, the city decides to relocate the encampment to a place, they say, that is better suited to the needs of the caravaneros: El Barretal, a large, concrete esplanade, usually reserved for massive outdoor concerts, way on the other side of Tijuana, on the outskirts of the city. Farther from the wall. But many of the caravaneros are reluctant to relocate. They want to stay close to the wall; they want to be able to *see* the border. If a miracle is going to happen, one woman tells me, she wants to be there for it.

While the caravan has been mentioned in the preceding chapters, here I turn to the caravan as a phenomenon and as an idea directly.

Much of the scholarship that has sought to analyze migrant caravans takes the events of 2018 and their replicas in early 2019 as unique moments in the history of undocumented transit migration across Mexico, focusing on the novelty and difference of this cluster.[1] I have been part of migrant caravans as some combination of observer, volunteer, activist, accompanier, researcher, and ethnographer since 2011. This relationship to migrant caravans puts me in the position of having both the possibility of and perhaps the responsibility to discuss them. In this chapter, then, I am less interested in thinking about caravans as new or particularly distinct from other migrations and instead want to explore their history and meaning for what this can tell us about migration more broadly. This collective, hypervisible migration movement encapsulates the culmination of and is a legible window into many of the dynamics I attempt to lay out across this book.

I was present for one of the first migrant caravans in January 2011, helped organize a second phase of that caravan in summer 2011, and then accompanied multiple caravans of various kinds in 2012, 2013, and 2014.[2] I joined the 2018 caravan for pieces of its journey, from Arraiga, Chiapas, to Juchitán, Oaxaca, and then spent a week in November and a week in December 2018 with the caravan-turned-encampment in Tijuana. I was there the day many protesting caravaneros tried to make a break for it and breach the US border wall and were met with Mexican police and US forces firing tear gas into Mexico. I spent Christmas with the caravan.[3] Adding to the growing body of caravan-centered scholarship, then, I draw from this long-term entanglement with caravans across space and over time to make sense of, give depth to, and narrate the context of the caravan that grabbed the world's attention in 2018.[4]

I have discussed throughout this book how people circulate through processes of displacement, migration, detention, and deportation while also stressing that violence, marginalization, and strategies of survival circulate as well. I add here that the idea of group migration, a caravan, as a way to get through hostile space and at once protest against the structures that produce that hostility, has also circulated over the years, along with the young people who criss-cross Mexico and get sent back to Honduras and elsewhere over and over again. Despite the spectacular novelty of caravans for many observers (politicians and journalists among them), caravans have a deep history and build on preexisting networks, forms of movement, and migrant knowledge.

Caravans coalesce in response to conditions on the ground, in the moment; these conditions—mobility control, interdiction, policing, criminal control of territory, and so on—also shift and evolve in response to the presence of migrant protest and tactics. The interplay among these opposing forces produces the possibility of moments of mass, collective migration movements. This is not a linear shift from one kind of migration to another but rather an ongoing, iterative social process embedded in the changing entanglements that people experience as they move through displacements, detentions, and deportations. Sometimes, in order to keep moving, they protest/migrate along the way. In the words of anthropologists Nadia El-Shaarawi and Maple Rasza, who have documented similar interplays in migration in the Balkans, caravans can be thought of as "movements upon movements," where "a demand and a concrete practice of freedom of movement" becomes social movement.[5]

Caravans Are Coming

The 2018 caravan pushed its way into Mexico and international headlines right in the middle of the fieldwork I was conducting in Honduras. I was in La Ceiba, on the country's northern coast, when news broke of a few hundred people gathering at the San Pedro Sula Bus Station to migrate together toward the United States. While HCH,

Honduras's twenty-four-hour, everything-is-always-breaking-news station, unsurprisingly covered the caravan in superlative, crisis-laden terms, I did not think much of it at first. Caravans were not, despite what the breathless reporters said, big news.

A few months earlier, I had been standing on the rooftop balcony of the building housing Fe en Acción (FeAc) when I got a call from a longtime immigrants' rights activist in Mexico. He wanted to organize a big caravan, he told me. He knew I was in Honduras; he wanted me to lend a hand. I brushed him off. I had too much work to do, research plans to complete, and at the time I felt like I already knew caravans—their scope, their power, their meaning—well enough. Over the years, I would receive calls like this from Irineo from time to time;[6] he was always organizing something, pulling together protests, events, caravans. Sometimes they took off; sometimes they didn't.

I had first met Irineo at a shelter for migrants in Arriaga, Chiapas, in southern Mexico, just a few days after New Year's in 2011. I walked into the shelter's dining room, which had been turned into a kind of center of operations and introduced myself to him. He greeted me with a warm hug, as though he had been expecting me, as people from the shelter for migrants in Ixtepec, Oaxaca, had told each of us about the other. I was a somewhat new researcher/volunteer/activist, who had been coming to the Ixtepec shelter for just a few months, but I had been swiftly folded into the shelter's small team. Irineo was a relatively well-known activist (at least within migration circles), friend of the shelter, sometimes photographer/photojournalist, who had gone on a hunger strike to get his camera equipment returned to him after he photographed federal police violently raiding a train and assaulting migrants.[7] He chained himself to the Instituto Nacional de Migración (INM; National Migration Institute) offices in Puebla, Mexico, and eventually got a little bit of justice and his equipment— memory cards included—returned.[8] A photo of Irineo's that showed a uniformed police officer with baton-wielding arm raised high in preparation to strike a cowering migrant, all in the shadow of the train tracks, became emblematic of the abuses of authority against migrants in Mexico. After this, Irineo became a kind of small-scale folk hero and an ardent believer that righteous suffering and press attention move those in power.

December 2010 had been a particularly alarming period in Oaxaca for migrants. The execution of seventy-two migrants at a ranch in northern Mexico in August of that year brought international attention and scrutiny to the violence migrants faced.[9] While receiving less press coverage, two mass kidnappings had taken place in the state of Oaxaca in southern Mexico, and the shelter volunteers had documented a pattern of assaults that invariably involved some of the local police units. People were arriving in Ixtepec, the first stop on the freight train lines in the state of Oaxaca, with bruises and wounds and trauma, telling stories of beatings, robberies, and brutal abuse on their way there. In addition, both the priest who founded the shelter in Ixtepec, Padre Alejandro Solalinde Guerra, and Alberto, a young Guatemalan man who coordinated its operation and was becoming a well-known defensor de derechos humanos, had received alarming death threats.[10]

In response, a small group of activists, Irineo among them, put together what would become this migrant caravan. Irineo was joined by Elvira Arellano, a young woman who had become well known among migrants' rights activists for publicly seeking sanctuary in a church in Chicago in order to protest and challenge an order of removal. Documentaries had been made about her and her fight;[11] folk songs had been written about her.[12] Despite her campaign's initial success, she was eventually made to return to Mexico, and I was a bit star struck upon encountering her among the small group of activists organizing this protest march out of Ixtepec. Irineo and Elvira were also working with a young Mexican activist who had once been undocumented in the United States himself and who would later become a key figure in the migrants' rights movement in Mexico, especially in the search for missing migrants and the reunification of families. They consulted closely with Padre Alejandro and Alberto—and I just happened to be there and got pulled into the planning and execution.

They called it "Paso a paso hacia la Paz"—Step by step toward Peace.[13] The activists gathered in Ixtepec understood something fundamental about the violence with which undocumented people everywhere contend. It is a direct consequence of the fact that, in order to evade immigration enforcement, migrants frequently try to avoid detection, becoming as invisible as possible by staying in the margins, away from the light. This strategy, however, can be rife with danger, as those who would exploit migrants' vulnerability thrive in the darkness. The activists—drawing from Irineo's hunger strike experience and Elvira's protest actions—reason that accompaniment by human rights activists, clergy, journalists, academics, politicians, and community leaders, by people who are not in danger of deportation in general, would help undocumented people move across a stretch of Mexican territory more safely. It would also be a protest, meant to bring visibility to the issue of the violence facing migrants, decry the immigration policies of the Mexican and US governments, and demand that the human rights of all people, regardless of immigration status, be guaranteed. Step by step, they imagined, they would walk toward a more peaceful future.

Their initial plan was to accompany the migrants from Arriaga, Chiapas, to Ciudad Ixtepec, Oaxaca, riding with them on top of the freight train. The train company, however, got wind of the planned protest and moved the train's schedule forward. There was no train to be ridden from Arriaga north on the intended day.

When I arrived in the *comedor*, Irineo and the others gathered around the table were discussing what to do instead. The best plan at the moment was for everyone to walk the eight hours from Arriaga to Chahuites, the first town the train passes after crossing from Chiapas into Oaxaca and the town where many assaults on migrants had taken place. Though an eight-hour walk along the rail lines in the dark seemed like a daunting prospect to some (myself included), the migrants who were at the table were not deterred. Then word came that we would be given transportation—at least as far as the next state. Padre Alejandro, the priest from Ixtepec, had arranged with the governor of the state of Chiapas to come to Arriaga, greet the migrants at the *albergue*, the migrant shelter, and provide transportation to get the entire group safely to the border of Chiapas and Oaxaca.

At this point, we were hundreds of people. This action, if any money was to be used to pay for the transportation, could have been construed as illegal under Article 66 of the Ley General de Población—the Mexican law governing migration matters at the time. This potential legal issue caused a momentary hiccup, but Padre Alejandro made the case quite plainly to a member of the governor's team. "I understand the law," he told him. "But tell the governor it will be more of a risk politically to not let us do this."

Within an hour a small fleet of large vans arrived, along with the governor and his wife and journalists from a variety of Mexican news outlets. There was a pleasant photo-op, a short press conference, and then all the activists and migrants piled into the vans and headed for Oaxaca. The vans dropped us off just before crossing the state line. After waving goodbye amicably to the drivers, we set off on foot, to complete the walk to Chahuites.

.   .   .

Spirits are high. I find myself walking along the highway next to Alberto, who had already been deported four times from the United States but was outraged after being assaulted by law enforcement on his way through Mexico on his fifth attempt. His sense of injustice inspired him to stay in Ixtepec and file complaints against the police.

He turned his personal anger into a vocation and would go on to encourage and support many other migrants to seek justice for crimes committed against them. Walking down the highway at night, Alberto's full of that righteous anger, almost giddy with the feeling of triumph as we march past an immigration checkpoint. Led by Elvira Arellano with a megaphone, we sing:

Si tuvieras fe como un granito de mostaza
Eso lo dice el Señor.
Tú le dirías a la migra,
muévase, muévase, muévase
y la migra se moverá, se moverá, se moverá.

If you had faith like a little grain of mustard
This is what the Lord says
You would tell them, tell the migra,
Get out of the way, get out of the way, get out of the way
And the migra will move away, will move away, will move away.

In Chahuites, the tired but triumphant caravaneros are greeted with warm food at a local parish and are given an empty auditorium to turn into a dormitory for the night. The next day, there are press conferences held and *comunicados* written. More transportation is arranged, and the three hundred or so migrants who happened to be in Arriaga at the moment of the caravan make it to Ixtepec safely. Once there, the gathered migrants regroup and then go their separate ways, returning to their individual networks and plans. And the caravan as an idea, as a possible way to navigate the rough terrain of Mexico, goes with them.

I describe this first caravan for a few reasons. First, a narrative account seems to be missing from the record, and I find myself in a position to offer my experience. Second, this caravan, of a few hundred people walking a few hundred kilometers, is one of the seeds that germinates and eventually produces the possibility of the moment in 2018 when thousands of Central Americans collectively cross Mexico. And third, the emblematic elements of this first caravan—a mix of a practical tactic of mobility and a protest, the shift from invisibility to hyperinvisibility, and its emergence as a response to the collateral violence of immigration enforcement—become part of the repertoire of migration. The idea of the caravan as a possibility, as a tool, circulates through the circuits of migration (and detention and deportation) along with the people who constitute it.

In the world of transit migration in Mexico, the tactic starts to become familiar: When people hoping to migrate get stuck somewhere, when the road ahead becomes especially treacherous, or the costs (both economic and otherwise) too high, people come together and form a caravan. The strategy often worked as Mexican authorities, as well as organized crime groups, did not quite know how to deal with unapologetic yet still unauthorized migration, buffered by human rights activists. Scholars recognize the fundamental fact of the caravan as a way for people migrating to collectively protect themselves from both detention and deportation and the myriad dangers faced when trying to evade detection by staying in the margins and moving through the shadows.[14] The caravan is intentionally, defiantly hypervisible, turning the typical logic of clandestine migration on its head, finding safety in attention and in numbers, seeking the limelight rather than the shadows to facilitate unauthorized movement.[15] This turn takes everyone by surprise and forces a corresponding reorganization of the tactics of deterrence. In the space provided by that moment of reset and reorganization, the caravan advances.

In chapter 2, I wrote about the shifting terrain of immigration enforcement in Mexico, as the United States pushes its bordering logics ever farther from its territorial boundary, and, as a consequence, the dangers for people in transit multiply. As this process unfolds over time, people are not only detained and deported more frequently and earlier in their journeys; they are also, always, inventing new ways to circumvent and challenge the obstacles to mobility.

Caravans-as-Protest and *Las Luchas Migrantes*

Over the years since the first caravan in 2011, there have been many more migrant caravans, expanding in size, demands, and the extent of territory covered. I participated in organizing a second caravan in 2011 that focused on decrying the kidnapping of migrants in Mexico.[16] After an audience with a Special Rapporteur from the Interamerican Human Rights Court in Tierra Blanca, Veracruz—the epicenter of migrant kidnappings at the time—many of the caravan participants decided to stay together and go all the way to Mexico City. Once there, after protesting in front of government actors, the caravaneros were able to get a *salvoconducto*, a thirty-day transit document that allowed everyone to keep crossing Mexico without fear of deportation.

In 2012, when a railroad bridge collapsed near the port city of Coatzacoalcos, Veracruz, stranding migrants there for weeks, human rights activists showed up and organized the waiting migrants into a caravan, collectively making it past the broken-down bridge, finding safety in their gathered numbers and press attention. In 2014, there were at least three back-to-back caravans, starting with the Viacrucis turned caravan of Holy Week that year. Over this period, other protest movements in the public imaginary got translated into a caravan in the migration context: Toma la Bestia (Occupy the Beast, as the freight train is often called), a migration-related spinoff of the Occupy movement; Los Migrantes Tambien Estamos Hasta la Madre (We Migrants Are Also Fed Up), a gesture to the movement against the drug war–related violence in Mexico; and Los Migrantes Somos 132 (We Migrants Are 132), a reference to student protests directed at then-presidential candidate Enrique Peña Nieto in 2012. In 2014 and

2016, two small caravans made up of migrants who had lost limbs during previous migration attempts, crossed Mexico together, as a group, to raise the issue of the "mutilation" of migrants by the freight train and then sought asylum in the United States.[17] Smaller caravans of queer-identified migrants have also formed to cross Mexico together and cultivate safety from myriad dangers and exploitations, including those at the hands of other migrants and actors within the shelter-based migrant support infrastructure.[18] In all these actions, activists and migrants gathered, moving forward on the migration journey together, bringing attention and press to the plight of migrants but also advancing toward their goals. Caravans, with this dual aspect, become the shape of migrant protest.

Caravans also become a familiar idea among people on the move. Whenever migrants gathered and started to feel stuck in one spot, the idea of a caravan would emerge as a way to, collectively, get unstuck. Sometimes the activists from 2011 or others like them initiated the strategy, but, increasingly, it was the people migrating who started to talk about doing a caravan to get across some part of Mexico. Just like that early caravan, the tactic resurfaced in response to the changing contours of clandestine immigration across Mexico. As crossing becomes more difficult and more violent due to heightened enforcement, new fights over territory between organized crime groups, or the overwhelming of humanitarian infrastructure leading to years-long wait times, people who are trying to migrate band together and, drawing on this now-lengthy history, form a caravan.

Beyond the specific context of migration, the caravan-as-protest has a long history in Mexico; the idea of people coming together and traversing long distances to bring attention to their cause is not new. In 1951, the Caravana del hambre (Caravan of Hunger) saw four thousand striking miners and their families walk from their home in the northern state of Coahuila to Mexico City.[19] Over the nearly two months it took for them to reach Mexico City, these caravaneros were supported by the solidarity of people along the way while also having to contend with the attempts of authorities to thwart their progress.[20] In Mexico City, they met acclaim and repression, eventually returning to Coahuila defeated but having left a mark on Mexican social movements.[21] Since then, across time and region, striking workers, Indigenous rebels, students, peasants, and peace activists have implemented the caravan-as-protest as a tactic to showcase different kinds of suffering and to pressure the Mexican government.[22]

The migrant caravan draws on this long repertoire of caravans-as-protest as well as the broader landscape of what scholars have called *las luchas migrantes*,[23] or the migrant struggles, indicating a larger, transnational fight to recognize a right to migrate as well as the struggle and resistance of those who migrate. This landscape in Mexico includes a network of shelters, mostly affiliated with members of the Catholic Church.[24] Within this infrastructure, also drawing on a longer history of Catholic-linked social protest, the Viacrucis del Migrante—Migrants' Stations of the Cross—emerges as a method to bring attention to the plight of migrants, drawing from the Catholic repertoire of reenacting the Stations of the Cross during Holy Week, leading up to the crucifixion of Jesus. Organized first from the Catholic-led shelter spaces, the Viacrucis places the migrant as protagonist, with a cross-bearing migrant at the helm, demanding that Mexican Catholics and society at large see the face of Christ in the migrant's suffering.[25] Priests and nuns who draw on the gospel to proclaim the righteousness of protecting migrants work in tenuous and sometimes contentious communion with anarchist activists, human rights NGOs, and civil society organizations. Going back to at least 2011, the Viacrucis del Migrante has been a recurrent public act of faith, vigil, and protest, and at certain moments it starts to merge with the onward movement of the caravan-as-protest.[26]

In 2014, for example, the Viacrucis del Migrante expanded into a caravan that ended up with around a thousand people staging a sit-in in front of Los Pinos, Mexico's presidential residence, demanding freedom of transit. The caravan started from a shelter in Tenosique, Tabasco, where the Viacrucis had become an annual event during Holy Week that attracted activists and journalists from across the country, staging a powerful, public reenactment of the Stations of the Cross along the town's train lines. Usually, after Holy Week concluded, the gathered migrants would each go their own way. In 2014, however, the train refused to move, and the group of migrants who happened to be there at the time decided to advance, together, *en caravana*. This caravan inspired replicas, and, foreshadowing what would come in 2018–19, over the course of two months more caravans were organized. During these caravans, activist accompaniers started to work with caravaneros to prepare for the asylum process in the United States. Since 2014, many Viacrucis del Migrante (though not all) have become caravanas, and the terms bleed into one another in coverage and analysis, especially as some factions within the migrants' rights coalition in Mexico preferred the language of Viacrucis and the religious righteousness it conferred to the unruly caravan.

Another thread of the luchas migrantes that contributes to the circulation of the caravan as an idea within migration is a long-standing "caravan" of Central American mothers who organized themselves to travel to Mexico to search for their children who had disappeared while trying to migrate.[27] In El Progreso, Yoro, Honduras, Hemeteria, Rosa Nelly, and Edita had each experienced the ambiguous loss of a family member when a child left home with the intention of making it to the United States and was never heard from again.[28] In the late 1990s and early 2000s, this experience was becoming increasingly common in Central America, ushering in a new era of disappearances from the migration context.[29] Hemeteria, Rosa Nelly, and Edita first tried to get answers and action from their own government in Honduras—where they were roundly dismissed.

Drawing from another long-standing Latin American history of protest, mothers searching for their disappeared children, the three women formed Cofamipro, the Comité de Familiares de Migrantes de El Progreso, Yoro, (Committee of Families of Migrants of El Progreso, Yoro). Their challenge was novel, however, as the context of disappearance was different: Their children went missing while engaging in clandestine migration, moving through Mexico in a context where invisibility is often cultivated, where people often strive to strategically disappear themselves at least for a moment in order to evade detection. Given this complication and the fact that their disappearance happened outside the bounds of Honduras, the Honduran government easily washed its hands of responsibility; the mothers decided to take their fight to Mexico. In the first caravan, a small group of mothers from Cofamipro journeyed together to Chiapas and tried to knock on doors of churches and shelters to see if anyone could give them any answers about their children.

Over the years, the caravan of mothers grew. Committees similar to that of Cofamipro formed in Guatemala, El Salvador, and Nicaragua, and a Mexican organization, the Movimiento Migrante Mesoamericano (Mesoamerican Migrant Movement), joined forces with the Central American committees and started organizing bigger, longer, and more comfortable annual caravans. While increasingly including other family members, it has retained the moniker of being a caravan of *madres*, turning into a yearly pilgrimage "to raise awareness of the brutalities of the migrant journey by physically retracing the steps of their missing loves ones."[30] These caravans—and this idea of winding one's way through Mexico to make demands on the Mexican state—contributes to the growing familiarity with a caravan as a rebellious, turbulent, and effective feature of transit migration in Mexico.

Since 2018, caravans have captured the attention of many scholars, especially in Mexico, producing a new, robust body of literature. The caravan has been theorized as a "transnational social movement on the move" or "coalitions in motion."[31] Many authors start from 2018–19 and then look back at antecedent events, attempting to fix a clear, linear, evolution—from Viacrucis to caravan, from religious symbolism to human rights movement, from protest to mobility tactic.[32] While their work reconstructing a history that was little documented in real time is worthwhile, the backward-looking perspective allows for a misrecognition of the preexisting entanglements of every element. The caravan has always been both protest and mobility tactic; the Viacrucis and the Mothers' Caravans intertwine with the caravans-as-protests to shapeshift and merge branches. Religious leaders and civil society groups and anarchist no-borders activists are always already in contentious coalition, resulting in a tension that sometimes bubbles to the surface over the meaning and merit of caravans.

In 2014, during the Viacrucis turned caravan, I was part of a small meeting during which the head of the Catholic Church's Pastoral de la Movilidad Humana at the time, Hermana Leticia, turned to Padre Alejandro, the same priest who had been the protagonist of the early caravans, and admonished him, saying, "These are your flock, Alejandro, they need you to lead them." He had been grumbling about this iteration of the caravans, doubting their efficacy, frustrated with the unruly and insistent drive to move forward. He eventually agreed to accompany a subsequent, "surgical" caravan whose intention would be to get to Mexico City and meet with policy makers to lobby for reform. The priest was convinced of this idea; many of the migrants who had found themselves in Ixtepec as this caravan gathered were not. While they were enthusiastic about the idea of calling on the Mexican government to change policies, they also wanted to move forward in their journeys. Walking together, with this famous priest at the helm, seemed to them like a good way to advance. As this caravan left Ixtepec, Irineo was already in Tapachula, gathering another group to form a new caravan.

Exodus, 2018

Arriaga is bustling. There's so much more activity than the last time I was in this small city in Chiapas for a caravan. Then we were a few hundred, gathered in and around the parish-affiliated shelter a few blocks from the train tracks. This time, when I connect with the caravan, the central plaza looks like a cross between a music festival and a refugee camp. Later people would estimate around seven thousand people made up the caravan at this point. The atmosphere is bristling with energy. People are setting up makeshift tents, stringing tarps from park benches, careful to leave the sidewalks clear. The caravan has been moving together for a while at this point, and they've already got a kind of template for how they set up in a new place. Local groups arrive to give out food, and street vendors find eager buyers for their wares among the caravaneros. There is such an outpouring of solidarity that caravaneros laugh that they eat better as part of the caravan than they did at home.

As I walk through the gathered crowd, which is just starting to settle in for the evening, I run into a familiar face. Omar had been a participant in the FeAc programming for deported youth in San Pedro Sula; I met him during a visit to one of their cycles of barbería courses. He had been the star of the class, but the support offered by FeAc wasn't enough to get his own business really going and—I learned that evening in Arriaga—he had decided to leave Honduras for a second time. He was already in Tapachula when this caravan movement arrived, and he thought he would join in to get across Mexico. A little while later the gathered caravaneros hold an *asamblea*—an assembly, a form of direct-democracy decision making where everyone who wants to can participate as much as they want—to decide what their next steps will be. The president of Mexico at the time, Enrique Peña Nieto, had made them an offer: work visas in Mexico in exchange for staying in the southernmost state, Chiapas. The caravaneros unanimously reject the president's offer and decide instead to keep going. They will leave for Oaxaca the next morning, starting out at 3 a.m., with the hope of advancing many kilometers before the sun gets too hot. The next town is Tapanatepec, in Oaxaca, 44 kilometers away. That's where they'll regroup.

As I try to get a few hours of sleep that night, I am struck by how much I am reminded of that first caravan; both these roads and the constant negotiation between repression and welcome have become familiar to me in the intervening years. Yet much is different: There is a blueprint now for how this works. There are veteran migrants—like Omar—who are part of the caravan; there are also veteran caravan organizers in accompaniment. Irineo is here again, but a whole new generation of migrants' rights activists are as well. The *auto-gestión*, the self-organization, of this caravan is notable. People have formed committees, by department in the case of Honduras, by country for the rest of Central America, and the committees have appointed spokespeople to engage in the asambleas and general decision making. There's a security committee too—they wear flimsy neon vests—made up mostly of veteran caravaneros, migrants who have made this journey, in this way, previously and know each other and what the road ahead may hold. And, of course, the sheer numbers. The feeling of massive collectivity is like none of the other caravans I had been part of in the past, and this makes the whole movement feel more powerful, more inevitable, than any previous caravan.

After a few hours of restless sleep, I head out on the dark highway to scout the road ahead. I have a rental car this time (another substantial difference from 2011), and a few of us have gone ahead of the groggy caravaneros who are starting to stumble toward Oaxaca. The trajectory the caravan is intending to cover today includes a long, remote stretch of highway, the same stretch that the governor of Chiapas had provided vans for us to cross in 2011. Just before we reach the border between the two Mexican states, we hit the obstacle we were hoping not to find: a blockade. There's a line of riot police waiting for the coming caravan, looking very much like they are ready to do battle.[33] The human rights commissioner from the state of Chiapas is also there—and he whispers to me, urgently, "Get the press here." I am able to post a few tweets, send a handful of WhatsApp messages before the cell phone signal disappears. I suspect—as do the Mexican activists who are there—that the police have blocked the signal; we reason that the police do not want anyone to witness what they are planning to do. At least not in real time. It's a familiar tactic used against direct action protesters, but since we are in the middle of nowhere, it is also entirely possible that the internet has just cut out.

Some press and human rights defenders arrive. They make a line, linked arm in arm, to mirror the line of police in riot gear. When the first group of caravaneros start to arrive, they do not engage in confrontation or try to push their way past the blockade. Instead, they sit. More people arrive; they sit. As the sun starts to come up over the mountains, there are people filling the highway, as far back as my eyes can see. They do not react to the blockade with aggression, but neither are they deterred. This seemingly spontaneous sit-in is the product of the asambleas held the nights before—and the product of the caravans-as-protest that have been happening for nearly a decade. The crowd appoints spokespeople—two men and two women—to go negotiate with the police. They know their direction from the decision made last night: The caravaneros will not accept any proposal that keeps them in Chiapas. They might each have different individual destinations, but they were all in agreement on one goal: onward.

I don't participate in the negotiations. I talk with the waiting crowd. We compare neighborhoods we have in common back in Honduras; we make jokes about how we could have gotten a few more hours of sleep. Some people do nod off. The committee returns and, using a megaphone, announces the deal: The police will distrib-

FIGURE 3. The caravaneros respond to the police blockade by sitting and waiting, Chiapas, Mexico, 2018. Photo by author.

ute information about Enrique Peña Nieto's proposed plan, and the caravan will be allowed to proceed. Slowly—with the sun now bearing down overhead—the caravan heads forward once again. One of the negotiators, Lucas, climbs into the car with us and almost immediately falls into a deep sleep. He had been a police officer in Honduras, a true believer in the rule of law. He was fairly new, very young, and had been removed from duty as part of the *depuración*—purge—of the police force that happened in 2016. While the purge was touted as a tool to combat corruption, it was done with suspicious secrecy. Lucas says he was targeted because he was honest and would not get involved with or cover for the corrupt officers around him. He gave up, decided to leave, and found himself in the caravan.

I stay with the caravan through the next two towns—Tapanatepec and Niltepec—saying goodbye to them after a few days in Juchitán.

I'll rejoin the caravan later, in Tijuana, but it is in Juchitán where I get to know Edgar, a taxi driver from the Tegucigalpa area who had been deported many years earlier from the United States and who had become the head of the caravan security committee. Edgar is so high profile as part of the caravan that he later gets an *alerta migratoria*, immigration alert, placed on him by the United States and is deported back to Honduras despite having legal presence in Mexico. I host him for a few days in San Pedro Sula before he starts the walk north again.

I meet Juan David, a budding economist from San Pedro Sula, who was blacklisted for his anti-JOH protest activity after the 2017 electoral fraud. He gets labeled a *ñángara*, a communist, a *revoltoso*, someone who stirs things up, and he can't get hired anywhere. "I believe in the capitalist system," he tells me, "just not the people who are applying it in my country." He had also been identified by the gang that controlled his neighborhood as a gifted student, and they wanted him to go to law school, for them. He declined their offer. Juan David settles in Tijuana and starts a family. He had thought about applying for asylum in the United States, but the possibility of getting deported terrified him. "If I'm sent back," he tells me, "I'm a cadaver."

In Juchitán, I take Rey with me to buy supplies for the new encampment at a big-box store. As we push a giant cart up and down the aisles, he tells me how he and his wife were getting threats from the gang that controlled their neighborhood in La Ceiba—threats that were increasingly targeted at their three preteen daughters. They had been saving for a coyote but decided to try their luck with the caravan when they saw it on the news. Rey and his family part ways with the caravan in Mexico City, and I don't know what happens to them after that.

I find Omar again in Juchitán and wish him luck, hoping that he fares better on this, his second try. A few months later, I'll pick up Omar when he's deported for the second time and take him to the Gran Central Metropolitana, the Sula Valley's transportation hub, so he can exchange the voucher they gave him at CAMR for a bus ticket and make his way home, again. He's exhausted but already saying that the third time he'll make it.

When I make the mountainous drive from the isthmus to the airport in Oaxaca City, my heart feels both full and like it is breaking, all at once. There is so much hope in the air around the caravan; there is also so much suffering. More than one caravanero has been injured and died in traffic accidents; many people are ill. There's a *tos caravanero*, a hoarse, wet cough, going around. A group of nuns have been providing first aid in the caravan encampments along the way, but there's never enough supplies and it's hard to stick to a medical regimen while walking for hours on end and sleeping on the ground night after night. I'm prescribed antibiotics once home in Honduras.

The enduring image of the caravan is lines of people walking, slowly, along the highway. Shuffling, limping, on blistered feet, in shoes that are too small. Women in flip flops. Flip flops! Pushing baby carriages along the highway. And they just keep going.

One boy is wearing high-top sneakers, like knock-off Converse, black. They appear to be in good shape. I ask him about his shoes. He says, good-naturedly but not as a joke, "If I take these shoes off you don't want to see my feet . . . if I take these shoes off, I won't be able to put any shoes back on again ever."

Anthropologist Julie Kleinman, in her discussion of migrants as adventurers, encourages those of us who study migration to propose new models and narratives based on the way in which migrants themselves understand what they are doing, why, and what it means.[34] Hondurans do not typically use the language of circulation that I use throughout this book; however, there is a growing shift in how people talk about their own, channeled mobility. The discourse around and from migrant caravans highlights this. From 2011 to 2014, the multiple caravans that occurred called for *libre tránsito*—freedom of movement—and involved the frequent chanting of slogans like, *Los migrantes / no somos criminales / somos trabajadores / internacionales.* (The migrants / we are not criminals / we are international / workers.) By 2018, there were arguments about whether it was even appropriate to call the caravan a caravan; both internally and externally, the word *exodus* was sometimes used in replacement or in addition.[35] The committees formed by the caravaneros to negotiate dubbed themselves the Comité de Diálogo del Éxodo—the Exodus Dialogue Committee—and people started referring to the entire endeavor as the *caravana del éxodo*, the exodus caravan. The exodus, however, extends beyond the caravan and includes all the people who are looking to leave Honduras every day in less visible ways.

An important feature of thinking about one's own migration as exodus is the kind of biblically derived righteousness with which an otherwise illegalized form of mobility becomes imbued. Unauthorized migration has historically been most "successful" when done on the margins and in the shadows. In Mexico, most people who engage in it try to make themselves as invisible as possible in order to make it across the country. One migrant explained his own approach to migration to me as such years ago: "I enter Mexico, and I prepare myself to be invisible." The clandestine nature of migration in this context pushes people into shared space with other illicit actors, contributing to the idea that migration itself is criminal. The language of exodus turns this around and constructs those who are attempting to move across foreign territory as following a higher law. Migrants frequently remind us, *Dios no hizo fronteras*, God did not make borders. In the caravan, instead of keeping a low profile and moving along the literal margins, this ethic of a higher right to migrate is made manifest as migrants walk into the town square, en masse, and negotiate accommodations and aid, as equals, with authorities.

This language of exodus reflects how those who migrate from Honduras feel about their movement, its motivations and meanings. The ongoing, unwanted circulation I identify in the experience of

Honduran deportees in this book is not presented as a counterpoint to the affect of exodus that infuses out-migration but rather to complement it. Exodus implies a mass movement outward that is compelled but blessed, perhaps even divine; circulation describes what people who have engaged in exodus experience when they are forced back to where they started. If people think about leaving their country of citizenship as a kind of exodus, how could they do anything else but leave again (and again) if—and very likely when—they are made to return?

Alerta que Camina (Warning on the Move)

Someone cups their hands around their mouth and starts the chant, extending the middle vowel sound:

> *Aleeeeerta*
> *Aleeeeerta*
> *Aleeeeerta*

It has the same effect as a siren might, alerting everyone within hearing range. Those who hear join in as the pace of the familiar protest chant picks up.

> Alerta
> Alerta
> Alerta que camina
> La lucha del migrante
> Por América Latina

> Warning
> Warning
> Warning on the move
> The struggle of the migrant
> For Latin America

In this version, the chant alerts the world around the marchers to the struggle of migrants, a struggle done on behalf of, to save/protect/improve, Latin America. But "migrants" is just one version; that part of the chant can be switched out for any protagonists of social struggle: students, workers, women, all on behalf of Latin America (which rhymes with "on the move" in Spanish). The "on the move" part, in other contexts, would make reference to the movement, the social movement, and the march during which the chant is repeated.

Transposed to the context of the migrant caravan, where social struggle and literal movement forward are intertwined, the chant reveals and points toward something more. Here the alert, the warning, on the move both signals protesting for a right to transit embedded in the caravan and suggests the warning that the caravan serves to the world. It is a warning, an alert, literally on the move—or at least trying to be—to the increasing desperation that so many experience in Central America as elsewhere, to the crumbling possibilities of staying home even when one might wish to do so, and to places like the United States—the so-called global north—that they are going to have to contend with the displacements that this desperation will increasingly engender.

This book is premised on the idea that the shifting terrain of border enforcement, especially in its decoupling from the physical border and the infiltrating of border enforcement throughout Mexico, has changed the nature of migration and deportation for those who are engaged in the first and subjected to the latter. Migration, however, is not solely reactive. People are not just pushed around. They are always navigating, pushing back, circumventing too. The caravans and their ripple effects make this especially clear, but it is also the pulse of the insistent, transgressive mobility that is ongoing and more often unseen.

Scholars have proposed the "autonomy of migration" (AoM) as an alternative way of conceiving of the relationship between migration and power structures. The AoM framework moves away from dominant migration studies paradigms, by decentering the state, moving beyond the rational-actor model or push/pull frame, constituting a "copernican turn" in the foundation of migration studies.[36] Rather than start from an assumption that migration responds to migration controls, the AoM literature understands migrants and their "turbulent geographies" and "excess mobilities" as autonomous forces operating independently from, and in turn shaping, apparatuses of control and their corresponding institutions and practices.[37] This is not to blame migrants for the violent regimes of mobility control to which they are subjected, nor is it to romanticize the tenacity, power, and politics of migration movements.[38] AoM, rather, offers a framework for seeing the insistent agency of migration as pushing back, pushing against, pushing forward with such force as to produce new kinds of mobility controls in response. AoM takes mobility seriously as a starting point to understand border policies. The core idea here is that migration is autonomous, which is to say, it is a dynamic and creative force in its own right. The agency of migration precedes bordering;[39] "escape comes first, power and control follow."[40] Thinking migration through the lens of AoM means "training our senses to see . . . mobility before control (but not as disconnected from it)."[41]

The migrant caravan and its relationship to migration controls make the AoM frame seem almost prophetic. This body of scholarship mostly emerged in the 1990s out of a particular context in Europe: the changing relationship between labor, capital, and mobility.[42] It proposes the idea of understanding clandestine, unauthorized, irregular migration as a literal social movement,[43] but it recognizes that individuals engaged in migration are not necessarily revolutionary, vanguard subjects.[44] It focuses on the relationality between mobility and mobility control while identifying an "imperceptible politics" as necessarily contained within migration, which acts as a creative force within—and against—structures.[45] Papadopolous and

Tsianos, two of the leading theorists of the autonomy of migration frame, write that "migrants expose the limits of liberal citizenship without ever intending it."[46] They could be describing the migrant caravans only; instead this frame helps us understand how caravans reflect and amplify the already existing but suddenly visible "imperceptible" politics of migration.

As people gather in caravans in response to the diffusion and proliferation of bordering, so too does bordering change shape in response to caravans and the migration movements they represent. Mexico's "Plan Frontera Sur," which intensified migration interdiction efforts in southern Mexico, launched in 2014, after the so-called crisis of unaccompanied minors arriving at the US border and the overlapping period of back-to-back caravan movements. After the 2018 caravan, the United States threatened Mexico with tariffs and launched the Migrant Protection Protocols (also known as Remain in Mexico), which sent people seeking asylum in the United States back to Mexico to wait for their hearings, sometimes for months on end. The caravans provided additional fodder for fear-mongering nativist politicians in the United States, entering into the political lexicon to materialize an imagined invasion against which they could eagerly campaign. This could be read as a failure of caravans, a backlash so violent as to warrant the discarding of the tactic altogether. The AoM framework encourages us to also see in this relationship the power of caravans—and the larger migration they represent—in that their existence and their insistence produce new approaches to mobility control. This suggests an actual weakness at the heart of the border project, as it is forced to respond to the movement of people.

AoM identifies migration as a force that is not just reactive, but contributes to shaping the bordering practices that migrants, in turn, endeavor to evade. As scholars of migration Margarita Nuñez Chaim, Amarela Varela Huerta, and Valentina Glockner write, "By defying

FIGURE 4. Caravan, Oaxaca, Mexico, 2018. Photo by author.

these devices, the *caravaneros* reconfigured the tactics of disciplining and migration governmentality."[47] I think we can add to this that the consequences of the expanding bordering regime, in the form of the circulations of multiply deported young people, also contribute to the spread of creative, collective mobility tactics like the caravan. Not only can we draw a chronology of migrant caravans-as-protest that builds to the 2018 mass movement, but we can also think in circular socio-spatial development over time and space, as the idea of a caravan travels with people and filters through to inform the possible imaginaries of migration. The caravan is just a small window into a larger, ongoing, turbulent movement of people collectively inventing and enacting new ways to circumvent mobility control and leave behind an exhausting present in the hope of making their way to an otherwise future.

A Right to Migrate

The migrant caravan is not composed of people who are engaged in revolution, at least that's not how most caravaneros would describe themselves and what they are doing. Their collective action, transgressive as it is, is centered on a demand to be included in the world-as-it-is rather than a vision of changing that world. At the same time, however, the foundation of the idea of the caravan—that there is a right to move across space regardless of a person's citizenship or immigration status—is world *re*making. The foundation of the (neo)liberal order, where people are understood to belong to their country of citizenship and where rights mostly exist within the container of that citizenship, is challenged by the idea of the caravan and the migration movements it represents. The caravaneros proclaim a *derecho a migrar*, a right to migrate, which is at its core a right that explodes the organization of nation-states and citizenship itself. The caravaneros want to move across space, to get to a place where they can work, to participate more fully in the world's economy. They are not, by and large, aiming to upend the system. And yet their transgressive mobility challenges the socio-spatial organization on which the system is built. Here scholars have focused on the *refusal* of the caravan and the challenge to the order of sovereignty that's embedded therein.[48] Jorge Cuéllar argues that the caravans reveal what he calls "a mobility of refusal," as Central Americans abandon their countries of citizenship in a reflection of the profound abandonment that conditions everyday life there.[49] Margaret Franz takes this idea of refusal further, arguing that "caravans, as opposed to other forms of migration, mark a distinctly political representation of transnational mobility."[50] Yet this appraisal of the caravan overdetermines, I think, the extent to which the caravan is fundamentally different in this challenge, in its refusal, from the everyday, massive migration that is mostly occurring far from the spotlight.

The politics of movement-as-transgression are always present in migrations; the caravans render this exceedingly visible, providing an accessible window into a much larger phenomenon. The thousands of people who have been caravaneros as part of their migration journeys over the years are but a fraction of the hundreds of thousands of Central Americans who try to migrate each year. The caravan alerts us as to what is going on all the time in less visible and less documented ways. The insistent mobility, the refusal to be turned back, to be forced to stay put, animates migration journeys; the rerouting, regrouping, and determination to move forward is always present. The very challenge of the caravan, the circulating idea that there is a fundamental right to migrate regardless of visas and status and citizenship—this also permeates and emanates first from migration that is done in the shadows.

In the years since I've been on the ground with caravans myself, the back and forth of creative, insistent mobility and shifting, expanding mobility control efforts continue. The caravan experience of Ezra, described in chapter 2, is one example of this. After caravans in 2018 and 2019 had made it into southern Mexico, the United States enlisted the Guatemalan military to make sure groups could not form before reaching Mexico and make it there en masse. Mexico also retooled its enforcement approach, learning to wear out a moving caravan rather than try to stop it with force. The new militarized national police force, the Guardia Nacional, would come to count on attrition to break up caravans.[51] They would let these caravaneros walk along the highways but would not let them rest, enter towns to buy food and water, or flag down trucks to get a lift. Mexico has also increasingly tried to contain people in its southernmost state through more sophisticated mechanisms than an "offer" from the president. Caravans have also evolved, shifting from being a tactic connected to moving through remote areas safely to one where large groups of migrants come together to break out of the containment zone of

Tapachula.[52] Venezuelans, for example, newly stuck after Mexico began requiring visas of them in 2022, organized caravans like these.[53] People from all over the world, who are increasingly present in the migration routes being trod across the Americas, have become caravaneros as they entangle with the world of externalized borders and clandestine transit migration. The changing tactics intended to discourage, detain, contain, and repel caravans reconfigure the methods employed but do not deter the migration that propels them.

The caravaneros I have known throughout the years were already thinking about migration, already contemplating the possibility of needing to escape, already looking for a chance to leave if they could, already on their way. Rather than suddenly appearing from nowhere, requiring heavy-handed powers pulling some strings, the caravan, then, is utterly predictable in this context. Understanding the pressures producing migration in Honduras in conjunction with the growing costs—both physical and economic—of clandestine migration across Mexico leads us to see the caravan as a wholly unsurprising turn of an events, the spilling over into public view of an ongoing and massive movement of people. The stubborn refusal of the caravaneros in 2011, 2014, 2018, and beyond to be turned back, to be stuck in place, as well as their rerouting, regrouping, returning, and then moving forward regardless of the obstacles placed in their way and without any guarantee of success, is echoed in every step taken by all migrants whose journeys never make the news. The insistent, transgressive mobility of the caravan is everywhere within migration. *Alerta que camina.*

Conclusion

A Final Visit to CAMR

In April 2019, I have one final opportunity to be back at CAMR, the deportation processing center adjacent to the San Pedro Sula airport. Although the government's access rules haven't changed, there has been a change in leadership at the center itself, and one of the people who is running the center at this time invites me.

Although it has been more than a year since my last visit to CAMR, the place feels familiar, the process essentially the same. Deportees shuffle in and are directed to sit, in order, in tightly placed rows of chairs. Everyone gets a small Styrofoam cup of coffee and a baleada. They are given a flimsy green backpack with a *kit de aseo personal*, a personal hygiene kit, provided by USAID, with the words, "Del pueblo de los Estados Unidos de América," emblazoned below the logo. "From the people of the United States."

Once in, the crowd is restless, eager to get out of this place and get on to whatever comes next. But first they must wait to be called to retrieve their belongings, which were sent on the plane that brought them here in mesh bags, separate from the deportees. Then they must wait again to be called to get their *constancias*, the official piece of paper that serves as an interim form of identification. Then, yet again, they must wait, in line, to get interviewed and registered by the team of volunteers. Once they've gone through these steps, they are released into the blinding heat of San Pedro Sula. Those who want it are given a lift to the bus terminal; from there they are on their own.

Every time I come here, I think to myself, "I wonder if I'll see anyone I know." The thought comes with both a bit of hope and a sinking feeling—how nice it would be to see a familiar face, how sad it would be. For some reason I always think I see Milton, a young *pollero*—a low-level people smuggler—I met in 2012 on the train tracks outside of Mexico City. It's never him, but every time I'm at CAMR, it's his face I'm scanning the crowd for.

This time, I help distribute the bags of belongings to the deported men—it's all men today—calling their names from a little table set up in the front of the room. Then it happens. First, I notice the two-toned puffer jacket, brown and cream, just like when I had met him in Tijuana, just a day or two before he turned himself over to US border agents to ask for asylum, when we talked about his life in Honduras over french fries at a Carl's Junior. It was cold in Tijuana in December, and he never took off the puffer jacket. Ulises. He's across the room from me, holding the Styrofoam cup of coffee in his hands. Noticeably thinner than he was in the caravan. Eventually he looks across the room, and I catch his eye—and that same big smile spreads across his face. He makes his way through the rows of chairs, and I give him a giant hug. I don't know if there are rules against personal interactions, but no one seems to care. I remind myself it's probably not the first time an arriving deportee has had a connection to someone inside the center.

Ulises! He seems dazed, disoriented, but happy to see a familiar face. We can't talk much in the center; the process of registration is slow but precise, and there's no room for chitchat. I give him my number so we can reconnect later. He returns to his spot in the line of chairs, but he catches my eye and grins broadly from time to time for the rest of the day.

Then, from the row of chairs closer to me, another young man tries to get my attention. He asks, politely, "¿Verdad que Ud. estaba en Tijuana?" (You were in Tijuana, right?) "I was," I say. He turns to the boys around him, quietly triumphant. "Sí es ella. Les dije que ya la conocía." (It *is* her. I told you that I already knew her.) Manuel, the young man whose story appears in the prologue, recognized me from the caravan activities in Tijuana. He reaches out to me the next day, and I go to visit him at his sister's house in Villanueva, just before he leaves Honduras again. Another caravanero, Hector, a bus driver from Choloma, also messages me on Facebook that evening. He too had seen me in the deportee reception center that day.

The cultivated serendipity of ethnographic research facilitates these moments, when I happen to be at CAMR the day that three caravaneros who I had met in Mexico are deported. This book has been about how people and processes circulate through these spaces, channeled and shaped by an expanding and hardening migration management regime. My circulation as a researcher through the circuits and moments of migration intersects as well with that of Manuel, Ulises, and so many others. We reconnect, reappearing after taking different routes, but finding ourselves thrown together, again, in the same spaces of migration.

An Anthropology of Deportation

I began this book with an overview of the situation in Honduras, the data that tell us one piece of a larger story—of an enduring epidemic of violence, of a clear pattern of increasing deportations—and suggested that we can understand another layer of this story if we approach deportation and migration ethnographically. My research offers this additional insight, where deportation becomes an extension

FIGURE 5. Caravaneros, one carrying the backpack distributed to deportees, Chiapas, Mexico, 2018. Photo by author.

of a life already lived at the margins, where criminalization and displacement entwine both inside and outside a person's country of citizenship.

Across these chapters, I have endeavored to describe intersecting regimes of mobility control that shape the contours of daily life for young Hondurans in Honduras and also shape their experience of unauthorized migration, detention, deportation, and return to the country from which they had fled. I have offered analysis across multiple scales of inclusion and exclusion, from the neighborhood level out to the nation and across international borders. I have shown how poor young people in Honduras belong in their colonias (until they don't) and are simultaneously structurally excluded and marginalized. In part, that exclusion looks like being unable to circulate freely in Honduras beyond their colonia, and in part, it looks like being treated as a likely criminal, both in Honduras and beyond, for growing up in that colonia in the first place. I have shown how deportation in Honduras entails being sent back to the familiarity of treacherous mobility and layered precarities and how, given this, deportation fails to discourage repeated migrations.

For the young people with whom I worked, deportation is not a singular event; it is not a moment of rupture leading to upended lives. To the contrary, deportation for them is coherent with a prior condition of exclusion and circumscribed mobility, extended now across international borders. This results in a differently situated trauma, as deportation continues to be violent not in its exceptionality but in its very ordinariness. As anthropologist Nicholas De Genova writes, "Inasmuch as deportation is never reducible to a single act or event, we should likewise underscore that deportation seldom signals a genuine closure, is never truly a conclusion, and never signifies the last word."[1]

When I first began designing the research for this project in Honduras, steeped as I was in the literature on the post-deportation experience elsewhere in Central America, I planned to answer a clear research question: How do people remake their lives and reimagine their futures after being deported back to neighborhoods that are labeled as being among the world's most violent? What I learned, however, was that the premise of my question was incongruous with the contours of deportation for many in Honduras today. In short, Hondurans like the young people whose stories shape this book are not remaking or reimagining lives in a new way after deportation because, quite simply, the conditions around them in Honduras have not yet had the chance to change. Most of the deported young people I came to know had not been gone long enough for the ground to shift beneath them, for their neighborhood to have forgotten them, or for them to have grown accustomed to the shape of life elsewhere. They were sent back instead to the same streets, the same neighbors, the same pulpería, the same pandilleros.

In this way, this book responds to a call put out by anthropologist Shahram Khosravi for more ethnographic work to be done in the post-deportation context, noting the risk that a "lack of attention towards what happens after deportation would naturalize and reinforce the idea of nation-states."[2] He argues that we see an increasing stretching—both spatial and temporal—of deportation, linking deportability in the "host" country with what he calls the "estranged citizenship" of the deportee in their country of origin. He reviews the ill-equipped, hypervisible, stigmatized condition of deportees who are returned "home," noting possibilities of continuities of exclusions, even as the ethnographic content still largely focuses on the kinds of deportees who have lived long lives elsewhere and are sent to unfamiliarity. Khosravi gestures toward the forced return of people to conditions that might have been part of their reason for leaving in the first place; this book centers this aspect of the condition of deportation. "We should not look at deportation as a discrete event," he argues, "but investigate how the condition of protracted, multiple, and ceaseless abandonment before, during, and after deportation constitutes normality in the daily lives of deportees."[3] By starting from deportation and connecting it with the premigration navigation of mobility control through the idea of circulation, I offer one approach to focusing on this "ceaseless abandonment" and the normality of deportation.

More broadly, this project raises questions about the nature of mobility, why people move, and what it means for them to do so.

Thinking about deportation beyond the event of it, my approach revises the geography, the temporality, and the nature of the trauma associated with being removed and returned. It also further blurs any enduring idea of mobility as either forced or chosen, understanding a kind of freedom to move and being made to move as nested, connected, and simultaneous conditions. This troubles an association with mobility as the domain of the privileged and immobility as the condition of the subaltern, as I identify a transgressive and insistent mobility that people engage in both at home and when they strive to cross international borders without authorization.

This exploration of the Honduran case points us toward the future of deportation and migration more broadly. The dynamics I start to address here will only intensify as people in different parts of the world continue to find life at home unlivable while borders expand and militarize and the basic idea of seeking refuge from persecution is undermined and attacked. Khosravi notes that "the condition of post-deportation characterized by fear, anxiety, uncertainty, and insecurity, resembles the condition of undocumentedness prior to the deportation."[4] Extending this insight, one aspect of the argument I offer here is that, essentially, even prior to migration, many Hondurans are already living with an instability and exclusion that is akin to that which has become a feature of life for the undocumented in the United States—the ever-present potential of emergency, the perennial possibility of displacement. The vast literature on liminal subjectivity theorizing the partial, contingent belonging for undocumented communities within the United States could aptly describe daily life for Hondurans in Honduras. This raises further questions about what citizenship confers, what meaning it holds, and how the illegalization of immigrants might be a process that begins and a condition that is acquired well before migration, decoupled from legal status.[5]

And this decoupling has reverberations that reach back into the United States as well. In this book, I identify a "new" era of deportation, where people are caught up in ongoing cycles of unwanted, unending circular motion, unable to arrive but also not really able to stay home. I link this to a qualitative change in the way that immigration and border controls have hardened and expanded while also bleeding into an intensified focus on limiting access to international protection mechanisms. This iteration of the deportation regime, where hardening, criminalization, externalization, and the attack on asylum converge, also augurs the increasingly hostile turn immigration enforcement has taken, sending people to third countries not of their birth, disappearing them directly into foreign prisons, making them wait endlessly in dangerous, inhospitable in-between places, and reasserting the power to remove all immigrants, including those with legal status. The unauthorized, criminally coded migrant subject, especially those who hail from countries associated with organized crime or terrorist threats, is the easy, first target. But in an era of rising nationalisms and resurgent nativisms, the violent suspicion that justifies removal of the other, first constructed as the migrant outsider, will eventually also ensnare the dissident, deemed undesirable, citizen.

I write these pages as Donald Trump begins his second term as president of the United States, riding a wave of anger about migration back into the White House. He promises to build more walls, use more force, and do everything in his power to stop people from coming to the country. He's willing to wage trade wars and maybe actual, directly lethal wars to stop what he characterizes as an invasion, often invoking the specter of caravans. Trump is in it for the spectacle; he wields the image of tough-guy-against-invading-marauders well, serving up red meat to a base that he has contributed to whipping into an anti-immigrant frenzy. Trump, and those he represents, however, is not aberrant. Their gleeful cruelty might be a different tone, departing from one of tempered justification, but there is much continuation from one administration to the next, between one party and the other. The ground on which there is enduring, bipartisan agreement is that there is no fundamental right to migrate; that some people can and should have access to mobility, and others cannot and should not. Trump is the latest, cruelest version, but he is not a departure from the structural consensus. His return to power, however, widens the boundaries of who is constructed as being out of place and thus "legitimately" made removable.

This book is coming out, as most academic books do, quite a few years after the bulk of the on-the-ground research was conducted and a new era of deportation was coming into view. In the intervening years, the United States has returned to targeting anyone and everyone for deportation, including those who have lived here for many years, who are deeply invested in jobs and families and communities. The second Trump administration has made it a point to remove the Temporary Protected Status (TPS) that so many have had for decades, including Hondurans, making hundreds of thousands of people newly deportable. His fervor for mass deportation is once again wreaking havoc on the lives of long-established, mixed-status immigrant families. Exile is back.

This in-your-face violence, images of restaurant workers and day laborers being rounded up, of anguished children reaching for their handcuffed parents, of people being arrested while attending their court hearings, rightly sparks outrage. The stories in this book, however, tell us that deportation is always violent, including when it is carried out well before people ever reach the border, when it is done with far less spectacle. The current moment of state terror is, like so many aspects of Trump's agenda, backward-looking, a return to the logics and tactics of earlier eras: brute force policing, masked thugs, direct state violence in this case. But the broader agenda of keeping people out has evolved over decades in ways that do not force most US residents to reckon with the violence of their immigration regime, by immobilizing migrants, forcibly returning them to places they cannot stay, keeping them both stuck in motion and out of sight. Perhaps this book can serve as a reminder and a warning for the future, that even with a government that does not openly delight in terrorizing immigrants, a more "humane" approach has often amounted to shifting the terror southward, just beyond view.

Thinking Circulations "Otherwise"

Field Notes

A man from Honduras, looking at the wall from inside Estadio Benito Juárez one night, turns to me and says, "Yeah yeah, I know. But you know what? Here's the thing. For us, for Hondurans, now, life isn't worth anything. We'll get in, because we'll get in. And sure, they'll kill some of us. But we'll get in."

·   •   ·

In the years since the bulk of the fieldwork for this project was conducted, I sometimes slip into a register of hope—maybe even bordering on romanticization—as I write about and reflect on migrant caravans and all the people whose paths crossed with mine in our circulations. Yet when I dive back into my field notes and the audio recordings, I am reminded time and time again just how much a kind of hopeless determination inflects migration. There is a stubborn insistence on surviving and pushing through. A closeness to death, a frankness about the ever present possibility of violence. This is not, then, a conclusion where I want to suggest a romantic future and a harmonious vision of a borderless world.

Yet migration *is* an act of hope, of faith, of believing in the possibility of something beyond the constricted chances available at home. It is also a refusal, a refusal to accept the world as it is, along

FIGURE 6. "The sun shines for all." Border infrastructure between Tijuana, Mexico, and San Diego, California, December 2018. Photo by author.

with an insistent, transgressive, turbulent attempt to bet on the possibility of another world. Ramón explains to me, "Somos un pueblo que aguanta. Sabemos aguantar." (We are a people who endure. We know how to endure.) "Endure" isn't a perfect translation of *aguantar*; English doesn't have a single word that captures its layered meaning. Ramón is telling me that, in his assessment, Hondurans are a people who bear it, who survive through adversity, who keep going. Hondurans know how to keep going. Even when there's a wall in front of you. Even when confronted with death.

I depict a story here of people in continued circulation, cycling through circuits, again and again, as they keep going, yet some eventually *do* make it. At least somewhere. At least for a while. They build new families in Monterrey, fall in love with other migrants from halfway across the world. And find community. In movement. And, perhaps, in this they show us one possible future. A future that reduces the salience of borders and visas and stasis and rootedness. A future that is constructed with mobility taken for granted, rather than pathologized, as a state of things. Excessive movement, writes Gilberto Rosas, provokes deep unease while also perhaps "foreshadowing a coming political community. . . . It is they who live in the future[;] . . . we are anachronisms."⁶ Similarly, Nadia El-Shaarawi and Maple Rasza suggest that alternative social relations are modeled in border struggles; it is not that refugees are inherently less racist or xenophobic than anyone else but rather that the kinds of comings together and layered mobilities that emerge in movement might depict another way of human (self-)organization altogether.⁷

We might ask the question, too, as to whether this future does not already, at least in part, exist in the present. Miriam Ticktin encourages us to engage in speculative thinking when it comes to mobility, which in her formulation takes place at the edge of what we can see. This is not to suggest fanciful utopian imaginations but to "create room in public discourse . . . to enable *alter-visions*, or alternative political formations that exist alongside the current political order."⁸ In other words, this speculative thinking starts from the world as it is and thinks crosswise, reframing the real rather than negating it or imagining not-yet-existent alternatives. Taking the world as it is, then, we see one where people move regardless of the violence and uncertainties they face, the walls and cages built. People regroup, reroute, reimagine migration, but they don't accept a bordered world and just stay put. Taking *that* as the condition of the real, borders already do not matter insomuch as they do not deter, regardless of the violence they inflict. What would happen if we just accepted that as fact and moved on to other things?

This is the part of the book where some readers might wish for me to propose alternative solutions. Solutions, however, first require an honest assessment of the problem at hand, and the *problem* is not migration. The fine-grained, slowly immersive work of anthropology confirms that migration is a core feature of humanity itself—now, in the past, and into the future—the genius of our ability and willingness to seek new ground when the conditions around us become inhospitable. Migration is not driven by "push/pull" factors that might be adjusted, nor is it a response to political discourse of more or less welcome, more or less open borders. It is, rather, an expression of survival, refusal, desperation, aspiration, adventure, and that basic desire to try to make a life that is just a bit more livable, just a bit more of one's own design. The *problem*, then, lies in all the attempts to stop human mobility, to contain, detain, and deport people; the *problem* is everything that then happens to people who insist on their mobility, transgressive as it may be, despite those efforts. Real solutions, then, would need to address the conditions that make people feel like they have no choice but to move and would also need to reduce, rather than reinforce, barriers to that movement. The so-called crisis at the US-Mexico border is a "crisis" of our own making, one born of fencing and armed guards. The solution to *this* crisis is not to harden the borders and make deportation more palatable or more "sustainable" but rather to facilitate people's chosen movement across borders. Let people leave, when and if they want to. If we can reimagine mobility and circulation as a given, not as aberrant, perhaps then we can develop policies that are not designed around deterring migration or forcing people to stay put but that instead start from recognizing migration as a fundamental feature of the world, now as always.

Epilogue

Ramón knew what was coming.

2020

In the years since my long-term fieldwork concluded, Ramón was arrested and charged with cobrando la renta—collecting extortion payments. The police circulate the standard image of the culprits they've caught. There's Ramón, wearing a faded, secondhand T-shirt, with hands cuffed behind his back, and on the table in front of him the "goods" the police have seized: 300 lempiras and two very out-of-date cell phones.

2021

I visit Ramón in prison. He's still there under suspicion, hasn't yet had a hearing, is hopeful that the witnesses, who, he insists, must all be police officers themselves, can be convinced to recant. He and his long-term partner, Tatiana, have raised substantial funds to hire an attorney who, they think, will be able to negotiate—quite likely through bribes—Ramón's release. Ramón's positivity fails him in prison. He greets me with warmth and the same friendliness he has extended to me since the day we met on the cancha of La Libertad, but he's agitated and frustrated and, understandably, brimming with negativity. He introduces me to other inmates and shares with indignation the stories of the even more outrageous arrests and convictions of those around him. A campesino father and son from Olancho; a few non-gang-affiliated kids from La Libertad; someone whose sentence has been completed and yet, inexplicably, has not been released. Ramón also introduces me to people who admit their guilt, recognize that they've earned their spot in Támara. He's still a leader, a leader of lost and violent kids. He's worried that his neighborhood will be lost, too, without him there; he thinks his arrest was a plot between MS-13 and the police to get him out of the way so that the gang could take over La Libertad.

2022

When I'm back for a short visit in San Pedro Sula, Tatiana invites me over for lunch in their home in La Libertad. I realize that I had never been inside before, not when Ramón was around. She still goes to visit him in prison; there's no real movement on his case.

2024

I haven't been able to get in touch with Ramón or Tatiana this time around. The cell phone that Ramón had access to in Támara seems to no longer be connected. Even so, I send a vague message to the number—just in case he is still somehow able to communicate there.

I'm not worried, not at first. Cell phones and SIM cards come and go in Honduras generally, and they are even more ever changing inside a prison where they are technically prohibited in the first place. Ramón always found a way to pick up communication with me. I assumed, eventually, I would hear from him. I think maybe I'll just pop over to Tatiana's house when I'm back in Honduras.

When I do arrive in San Pedro Sula in August 2024, I meet with Pastor Luis first. It has been a few years since we've seen each other; our schedules just weren't syncing the last few visits. We have coffee and pastry at a favorite coffee shop in one of the nicer areas, the *zona viva*, of San Pedro Sula at Luis's suggestions. It's so nice to catch up. We recount the adventures we had had together; we update each other on our families; he tells me about his numerous failed business ventures. Uber has recently started in San Pedro, and he's enjoying driving people around. He's always been an eager, warm talker, and I can see how Uber would suit him. He's enthused about getting to know people from outside of his neighborhood, outside his country. Eventually we turn to Ramón and Tatiana and La Libertad.

It has all changed. He's not sure where Tatiana is now. Ramón is still in prison, as far as Luis knows, but he hasn't heard from either of them in a while. It's too dangerous. The gang that controlled La Libertad finally fell to MS-13—with the help of the police, Luis insists—and Tatiana and her whole family, what's left of Ramón's family, had to flee the area.

The last four pandilleros left alive were given the option to flee, Luis tells me.

And Tatiana and Ramón's house is now a brand-new *posta*, a police outpost. Now the police and MS-13 coexist in and co-govern La Libertad.

In December, I share a photo of my Christmas Eve gathering on WhatsApp—my husband and me, my parents, my in-laws. Tatiana messages me in response. She says she thought I had been the one who changed my number, but she saw the photo and knew the number still belonged to me. We catch up through alternating voice notes. The mareros ran her out of La Libertad, she says, confirming Pastor Luis's version of events. She has left the Sula Valley altogether. She tells me where she's living but notes that most people in San Pedro don't know where she is; the gang threatened her, and she would rather people not know. She and Ramón have gotten married legally, but they moved him to a prison farther away, in Danlí, and they only allow a single hour for conjugal visits there. She hopes that next year he'll be released, and they can resume their life together.

Ramón knew what was coming. He was targeted, arrested, jailed, removed from the neighborhood. He was not all-powerful, not in any absolute way, but his presence was a bulwark. With him gone, the muchachos of La Libertad were more vulnerable, more exposed. And slowly but surely, the big guns came in and ran them out. The neighborhood isn't theirs anymore. And a new generation of locally grown MS-13-affiliated mareros will replace them. But Ramón and Tatiana and their kids and grandkids can never go home.

The last time I talked to Ramón he told me that as soon as he gets out of prison, he is going to leave Honduras again. This time for good. He had tried, in the best way he knew how, with the limited and complicated tools available to him, to make his little corner of the country better, but he lost. And now, he says, frustrated and exhausted, he's given up. With no home to return to, once Ramón is released from prison, if he survives prison, he and Tatiana will leave Honduras. If they can.

Acknowledgments

This book is the result of so many years and so many people. First, always, my profound thanks to the many people who shared their time and their stories with me. It has been an honor to be welcomed into your homes and your lives. I hope you see reflected in this work the deep admiration I have for each of you.

Carolyn Gallaher and Oliver Fröhling facilitated my first immersive visit to Oaxaca, where I had the good fortune to meet and be welcomed by Padre Alejandro Solalinde and Alberto Donis at the Albergue Hermanos en el Camino in Ixtepec. This book started there, though I did not know it at the time. Beto, I wish you were still here to see what all you patiently explained to me over the years has turned into.

In Mexico, the support, guidance, and friendship of Emiliano Ruiz Parra and Carmen Parra opened a whole world to me beyond the small sliver I knew of the Isthmo. I learned the ropes and the rails from many activist researchers but especially Cristóbal Sánchez Sánchez and Arelí Palomo Contreras, who continue to inspire me as the best teachers on how to do research in community, with people, and for a better world. I was very lucky to be welcomed into a tangled, beautiful community of migrants' rights activism, research, and journalism in Mexico, including Carolina Feldman, Ruben Figueroa, Irineo Mújica, Faba Mancilla, Magui Nuñez, Las Patronas, Hermana Lupe, Padre Pantoja, Padre Prisciliano, Sara Soto, and the banda caravanera, Gina, Alex, Tristan Felipe, and so many others. Thank you for bringing me into your worlds. Ana Enamorado, more than anyone else, you have shown me what it means to fight tirelessly, against all odds. Even though my research moved south, Mexico continues to feel like my anchor and because of you all, very much like home.

En Honduras, tengo que agradecer a mucha gente, quienes me abrieron sus casas y sus corazones y me enseñaron las cosas que son el alma de este libro. Los jóvenes del programa, gracias por todo lo que me enseñaron: Paola, Nicol, Victor, Everlides, Lesly, Fanny, Melissa, Flor, Jennyfer, Aris, Kervin, Nahín, Kevin, Tania, Heidy, Carmen, Eduardo, Bryan, Dulce, Maryuri, Genesis, Willians y muchos otros. Gracias a mi querida Doña Marcia y Glenda, junto con Rosa Nelly, Doña Edita y Pilar y todas las mamás de Cofamipro. Mi amiga Suany, quien me ha acompañado desde mi primera visita en Ixtepec, de frontera a frontera. Gracias a mis guías en el Valle de Sula, David, Miguel, Jeremías, Denis, Reina, Heydi, Claudia, Wendy, Miriam, Cindy, Julio y Carmen, se los debo todo; Oricela y las mujeres de Momuclaa; Doña Teresa Campos y la gente del museo; mi taxista de confianza Hugo; y Javier, Mercedes, Cinthia, María Isabel, Jerson, Yanina, César, no pudiera haber realizado este proyecto sin su apoyo. De igual manera, agradezco a Karla Rivas del ERIC; Rolando Sierra, César Castillo, Paola Pineda y Rosa Funes del Observatorio; mis colegas de la UNAH, Luis Martínez, Eva Lilia Martínez, y Ana Hasemann Lara. Jennifer Ávila, Sally Valladares y Tomás Ayuso, desde sus diferentes posiciones, me abrieron espacios, me brindaron confianza, y me tuvieron mucha paciencia explicándome cómo son las cosas en Honduras. Los amigos de San Pedro, Massiel, Lucía, Germán, Julio, y Carlos (amigo de mi alma), me dieron vida. Gustavo y Miguel, los recuerdo con tanto cariño. Pero la persona, quien me hizo todo posible en Honduras fue Sandra Ivett. Simplemente no sé qué hubiera hecho sin vos.

This project would not have been possible without the support of the School of International Service at American University; the Institute of Current World Affairs; Rackham Graduate School, the Department of Anthropology, the Center for Latin American and Caribbean Studies, and the Weiser Center for Emerging Democracies at the University of Michigan; the Inter-American Foundation; the Fulbright Foundation; the Wenner-Gren Foundation; the Social Sciences Research Council; and the American Council of Learned Societies. I finish this book at a time when so many of these programs have ceased to exist, and I worry about the future of experimental, complicated, on-the-ground research without this kind of backing.

I was fortunate to have had the collegial support of transit migration scholars Noelle Bridgen and Wendy Vogt since before I started graduate school. Scholars of Central America Ellen Moodie, Miranda Cady Hallet, Rebecca Galemba, and Jennifer Burrell offered me valuable guidance and encouragement as this project came into being. I have been honored and humbled by the kindness with which scholars of Honduras have received me. I had long admired Juan Martínez, Adrienne Pine, Jon Carter, and Darío Euraque, and I cannot believe my good fortune to have been able to discuss my work with each of them along the way.

The best part of academia is, for me, working collectively, not on the same project necessarily, but side by side. A wonderful group of colleagues contributed to this work in this way: my IAF-mates Jose Hasemann Lara, Camilo Ruiz, Amarylis Estrella, and Andrea Baudoin Farah; my companions navigating Honduras and visiting police stations and fiscalías, Elizabeth Kennedy and Marna Shorack; my peers at Michigan, Zehra, Sam, Ben, Magdalena, Huatse, Ozge, and Sheng; and my fellow early career, engaged Central America and migration scholars who are always ready to think together, to write together, and to encourage each other, Pam Ruiz, Bill López, Soledad Álvarez Velasco, Yaatsil Guevara, Martha Balaguera, Alejandra Díaz de León, Deniz Daser, Liz Rubio, and John Doering-White. I learn so much from each of you.

At Michigan, I had a team of dedicated, supportive, and enthusiastic mentors. Damani Partridge, Jesse Hoffnung-Garskoff, and Ruby Tapia were each generous with their expertise and feedback. Jatin Dua and Mike McGovern both read many early versions of what would become this book and patiently shaped my theoretical engagement. I went to Michigan, however, because Jason De León believed in me and my approach to ethnography before almost anyone else did. Jason, I'm endlessly grateful for your tireless mentorship, your careful editing eye, and your trust in me to do this work. This project and this book would not exist without your support and friendship and the path you have paved for anthropology. I am a better writer, a better thinker, a better anthropologist, and a better human for having you guide me.

Much of this writing was done during a pandemic. I'm not sure I would have survived that period intact, let alone produce the dissertation that would become this book, without the care, humor, and ride-or-die support of Kath Byrnes. I am incredibly grateful for the mix of friendship and mentorship from Lauren Heidbrink and Nara Milanich, who have both graciously and enthusiastically read many versions of what would become this book and supported my research ideas before they even knew me. Having them as compañeras is a true gift. My generous, brilliant colleagues Onur Günay and Grazzia Grimaldi each took the time to read the manuscript and offer me thoughtful, generative feedback. This book is worlds better for it. Mi comadre and the madrina of so many of us, Gabriella Sanchez, I am profoundly grateful for your careful reading. That each of you gave me your vista buena to proceed—along with precise suggestions for improvement—was critical to getting the book to print. The incomparable Catherine Calderón, of *Contra Corriente*, did me the great honor of designing the very special maps that appear in this book.

When about half of this book was drafted, I held a virtual book workshop through the support of the Program in Latin American Studies at Princeton. Susan Bibler Coutin, Elizabeth Velazquez Estrada, and Otto Argueta each graciously read this work in progress and offered thoughtful, constructive, and critical feedback without which I would never have been able to develop the ideas with as much clarity and nuance as, I hope, the final book contains. I deeply admire the work that each of you do, and I hope I have done your comments justice. I'm equally grateful to the anonymous reviewers who offered insightful, productive criticism. It was peer review at its best, reflecting my words back to me and pushing me to refine the ideas and write more clearly.

Years ago, when I learned that UC Press had a series in Public Anthropology, I dreamed that one day I might publish my own work there. I am so grateful to everyone at the Press who has made this into a reality: editor Kate Marshall, who trusted that I could write a book when I was not sure how and had the steady patience to wait for me for the years it took me to go from first conversation to proposal to manuscript; Sheila Berg, for her extremely careful editing; editorial assistant Natalie Gomez and senior project editor Emily Park, for walking me through each step of writing a first book; and the Public Anthropology series editor, Ieva Jusionyte, whose work I hold up as an example of the kind of anthropology I hope to produce.

At Princeton, I am extraordinarily lucky to have joined two departments, SPIA and Anthropology, that value public-facing ethnography. I am so grateful to be in an encouraging and challenging environment and to have had the early and enduring support of João Biehl, Carolyn Rouse, Gabriella Nouzeilles, and Miguel Centeno. I'm very thankful for the insightful reading and careful editing eye of Orla O'Sullivan and the feedback from students in my Anthropology of Borders class.

I, like so many, am the product of many migrations. I thank my Nonna and the bisnonni who I never got to meet for taking that leap to leave behind the worlds they knew in hopes of building a new life for their descendants. Vorrei che poteste vedere quanta strada abbiamo fatto. I dedicate this work to you and all the people who make that same bargain without assurances, without knowing what the future will hold.

To my parents: From a young age, you taught me to see difference as exciting, fascinating, and delightful, not threatening or scary. You wanted us to know the world, and you wanted us to care about the people in it, whether or not we would ever know them, whether or not we spoke the same language or came from the same place. If I am an anthropologist, it is because of who you taught me to be, first and foremost. Thank you.

And to my Saúl. The greatest fortune of my life was to have found you. Your brilliance, kindness, and remarkable ecuanimidad keep me grounded and keep me going. Te amo.

Appendix: Deportation Data

TABLE 1. Deportations to Honduras, 2015–2024

	US	Mexico	Other	Total
2015	19,321	56,554	0	75,875
2016	21,597	47,678	95	69,370
2017	20,841	26,991	190	48,022
2018	30,345	44,760	174	75,279
2019	40,984	64,649	3,552	109,185
2020	13,486	22,429	643	36,558
2021	10,527	41,774	667	52,968
2022	42,090	45,961	504	88,555
2023	42,581	15,814	364	58,759
2024	35,365	9,721	271	45,357
TOTAL	277,137	376,331	6,460	659,928

Source: Data from the Honduran government, accessed through Conmigho, the Observatorio Consular y Migratorio de Honduras, housed under the Secretaría de Relaciones Exteriores y Cooperación Internacional. Conmigho.sreci.gob.hn.

TABLE 2. Deportations to Honduras, 2015–2024, by Gender (as Recorded by the Honduran Government*)

	Deported from US		Deported from Mexico		Deported from Other		Total		
	Men	Women	Men	Women	Men	Women	Men	Women	% Men
2015	16,784	2,537	44,560	11,994	0	0	61,344	14,531	81
2016	19,286	2,311	37,178	10,500	62	33	56,526	12,844	81
2017	18,870	1,971	21,992	4,999	112	78	40,974	7,048	85
2018	27,532	2,813	34,928	9,832	99	75	62,559	12,720	83
2019	35,764	5,220	44,607	20,042	2,389	1,163	82,760	26,425	76
2020	11,200	2,286	18,700	3,729	455	188	30,355	6,203	83
2021	6,826	3,701	35,620	6,154	480	187	42,926	10,042	81
2022	25,721	16,369	38,969	6,992	293	211	64,983	23,572	73
2023	29,391	13,190	13,006	2,808	235	129	42,632	16,127	73
2024	25,708	9,657	7,520	2,201	161	110	33,389	11,968	74
TOTAL	217,082	60,055	297,080	79,251	4,286	2,174	518,448	141,480	79

SOURCE: Data from the Honduran government, accessed through Conmigho, the Observatorio Consular y Migratorio de Honduras, housed under the Secretaría de Relaciones Exteriores y Cooperación Internacional. Conmigho.sreci.gob.hn.

*These data include deportees of all ages; there is a higher rate of deported minor girls compared to deported adult women. However, as these disaggregated data are not publicly available for every year, I have included the full numbers.

Glossary

ACNUR Alto Comisionado de las Naciones Unidas para los Refugiados (UN High Commissioner for Refugees). See UNHCR.

AGUANTAR Roughly, to endure, to bear it.

ALBERGUE Shelter.

ALERTA MIGRATORIA Immigration alert.

ALUMBRADO/A Lit up, electrified.

ASAMBLEA Literally "assembly"; used to refer to the group meetings in the form of direct-democracy decision making held during migrant caravans.

ATOL DE ELOTE Sweet, warm, corn-based drink or pudding.

AUTO-GESTIÓN Self-organization, self-governance; frequently used in autonomous, horizontal social movement organizing throughout Latin America.

BALA Bullet.

BALEADAS Staple Honduran food, made of a soft, slightly spongy, freshly made flour tortilla, often filled with beans, cheese, and cream, sometimes with eggs or meat added.

BANDERA Literally "flag"; used to mean a gang-affiliated lookout, often a child; term mostly used by MS-13 in Honduras.

BARBERÍA Barbershop.

BARRIO Neighborhood; in Honduras, generally within the older, inner ring of the city; also shorthand to refer to one of the gangs, Barrio 18.

BORDO Informal settlement built up along the edge of riverbanks.

BUSERO/A Bus driver.

CAMR Centro de Apoyo al Migrante Retornado (Support Center for Returned Migrants); official reception and processing center for deported Hondurans, comprising CAMR-Lima, CAMR-Omoa, and Centro Belén.

CANCHA Soccer field, open empty space used to play soccer.

CALICHE Slang, used especially in El Salvador and Honduras.

CARAVANA Caravan, as in a large group of people attempting to migrate together.

CARAVANERO/A Participant in a caravan.

CAPITAL SEMILLA Literally, "seed capital"; mostly in-kind donations to get a small business off the ground.

CATRACHO/A Slang term for Honduran used by Hondurans.

CENTRO BELÉN Official reception and processing center for deported Honduran minors and their families.

CHELE/A Fair-skinned.

COBRANDO RENTA Collecting extortion payments on behalf of a gang.

COFAMIPRO Comite de Familiares de Migrantes de El Progreso, Yoro (Committee of Families of Migrants of El Progreso, Yoro).

COLONIA In Honduras, neighborhood, generally on the outskirts, in the newer parts of the city built beyond the historic inner ring.

COMEDOR Dining room, place for eating meals, cafeteria.

COMUNICADO Communiqué, press release.

CONSTANCIA Record, as in an official document recording that something has taken place.

COYOTE People smuggler or facilitator in the context of clandestine migration

DEFENSOR/A DE DERECHOS HUMANOS Human rights activist/defender.

DELINCUENTE Criminal, delinquent.

DENUNCIA Police report.

DENUNCIAR To file an official police report.

DEPARTAMENTO Department; in Honduras, juridical division similar to a province.

DEPORTADO/A A person who has been deported.

DEPURACIÓN Purge; in Honduras, an official process to weed out corrupt police officers.

DERECHO A MIGRAR Right to migrate.

DIPAMPCO División Policial Anti Maras y Pandillas Contra el Crimen Organizado (Anti-Gang and Organized Crime Police Division), established 2022.

EMBOLSADO/A Literally, "bagged"; used to refer to a body that has been left wrapped in plastic, burlap, or other material.

ENCERRADO Enclosed, locked in.

ENCHACHADO/A In handcuffs, shackled.

ENCIERRO Enclosure.

ENCUEVADO/A Encaved, as in living inside a cave.

FEAC Fe en Acción, or Faith in Action; a pseudonym for a Honduran NGO that offers, among other things, programming for deported youth.

FISCAL Public prosecutor.

FLACO/A Skinny.

FNAMP Fuerza Nacional Anti-Maras y Pandillas (National Anti-Gang Force), a now-defunct militarized police unit in Honduras specialized to go after gangs.

FRONTERA INTERNA Internal border, referring to the borders between neighborhoods within the territory under gang control.

FRONTERA INVISIBLE Invisible border, referring to the borders between neighborhoods within the territory under gang control.

GUARDIA NACIONAL National Guard; in the context of Mexico, a specialized, federal-level, militarized police force.

IMPUESTO DE GUERRA Literally, "war tax"; used to refer to systematic extortion payments demanded by gangs. Also *renta*.

IOM International Organization for Migration; multilateral UN-affiliated organization dedicated to promoting safe and orderly migration. Offers programming to support deportees in Honduras.

JEFE DE LA PANDILLA Local-level boss of the gang.

JOH Initials used widely to refer to Juan Orlando Hernández Alvarado, president of Honduras, 2014–22

JOMI From "homie," full-fledged gang member.

LLANTERA Tire shop.

LIBRE TRÁNSITO Free movement.

LOCOS Literally, "crazy people"; can be used to mean gang-affiliated people in a given neighborhood.

LOS DE LA RUMBA Those of the Rumba, a now-disbanded gang/drug cartel operating in the López Arellano sector of Choloma.

LUCHAS MIGRANTES Migrant struggles, migrant rights movement.

MADRE Mother

MANO DURA Literally, "hard hand," meaning iron fist security policies.

MAQUILA Light manufacturing plant; sweatshop.

MARA Gang; most often used to refer to the Mara Salvatrucha (MS-13) in Honduras.

MARERO/A Gang member; most often used to refer to a member of the Mara Salvatrucha (MS-13) in Honduras.

MINISTERIO PÚBLICO Public Prosecutor's Office.

MOTOTAXI Three-wheeled, covered, motorized taxis, used as short-distance, pay-per-ride transportation, especially in areas where the roads are not paved.

MUCHACHOS Literally, "boys"; in Honduras, a common euphemism for gang members.

ÑÁNGARA Communist, socialist, leftist.

NRC Norwegian Refugee Council; in Spanish, Consejo Noruego in Spanish. Tasked with assisting internally displaced people in Honduras.

OMBE Dude, man, in Honduran slang.

OIM Organización Internacional para las Migraciones. See IOM.

PAÍS TAPÓN Literally "stopper country," meaning a country that acts as a stopper, plug, or cork, keeping migration flows from moving through it.

PALMEAR The act of using your palms to flatten balls of dough into tortillas.

PANDILLA Gang.

PANDILLERO/A Gang member.

PATRULLA FRONTERIZA Border Patrol.

PAVIMENTADA Paved, main road (as opposed to a dirt road).

PILA In Honduras, refers to a large, deep, open container for water, often made of concrete, used to wash clothes and/or dishes.

POLLERO/A Literally, "chicken herder"; used to mean guide, smuggler, or facilitator in the context of clandestine migration from Central America, often a low-level actor.

PMOP Policía Militar del Orden Público, often simply called Policía Militar (military police); a unit in the Honduran Armed Forces tasked with civilian law enforcement and public security functions.

POSTA Literally, "post," meaning police outpost.

PRO-R Programa de Retornar y Reconstruir (Return and Rebuild Program); a project of FeAc dedicated to assisting deportees.

PRISIÓN PREVENTIVA Pretrial detention, up to two and a half years in Honduras.

PRODUCTOS DEL HORTO Garden produce and homemade goods derived from it.

PUEBLO The people; also town.

PULPERÍA Corner store, often in the front room of a person's home.

PUNTEANDO Standing guard, acting as a lookout, covering a "point" for drug sales.

RENTA Literally "rent"; used to refer to the systematic extortion payments demanded by gangs. See *impuesto de guerra*.

REVOLTOSO/A Rebellious; a person causing upheaval, protester.

RAPIDITO Literally, "small and fast"; in San Pedro Sula, the term is used to refer to the cargo van–size buses that make up the backbone of inner-city transportation.

RESIDENCIAL Literally "residential"; used to refer to a gated community where there is a guard at the entrance.

REVISIÓN DEL CARRO Vehicle registration.

SALVOCONDUCTO In Mexico, transit or exit visa

SAPO Literally, "toad"; in Honduras, a colloquial term for snitch.

SICARIO Assassin for hire, hitman.

TÁMARA A town in central Honduras; also used as shorthand to refer to the nearby prison.

TERCERIZACIÓN Third-partyization; refers to outsourcing, as in public-private partnerships.

TIERRA DE NADIE No-man's-land.

TIROS Gunshots.

TPS Temporary Protected Status, a short-term, contingent, legal status offered in the United States to specific nationalities in the wake of a specific crisis in their home country.

TRANQUILO/A Tranquil, calm.

TOS CARAVANERO Caravan cough.

UNHCR United Nations High Commissioner for Refugees. See ACNUR.

VIACRUCIS Stations of the Cross.

VIACRUCIS DEL MIGRANTES Migrants' Station of the Cross.

VOS Spanish second-person singular pronoun. In Honduras, used instead of "tú," with an extremely informal connotation.

Notes

Introduction

1. Khosravi, "Introduction."

2. Zilberg, "Fools Banished from the Kingdom"; Andrews, *Banished Men*; Brotherton and Barrios, *Banished to the Homeland*; Coutin, *Exiled Home*; Dingeman-Cerda and Coutin, "The Ruptures of Return"; Schuster and Majidi, "Deportation Stigma and Re-Migration"; Golash-Boza, "Forced Transnationalism"; Boehm, "US-Mexico Mixed Migration in an Age of Deportation."

3. In *Lives in Transit*, anthropologist Wendy Vogt also notes a continuum of violence that exists across migration journeys and historical processes in migrants' home countries.

4. Carter, "Gothic Sovereignty"; Arce, *Blood Barrios*.

5. Olivo Diaz López, "Relocating Morolica."

6. Another inflection point occurred right after I began my long-term fieldwork, when incumbent Honduran President Juan Orlando Hernández Alvarado declared victory in the elections of 2017. While the results were widely considered dubious, the United States congratulated Hernández on his reelection, and he was able to remain in power for a second term. The Honduran constitution prohibits reelection, but Hernández had stacked the Supreme Court to ensure that it ruled in his favor, deciding that a prohibition on reelection violates an individual's rights, without actually changing the letter of the constitution. Hondurans took to the streets after he declared himself the winner. Much of the country was shut down, and I spent my first months in San Pedro Sula visiting barricades and street protests and navigating a military curfew. Surprising no one, out-migration again increased after it became clear that Hernández would not be relinquishing power.

7. The history of Honduras here is complicated. As mentioned, Honduras was home to US counterinsurgency efforts in the region during this period, even dubbed "The U.S.S. Honduras" by Washington. Its small Marxist-inspired group of revolutionaries was essentially exterminated before it became a guerrilla force, with the recorded forced disappearance of activists and others at the hands of the US- and Chilean-trained Battalion 3–16. Honduras avoided some of the pressures that fomented into revolution in neighboring countries, including the institutionalization of some reforms and protections as a result of a general strike by banana workers in 1954.

8. Frank-Vitale, "From Caravan to Exodus, from Migration to Movement."

9. Moslimani et al., "Facts on Hispanics of Honduran Origin in the United States, 2021."

10. See the full breakdown of deportation numbers year over year in table 1 in the appendix. After the United States put added pressure on Mexico to stop Central Americans from reaching their shared border in the wake of the arrival of unprecedented numbers of minors in 2014, Mexico began to deport more Central Americans year after year as compared to the United States. This trend reverted in 2023, however, as more Hondurans were once again deported from the United States than from Mexico. This coincides with the expansion of the CBP One Application, a mechanism developed during the Biden administration (2021–25) through which migrants in Mexico could first request exemptions to the Title 42 restrictions and then request an appointment to begin asylum proceedings at a US Port of Entry. As people would often wait for months on end between applying for an appointment and the date of that appointment, Mexico honored the pending appointment without detaining and deporting people.

11. Igarapé Institute, "Homicide Monitor."

12. Igarapé Institute, "Homicide Monitor."

13. Igarapé Institute, "Homicide Monitor."

14. Silva, "Cristina y Josiris en Honduras, el país al que regresó la desaparición forzada."

15. Shorack et al., "A State of Mistrust."

16. Speed, "A Dreadful Mosaic."

17. Frank-Vitale and Martínez d'Aubuisson, "The Generation of the Coup."

18. Honduras is home to a variety of gangs, the Mara Salvatrucha (MS-13) and Barrio 18 being the most famous and numerous, but smaller, more local gangs also operate. At the time of writing, this includes but is not limited to the Vatos Locos, the Aguacates, the Olanchanos, the Tercereños, the Terrazeños, the Chirizos, El Combo Que No Se Deja, the Tacamiches, los Pumas, and the Benjamins.

New groups form all the time, and some groups—especially the smaller ones—fall, get taken over, absorbed into, or exterminated by the larger, more powerful groups. The continued emergence of new, neighborhood-based gangs (many of which start as vigilante, antigang gangs) demonstrates just how much the gangs' existence responds to a prior condition of disorder, abandonment, and distrust in the forces that are supposed to guarantee security and enforce norms of justice.

19. Ahmed, "Inside Gang Territory in Honduras"; Frank-Vitale and Martínez d'Aubuisson, "On Covering San Pedro Sula and Why Global Media Outlets Will Always Dangerously Get It Wrong."

20. Drawing from my research in Honduras, I frequently offer expert testimony in asylum hearings of Honduran nationals regarding country conditions in Honduras. A judge during one of these hearings remarked that the gang dynamics of control that I was discussing might be "tangential" to life in Honduras.

21. Peutz, "Embarking on an Anthropology of Removal," 219.

22. See Brotherton and Barrios, "Displacement and Stigma"; Golash-Boza, "Forced Transnationalism"; Schuster and Majidi, "Deportation Stigma and Re-Migration."

23. The Honduran government was deeply invested in maintaining an image of bringing greater security to the country, and official reports indicated that those who were migrating were doing so because of a desire for family reunification. Casa Alianza issued reports that contradicted that claim, insisting that their data suggested that many minors were trying to leave due to violence and insecurity.

24. The decision to expel the NGOs was only reversed in 2020 in the wake of the COVID-19 pandemic, when the Honduran government desperately needed the assistance of nongovernmental actors to deal with those who were deported while the country was in lockdown.

25. Reichman, *The Broken Village.*

26. Khosravi, "Introduction," 5.

27. I reflect more fully on the practice of taking field notes in this manner in Frank-Vitale, "Writer's Block."

28. Tavernise, "Reading, Pa., Knew It Was Poor."

29. Herrera, "Trump's Gains with Pennsylvania Latinos Are Real.."

30. Slack, *Deported to Death,* 209.

31. Berry et al., "Toward a Fugitive Anthropology."

32. For a longer discussion on how my research methods evolved, including the idea of cultivating distance as a research strategy, see Frank-Vitale, "Rolling the Windows Up."

33. Golash-Boza and Hondagneu-Sotelo, "Latino Immigrant Men and the Deportation Crisis"; Goodman, *The Deportation Machine*.

34. López, *Separated*.

35. For a full breakdown of deportations to Honduras by year, country, and gender, see table 2 in the appendix.

36. The Department of Homeland Security does not always record the gender of asylum applicants. These data have gotten more reliable in recent years, but, for example, in FY 2023, 25% of all cases decided list the applicant's gender as "unknown." Of the Honduran applicants whose cases were decided in FY 2023 and who have a gender recorded, women were denied asylum or other relief in 67% of cases and men were denied relief in 75% of cases. Across all nationalities, about 50% of both men and women (of those whose gender is recorded) are denied relief.

37. Abu-Lughod, "Do Muslim Women Really Need Saving?"; Spivak, "Can the Subaltern Speak?"

38. Herrera, "Femicide in Honduras"; Menjívar and Walsh, "The Architecture of Feminicide"; Nazario, "Someone Is Always Trying to Kill You."

39. Babb, "Feminist Anthropology."

40. Davis, "Border Crossings."

41. Scholarly work that explores masculinities in this vein include Fuller, *Difícil ser hombre*; Gutmann, "Introduction"; Gutmann and Viveros Vigoya, "Masculinities in Latin America"; Theidon, "Conclusions"; Velásquez Estrada, "Intersectional Justice Denied"; Viveros Vigoya, "Contemporary Latin American Perspectives on Masculinity."

42. Rutherford, "Toward an Anthropological Understanding of Masculinities, Maleness, and Violence"; Thangaraj, "Masculinities."

43. Gutmann, "Remarking the Unmarked," 62.

44. Scholarly work on women in migration with a focus on the borderlands includes Donato et al., "The Cat and Mouse Game at the Mexico-U.S. Border"; O'Leary, "In the Footsteps of Spirits"; O'Leary, "Mujeres en el cruce"; O'Leary, "Of Coyotes, Crossings, and Cooperation." Others have written about gender, migration, and remittances, including Petrozziello, "Feminised Financial Flows"; Mckenzie and Menjívar, "The Meanings of Migration, Remittances and Gifts." The relationship between violence at home and the violence of migration for women has been explored by, among others, Stephen, "Gendered Violence and Indigenous Mexican Asylum Seekers"; Speed, "A Dreadful Mosaic"; Menjívar, *Enduring Violence*; Cook Heffron, "'Salía de uno y me metí en otro.'" In addition, much scholarship has been produced in recent years on the experience of Central

American women in transit through Mexico, including Angulo-Pasel, "The Journey of Central American Women Migrants"; Cortés, "Gender-Based Violence and Border"; Schmidt and Buechler, "I Risk Everything Because I Have Already Lost Everything"; and Varela Huerta, "La trinidad perversa de la que huyen las fugitivas centroamericanas."

45. I am grateful to Grazzia Grimaldi for her incisive reading of the manuscript and encouragement to make this point an explicit part of the text.

46. Salazar Parreñas, *Servants of Globalization*.

47. See Hill Maher, "Globalized Social Reproduction"; Kofman, "Gendered Migrations, Social Reproduction and the Household in Europe"; Salazar Parreñas, *Servants of Globalization*; Solís Vega, *Culturas del cuidado en transición*; Truong, "Gender, International Migration and Social Reproduction"; Willers, "Migration and Reproductive Strategies of Central American Women in Transit through Mexico."

48. Sanchez, "Portrait of a Human Smuggler"; Sanchez, "Women and Migrant Smuggling Facilitation in the United States."

49. Adrienne Pine also notes the commonplace nature of this saying, glossing it as "entra quien quiere, salga si puede." Pine, *Working Hard, Drinking Hard*, 71.

1. *Fronteras Internas*

This chapter is derived in part from the following articles: Amelia Frank-Vitale, "Rolling the Windows Up: On (Not) Researching Violence and Strategic Distance," *Geopolitics* 26 (1): 139–58. Copyright © 2021 (Taylor and Francis). DOI: 10.1080 /14650045.2019.1662396; Amelia Frank-Vitale and Jesse Hoffnung-Garskof, "Honduras, Gangs, and Asylum Law," *Latin American Perspectives* 52 (2): 105–24. Copyright © 2025 (Sage Publications). DOI: 10.1177/0094582X251321833.

1. I refer to Juan as "Profe," which is short for "Profesor," the title used for a teacher. It is both respectful and, especially in this shortened form, lightly affectionate.

2. *Loco*, literally, "crazy person," in this context refers to the gang members, gang leaders, who would be known to the residents as those who control the neighborhood in question.

3. Carter, *Gothic Sovereignty*; Martínez d'Aubuisson, *El que tenga miedo a morir que no nazca.*

4. There continues to be an array of smaller street gangs that hold onto control over a handful of neighborhoods. These include but are not limited to the Chirizos, the Benjamins, El Combo Que No Se Deja, the Aguacates, the

Tacamiches, the Olanchanos (a hybrid banda-pandilla), the Tercereños, the Terrazeños, Los Feos, Los Puma, La Banda del Cementerio, and Los Cantantes.

5. Carter, "Revolution Betrayed."

6. In Honduras, the landscape of organized crime is complex and multilayered. There are the maras y pandillas, neighborhood-based street gangs that control dynamics internally, in the colonia. There are also *bandas de sicarios*, or organized groups of assassins for hire, which are often, at least initially, family based. There are drug cartels dedicated to moving drugs across Honduras and into Mexico who also control territory, but their ends are distinct from that of the pandillas. There are also armed vigilante groups, mercenary-like private security groups, paramilitary groups, and death squads. Many of these organizations are involved in the drug trade and extortion at differing scales and to differing degrees. Rivalries are fierce and deadly, and alliances are often tenuous and shifting. Their fights over territory—over small swaths of poor neighborhoods—create the contours for much of the geography of violence in Honduras.

7. Bruneau et al., *Maras*; Brenneman, *Homies and Hermanos*; Gutiérrez Rivera, *Territories of Violence*.

8. Gutiérrez Rivera, *Territories of Violence*, 2.

9. Euraque, *Reinterpreting the Banana Republic*.

10. Gutiérrez Rivera, *Territories of Violence*, 50.

11. Pine, *Working Hard, Drinking Hard*, 19. While the extreme poverty of most Hondurans is perhaps a compelling explanation for the rise of the maras, if socioeconomic factors were the whole story, Nicaragua, Honduras's southern, poorer neighbor would be at the top, as Bruneau et al. (*Maras*) note. Nicaragua, however, while being the poorest country in Central American (and the second poorest in the western hemisphere, behind Haiti) is by far the safest country in the region, and the maras have not been able to establish a presence there.

12. Gutiérrez Rivera, *Territories of Violence*, 51.

13. Grillo, *El Narco*; Gutiérrez Rivera, *Territories of Violence*, 4.

14. Matta Ballesteros was also supported by the CIA as part of its counterinsurgency agenda in Central America in the '80s, until the DEA went after him when it was attempting to apprehend the traffickers responsible for the murder of one of its agents in Mexico. Matta Ballesteros had become a bit of a folk hero in Honduras, distributing resources liberally, and people tried to set the US Embassy in Tegucigalpa on fire in protest after he was arrested.

15. Bruneau et al., *Maras*, 2.

16. Bruneau et al., *Maras*, 93; Arce, *Blood Barrios*, 178–79.

17. Carter, "Gothic Sovereignty."

18. Carter, "Gothic Sovereignty." 485.

19. For a full discussion of mano dura in El Salvador, see Wolf, *Mano Dura*.

20. Bruneau et al., *Maras*, 91. *Mano dura* translates conceptually to "iron fist" and signifies a suite of policies including harsh prison sentences, guilt by association, increased visible state violence against suspected offenders, and the abrogation of rights in the name of security.

21. Brenneman, *Homies and Hermanos*, 45; Bruneau et al., *Maras*, 142.

22. Bruneau et al., *Maras*, 98; Arce, *Blood Barrios*, 176.

23. Pine, *Working Hard, Drinking Hard*, 45, 57; Amnesty International, "Honduras: Zero Tolerance . . . for Impunity."

24. Pine, *Working Hard, Drinking Hard*, 72, 193, 198.

25. Diario La Prensa, "Guerra entre diez bandas genera violencia en Choloma."

26. Menjívar and Walsh, "The Architecture of Feminicide"; Varela Huerta, "La trinidad perversa de la que huyen las fugitivas centroamericanas."

27. For more on the problem of generation in Honduras, see Frank-Vitale and d'Aubuisson, "The Generation of the Coup."

28. Observatorio Nacional de la Violencia, "Boletín especial sobre homicidios en Honduras, 2019."

29. Observatorio Nacional de la Violencia, "Boletín especial sobre homicidios en Honduras, 2019."

30. Skurski and Coronil, "Introduction," 6; Theidon, "'Terror's Talk," 23.

31. Besteman, "Representing Violence and 'Othering' Somalia."

32. Feldman, "Ethnographic States of Emergency," 245.

33. Drybread, "Writing About Violence," 128.

34. Skurski and Coronil, "Introduction," 15; Daniel, *Charred Lullabies*, 4; Bourgois, "The Continuum of Violence in War and Peace," 433; Daniel, *Charred Lullabies*, 4.

35. Feldman, "Ethnographic States of Emergency," 245.

36. Bourgois, "The Continuum of Violence in War and Peace," 433.

37. Swedenburg, "With Genet in the Palestinian Field," 414.

38. Galtung, "Violence, Peace, and Peace Research"; Farmer, "An Anthropology of Structural Violence." The concept of everyday violence was first proposed by Nancy Scheper-Hughes in *Death Without Weeping* to identify the "routinization of human suffering" (16) and the "mundane rituals and routines of humiliation and violence" (225). Scheper-Hughes and Bourgois, in their crucial volume on violence, *Violence in War and Peace*, situate everyday violence as emerging from that which is "inherent in particular social, economic, and political formations" (21).

Arthur Kleinman, in "The Violences of Everyday Life," uses an essentially identical operating definition, writing that "the violence such structural deprivation does to people" is both "mundane and multiple" and calling for attention to this violence across the social order (227).

39. Everyday violence is connected to other forms of violence—personal, structural, symbolic, and legal. This is not a new assertion. Theoretical approaches to understanding the interconnectedness of multiple kinds and registers of violence include Bourgois's "continuum of violence," in "The Continuum of Violence in War and Peace"; Auyero and Berti's "violent concatenations," in *In Harm's Way*; and Speed's "violent mosaic," in "A Dreadful Mosaic." Here I simply want to call attention to the twinned features of everyday violence and the violence of everyday life as they are present and mutually reinforcing—while being distinct and potentially extricable experiences—in Honduras. This is to say that the violence of structural deprivation and marginalization can exist without the quotidian experience of murder always in the background. And at the same time, brutal physical violence can be a feature of daily life without the routinization of suffering that is structurally produced through poverty and exclusion.

40. Das and Kleinman, "Introduction."

41. Vigh, "Crisis and Chronicity," 11.

42. "Who are you, who are you . . . I'm not anyone, but I know what's up around here."

43. "Don't think it doesn't, it hurts, it hurts when they kill a brother. It hurts. If I were the boss . . . "

2. *Mañana Me Mandan, Mañana Me Vengo*

This chapter is derived in part from Amelia Frank-Vitale, "'Better in Jail There Than Dead Here': Deportation and (Social) Death in Honduras," in *Migration and Mortality: Social Death, Dispossession, and Survival in the Americas*, edited by Jamie Longazel and Miranda Cady Hallett (Philadelphia: Temple University Press, 2021). Copyright © 2021 (Temple University Press).

1. Coutin, "Deportation Studies."

2. This focus emerges, in part, because the field is largely rooted in a framework of governmentality and the state of exception. For deportation scholars who have theorized how the state reasserts itself through the ability to remove, see Peutz, "Embarking on an Anthropology of Removal"; De Genova, "Migrant 'Illegality' and Deportability in Everyday Life"; De Genova, "Spectacles of Migrant 'Illegality'"; Walters, "Deportation, Expulsion, and the International Police of

Aliens"; Walters, "Expulsion, Power, Mobilisation"; Slack, *Deported to Death*. The modern order of citizenship and corresponding rights based on territorial belonging would not reproduce itself naturally; deportation is precisely the regime through which this order and citizens themselves are constituted and maintained. This body of literature has opened important avenues for analysis, understanding deportation not as the obvious and logical punishment for unauthorized presence but as a crucial element of how the state makes and displays its sovereignty in the context of a globalizing world and all its attendant blurring of national boundaries and power. For a key collection of this literature, see De Genova and Peutz, *The Deportation Regime*.

3. Kanstroom, *Aftermath*; Dingeman-Cerda and Rumbaut, "Unwelcome Returns"; Peutz, "Embarking on an Anthropology of Removal"; Coutin, *Exiled Home*; Zilberg, "Fools Banished from the Kingdom."

4. Schuster and Majidi, "What Happens Post-Deportation?"; Collyer, "Deportation and the Micropolitics of Exclusion"; Drotbohm, "On the Durability and the Decomposition of Citizenship."

5. Martínez et al., "Repeat Migration in the Age of the 'Unauthorized Permanent Resident.'"

6. Tanya Golash-Boza, for example, in *Deported*, found that in Guatemala adjustment to life in one's "home" country after deportation can be fraught, requiring learning different rules, navigating unfamiliar social cues, and contending with unfamiliar dynamics of violence. In addition, deportees are frequently doubly stigmatized, suspected of being criminals whether or not their removal from the United States was related to a conviction and facing the stigma of being former providers—when they were sending remittances—who are now unable to earn a living. Also see Brotherton and Barrios, "Displacement and Stigma"; Golash-Boza, "Forced Transnationalism." Others have found a widespread idea that deportees are inherently criminal and at least partly culpable for rising violence. For additional work in this vein regarding Jamaica, see Charles, "The Reintegration of Criminal Deportees in Society"; regarding Mexico, see Anderson, "Tagged as a Criminal"; and regarding the Dominican Republic, see Brotherton and Barrios, *Banished to the Homeland*.

7. These studies show that deportees are at risk because of their de facto foreignness. At the same time, that otherness is sometimes also capitalized on and repackaged into a kind of "opportunity" for those who are deported and the countries receiving them, as well as international business interests. Call centers have proliferated in places where there are large populations of these kinds of deportees, like Guatemala, Mexico, and the Dominican Republic, where companies

serving US customers can hire cheap labor that still "sounds" "American" on the phone. See Rodkey, "Disposable Labor, Repurposed"; Anderson, "Tagged as a Criminal"; Golash-Boza, "Negative Credentials, Foreign-Earned Capital, and Call Centers." Alternately, deportees are sometimes seen as a potential resource for "development," possibly returning with savings and skills acquired before being sent back, building on the expectation and reliance on remittances. See Scarnato, "Deportation Meets Development"; Wiltberger, "Beyond Remittances." In this scenario, where foreignness is seen as a potential advantage, deportees are still constructed as other than nationals, different from their co-citizens who have grown up in the country, who are understood to be those who are *really* from there.

8. Martínez and Martínez d'Aubuisson, *The Hollywood Kid*.

9. Zilberg, *Space of Detention*, 37.

10. Katie Dingeman-Cerda has described the process of adapting to life in El Salvador for those who grew up in the United States as "segmented reintegration," adapting a term used by migration scholars to describe the process of "assimilating" over time into a new country after migrating. See Dingeman-Cerda, "Segmented Re/integration." For other studies that illuminate the Salvadoran experience of familial rupture as constitutive of deportation, see Dingeman-Cerda and Coutin, "The Ruptures of Return Deportation's Confounding Effects"; Berger-Cardoso et al, "Deporting Fathers"; Hagan et al., "U.S. Deportation Policy, Family Separation, and Circular Migration."

11. Coutin, *Exiled Home*.

12. Heike Drotbohm and Ines Hasselberg, in their conceptualization of a "deportation corridor," highlight the social suffering of deportation, both for those who are "banished" and those who remain behind. See Drotbohm and Hasselberg, "Deportation, Anxiety, Justice." William López's *Separated* focuses on the webs of disruption in the wake of an immigration raid and the deportation of the male family members. Joanna Dreby, in "The Burden of Deportation on Children in Mexican Immigrant Families," details the layers of trauma for children whose parents are deported or could be deported, while Deborah Boehm's *Returned* shows how deportation affects transnational families across borders, sometimes compelling the "expulsion" of US citizens as they join their deported loved ones in Mexico.

13. For other scholars who have noted that while the legal fiction may have persisted, a political reality has also long been present where the United States relies strategically on the potential consequences of deportation functioning as a disciplining mechanism for undocumented labor, especially as criminal and

immigration law increasingly converge, see De Genova, "Migrant 'Illegality' and Deportability in Everyday Life"; Horton, "From 'Deportability' to 'Denounce-ability'"; Golash-Boza, *Deported*.

14. Goodman, *The Deportation Machine*. Furthermore, deportation is legally a civil procedure, so those who are subjected to it are not necessarily guaranteed all the due process rights that a criminal matter would entail. Most notably there is no right to have a government-provided attorney. Similarly, the idea of double jeopardy does not apply. See Bleichmar, "Deportation as Punishment." Being incarcerated for a criminal conviction in the United States and then being deported after the sentence is served is both common and legal.

15. Khosravi, "Introduction," 5.

16. Slack, *Deported to Death*, 26.

17. Kanstroom, *Aftermath*.

18. Other scholars have also examined the ways in which the criminal justice system, in pushing poor people of color to take plea deals, also funnels individuals toward deportation by encouraging them to plead guilty, whether or not they are, in return for a reduced sentence. The guilty plea, however, often unbeknownst to the person pleading, can then result in deportation.

19. For work that illuminates the intentional violence of US deportation policy and practice aimed at Mexicans in the US-Mexico border region, where deportation is used as a weapon to directly put people in harm's way, see De León, "The Efficacy and Impact of the Alien Transfer Exit Programme"; De León, *The Land of Open Graves*; Slack, *Deported to Death*.

20. Gibney, "Is Deportation a Form of Forced Migration?," 122.

21. The literature that highlights the violence of "civil" deportation after IIRIRA also shows how deportation, even when coupled with incarceration, fails to achieve the supposed goal of immobilizing people once they are banished to their estranged homelands. Like the failed logic of PTD, which relies on the inhospitable borderlands to do violence to the bodies of migrants and, in turn, serve as a deterrent effect, as De León shows in *The Land of Open Graves*, the harshness of detention and deportation fails to deter remigration efforts. Lauren Heidbrink, in *Migranthood*, argues that the debt-driven remigration of deportees highlights how heightened enforcement—which makes the costs of migration higher—actually perpetuates the very return migration it seeks to impede. Likewise, along the US-Mexico border, deportees who locate "home" in the United States are those who are most likely to try to remigrate, regardless of threats, risks, viability, and costs, as Martínez et al. show in "Repeat Migration in the Age of the 'Unauthorized Permanent Resident.'" Geographer Nancy Hiemstra has extended this

analysis to argue that US detention and deportation policy aims to make this disciplinary function work extraterritorially, counting on the threat of future incarceration to have a "pre-entry regulation value" for would-be migrants in Ecuador. She notes, in "Geopolitical Reverberations of US Migrant Detention and Deportation," that even as this is an unsuccessful strategy in terms of curtailing migrations, it is still the logic underpinning the entire US deportation regime.

22. Dingeman-Cerda and Coutin, "The Ruptures of Return."

23. García, *Seeking Refuge.*

24. For detailed explanations of the mediated statuses that became available to some Central Americans in the 1980s and 1990s, see Coutin, "Falling Outside"; Coutin, *Nations of Emigrants.*

25. Reichman, *The Broken Village.*

26. Coutin, "Being En Route"; García, *Seeking Refuge.*

27. Goodman, *The Deportation Machine*, 183.

28. Carlsen, "Armoring NAFTA."

29. De León, *The Land of Open Graves.*

30. Carlsen, "Armoring NAFTA."

31. US Department of State, "Merida Initiative."

32. Doering-White et al., "Chapter 4: Central America"; Vogt, "Dirty Work, Dangerous Others."

33. This pattern endured until 2023, when the CBP One Application allowed non-Mexican nationals to make an appointment while in Mexico to seek asylum in the United States. As Hondurans take advantage of this process, they are no longer detained and deported by Mexico in such high numbers. Rather their presence in Mexico is tolerated and managed, through coordination between the Mexican and US governments.

34. Kovic and Kelly, "Migrant Bodies as Targets of Security Policies"; Vogt, "The Arterial Border."

35. Varela Huerta, "México, de 'frontera vertical' a 'país tapón.'"

36. Leutert, *Migrant Protection Protocols.*

37. Cuneo et al., "What Counts As 'Safe'?"

38. Garibo García and Call, "Caravanas de personas migrantes como expresiones contradictorias de tácticas de sobrevivencia y prácticas de subjetivación política."

39. Coutin, "Confined Within"; FitzGerald, "Remote Control of Migration."

40. The Darién Gap is the undeveloped and inhospitable area at the Colombia-Panama border. This stretch of jungle terrain had become a notoriously dangerous, week-long crossing point for migrants making their way north.

41. Central Americans in general have high rates of asylum denial compared to other nationalities. Honduras, however, has consistently been among the nationalities with the highest rates of asylum denial overall, with over 87% of cases decided in FY 2020 being rejected. See TRAC, "Asylum Denial Rates Continue to Climb."

42. FitzGerald, "Remote Control of Migration."

43. Zilberg, *Space of Detention.*

44. Coutin, "Confined Within."

45. Anthropology does not have a single, unified theory of circulation. (See Rockefeller, "Flow.") The term has long roots in the discipline, however, being a central feature of the interpretations of the Kula Ring and kinship. Circulation is the movement of things and people, from givers to receivers, weaving society together through their ongoing exchange. The term gained renewed prominence as a way to refer to the imagined free flow of goods, ideas, and people across national boundaries at the end of the twentieth century. Circulation becomes the language of mobility, multicultural encounter, and hybridity associated with progress, yet the focus on the moving entities frequently obscures just how this movement is channeled. For this renewed focus on circulation from this angle, see, e.g., Tsing, "The Global Situation"; Tsing, *Friction.*

46. Basch et al., *Nations Unbound.*

47. Coutin, "Confined Within," 201.

48. Coutin, "Confined Within," 201.

49. Malkki, "National Geographic."

50. Coutin, "Deportation Studies."

51. Wimmer and Glick Schiller, "Methodological Nationalism, the Social Sciences, and the Study of Migration."

3. ¡Bienvenido a Tu Tierra!

This chapter is derived in part from Amelia Frank-Vitale, "'Better in Jail There Than Dead Here': Deportation and (Social) Death in Honduras," in *Migration and Mortality: Social Death, Dispossession, and Survival in the Americas,* edited by Jamie Longazel and Miranda Cady Hallett (Philadelphia: Temple University Press, 2021). Copyright © 2021 (Temple University Press); and from Amelia Frank-Vitale and Juan José Martínez d'Aubuisson, "The Generation of the Coup: Honduran Youth at Risk and of Risk," *Journal of Latin American and Caribbean Anthropology* 25, no. 4 (2020): 552–68. Copyright © 2020 (Wiley). DOI: https://doi.org/10.1111/jlca.12512.

1. Anderson, "'Tagged as a Criminal'"; Zilberg, "Fools Banished from the Kingdom."

2. UNESCO, "Honduras."

3. Ordóñez, "Analfabetismo, un problema viejo con nuevos actores en Honduras."

4. FEREMA, "Educación."

5. FEREMA, "Educación."

6. During the Trump administration, insiders at the US embassy in Honduras reported that the agenda there was primarily set by the Department of Homeland Security and not diplomats representing the State Department, as would usually be the case.

7. Funes, "Representantes de la ASJ habrían recomendado 'reestructurar' Salud y Educación."

8. Geglia, "The Roots of the National Strike in Honduras."

9. As part of my collaboration with Pro-R, I offered participatory photography workshops to the youth enrolled in the program. The workshops combined my interest in exploring ways to counter the hyperviolent narrative around San Pedro Sula and foster mechanisms of self-representation with an interest from Pro-R participants in having opportunities for fun activities that were outside of their normal routine. I taught the participants the basics of photographic composition, and we discussed the value of photographing everyday life. Participants took cameras with them to photograph as they wished, then we reconvened, reviewed the images, and collectively developed two exhibits that were shown at the Museum of Anthropology and History of San Pedro Sula. The opportunity to showcase their work at the museum and speak to the press themselves about what that work meant was exciting for many of them; they worked hard to choose the images, mount the printed photographs, craft a statement to explain the exhibit, and receive the public at the exhibit's opening. While the workshops and the photographic products do not figure in this book, running these workshops and building these exhibits was one small way of contributing my time, resources, and ethnographic sensibility to cultivating a counterdiscourse and providing space for deported and displaced youth to narrate their own experience.

10. Mercado, "Menores retornados tienen oportunidad de reinserción."

11. Khosravi, "Introduction," 10.

12. Fonseca et al, "Reintegration," 9.

13. US GAO, "Central America," 4.

14. US GAO, "Central America," 10.

15. El País, "ONU apoyará programas de reinserción de migrantes retornados."

16. Ruiz Soto and Mora, "El lado olvidado de la deportación."

17. Spear, "Disarmament, Demobilization, Reinsertion and Reintegration in Africa."

18. Theidon, "Transitional Subjects."

19. Holmer and Shtuni, "Returning Foreign Fighters and the Reintegration Imperative."

20. Golash-Boza and Ceciliano-Navarro, "Life After Deportation."

21. Dingeman-Cerda and Coutin, "The Ruptures of Return."

22. Brotherton and Barrios, *Banished to the Homeland*, 298.

23. Dako-Gyeke and Kodom, "Deportation and Re-Integration."

24. Golash-Boza, "'Negative Credentials,' 'Foreign-Earned' Capital, and Call Centers."

25. Hagan et al., "A Longitudinal Analysis of Resource Mobilisation among Forced and Voluntary Return Migrants in Mexico."

26. Khosravi, "Introduction," 5.

27. Giroux, "Neoliberalism and the Death of the Social State," 591.

28. Pine, "Forging an Anthropology of Neoliberal Fascism."

29. Rainsford, "Honduras Police Purge May Be Derailed by Alternative Agenda." For more on the Honduran police and the deep mistrust they engender in Honduras, see Shorack et al., "A State of Mistrust."

30. Later, the "anti-maras" force that Profe Juan mentioned, the FNAMP, would be disbanded after reports surfaced that among their ranks, officers essentially operated as a death squad on behalf of MS-13. DIPAMPCO, the new unit formed in the wake of this, included many former FNAMP officers. For more, see Olson, "How an emergency declaration deepened Honduras's crime crisis"; Redacción, "Escuadrón militar de ejecuciones arbitrarias en la FNAMP y sicariato desde la PMOP."

31. Geertz, "Deep Hanging Out," citing Clifford, "Anthropology and/as Travel," citing Rosaldo, "Anthropology and 'the Field.'"

32. "Jomi" is the term used locally to refer to full-fledged members of the gang. It is derived from the English "homie."

33. Aretxaga, *Shattering Silence*.

34. Collyer, "Deportation and the Micropolitics of Exclusion."

35. Schuster and Majidi, "What Happens Post-Deportation?," 234.

36. During my first visit to the migrant shelter Hermanos en El Camino in 2010, I was not initially inclined to ride the freight train; in fact, when a group of

migrants who had been staying at the shelter first suggested it to me, I balked. Then I heard the priest who ran the shelter encouraging a male journalist and another male visitor to ride the train with the migrants in order to experience what it's like. My reaction then was, if the men are going to do this, I am too. With a small group of resident migrants with whom I had developed a friendship—including Carlos—I rode the train from Ixtepec to Matías Romero, about two hours. When the train pulled into a depot just after Matías Romero my migrant accompaniers and I all got off the train and took a bus back to Ixtepec; the rest of the migrants continued on the train north to Veracruz.

4. Alerta que Camina

1. Gómez Johnson and Espinosa Moreno, "Transformaciones en las migraciones contemporáneas en México (2000–2019)"; Gramajo Bauer, "Dos crisis que explican las dinámicas migratorias más recientes en los tres países del norte de Centroamérica"; Marchand, "The Caravanas de Migrantes Making Their Way North"; Mariscal Nava and Torre Cantalapiedra, "Batallando con fronteras"; Rizzo Lara, "La Caminata del Migrante."

2. This January 2011 caravan was the first migrant caravan of the kind that became well known in 2018. There was a precursor caravan-like small protest movement in fall 2010, however, including many of the same actors, aimed at pressuring the government to change its laws regarding irregular immigration.

3. This chapter is not intended to narrate in detail the specific twists and turns of the 2018 caravan. For that kind of journalistic account, see *Caravana* by Alberto Pradilla and *Juntos, Todos Juntos* by Carlos Martínez. For a good history of the pre-fall 2018 caravan, see Martínez Hernández-Mejía, *Reflexiones sobre la caravana migrante*; and for the 2018–19 stretch, see Gandini, "Las 'oleadas' de las caravanas migrantes y las cambiantes respuestas gubernamentales"; Colín, "Caravanas de migrantes y refugiados en México." Caravanero Douglas Oviedo also published his own fictionalized memoir-novel based on his experience of the 2018 caravan, *Caravaneros*.

4. For similarly engaged work on caravans, see Núñez-Chaim et al., "Caravanas migrantes y el régimen de control fronterizo en México en Tiempos pandémicos"; Garibo García and Call, "Caravanas de personas migrantes como expresiones contradictorias de tácticas de sobrevivencia y prácticas de subjetivación política"; Balaguera and Gonzales, "On the Migrant Trail, a Refugee Movement Emerges."

5. El-Shaarawi and Razsa, "Movements upon Movements," 96.

6. In this chapter, a few individuals are referred to by their real names, as their profile and coverage in the media make them public figures, and I refer to them in that capacity.

7. CDHDF, "Presenta el reportero Irineo Mújica imágenes de agresiones sufridas a manos de agentes de migración"; Bachmann, "Photojournalist Accuses Mexican Immigration Agents of Robbery."

8. Galán, "Levanta fotoperiodista huelga de hambre frente al INM en precario estado de salud."

9. Martínez, "Los coyotes domados"; Soberanes, "La PGR identifica 60 cuerpos encontrados en San Fernando, Tamaulipas."

10. Amnesty International, "Mexico: Migrants' Rights Defender at Risk: José Alberto Donis Rodríguez"; Amnesty International, "Father Alejandro Solalinde Guerra—Mexico."

11. *Elvira.*

12. "Elvira's Song."

13. Mariscal, "'Ojalá nos acompañaran todo el camino'"; Moreno, "Pide caravana reconocer como grupo vulnerable a migrantes."

14. Gómez Johnson and Espinosa Moreno, "Transformaciones en las migraciones contemporáneas en México (2000-2019)"; Villalever and Schütze, "Caravanas Migrantes as Counter Strategies against Violence and (Im)Mobility"; Colín, "Caravanas de migrantes y refugiados en México"; Montes, "Fleeing Home"; Velasco Ortiz and Hernández López, "Salir de las sombras."

15. Frank-Vitale and Núñez Chaim, "'Lady Frijoles'"; Velasco Ortiz and Hernández López, "Salir de las sombras"; París Pombo and Montes, "Visibilidad como estrategia de movilidad"; Irwin, "The Migrant Knowledge of a Caravanero."

16. Frank-Vitale and Palomo Contreras, "Caravan Migrant Roots"; Rosas, "Paso a paso hacia la Paz."

17. Martínez Hernández-Mejía, *Reflexiones sobre la caravana migrante.*

18. Flotte, "Transmigrations"; Mejía, "Race in Trans and Queer Migration"; Zecena, "Migrating Like a Queen."

19. Bassols Batalla, *Caravana de hombres libres.*

20. Novelo, "Pequeñas historias de grandes momentos de la vida de los mineros del carbón de Coahuila."

21. Librado Luna, *A 70 años la caravana minera de 1951 de Nueva Rosita a la Capital en busca de justicia.*

22. The 1972 Caravan for Justice and Land comprised peasants and students who traversed from Tlaxcala to Mexico City to make their demands and their suffering known. For an account of this caravan, see Trevizo, "Dispersed Communist

Networks and Grassroots Leadership of Peasant Revolts in Mexico." The Zapatistas, the autonomous Indigenous rebels from the state of Chiapas, have also made use of caravans to pressure the Mexican government. For more on the Zapatista caravans, see Stahler-Sholk, "Globalization and Social Movement Resistance"; Neumann, "We Make the Road by Walking." More recently, the Wixárika, an Indigenous group from Central Mexico, undertook a Caravana por la Dignidad y Conciencia (Caravan for Dignity and Conscience), moving collectively from their territory in Jalisco to Mexico City to force a meeting with the Mexican president, as reported by Contreras, "Caravana de Dignidad y Conciencia Wixárika avanza con paso firme hacia la CDMX." Most well known, perhaps, were the Caravanas del Sur and Caravanas del Norte organized by Javier Sicilia's Movimiento por la Paz con Justicia y Dignidad, which saw busloads of people affected by violence in Mexico, peace activists, and journalists move together across large swaths of southern Mexico and then northern Mexico, articulating personal tragedies and local struggles with each other, across class and space in the country. For analysis of the Sicilia-led caravans, see Muñoz Martínez, "The Politics of Scale, Place, and Mobility in the Mexican Peace Movement, 2006–2012"; Gordillo-García, "Social Movements and Political-Emotional Communities"; Gallagher, "The Last Mile Problem."

23. Ramírez, "Autonomía de las migraciones"; Rho, "Ciudadanía y luchas migrantes"; Varela Huerta, "'Luchas migrantes'"; Varela Huerta and McLean, "Caravanas de migrantes en México."

24. Frank-Vitale, "'Fui migrante y me hospedaron'"; Doering-White and Díaz De León, "The Shelter Multiple."

25. Garibo García and Call, "Caravanas de personas migrantes como expresiones contradictorias de tácticas de sobrevivencia y prácticas de subjetivación política"; Innocente Escamilla, "Usos políticos del sufrimiento en el Vía Crucis del Migrante, Ixtepec, Oaxaca"; Varela Huerta and McLean, "Caravanas de migrantes en México"; Vargas Carrasco, "El Vía Crucis del Migrante."

26. Vargas Carrasco, "El Vía Crucis del Migrante"; Martínez Hernández-Mejía, *Reflexiones sobre la caravana migrante*.

27. Diego Rivera Hernández, "Making Absence Visible"; McLean, "A Question That Has No End."

28. Boss, *Ambiguous Loss*.

29. Stephen, "Los nuevos desaparecidos y muertos"; Ferrer, "Madres centroamericanas estiman en 70 mil los migrantes desaparecidos en México."

30. Vogt, *Lives in Transit*, 191.

31. Rizzo Lara, "La Caminata del Migrante"; Chávez, "Understanding Migrant Caravans from the Place of Place Privilege."

32. Torre Cantalapiedra, *Caravanas*, 60; Gandini et al., *Caravanas*; París Pombo and Montes, "Visibilidad como estrategía de movilidad"; Varela Huerta and McLean, "Caravanas de migrantes en México."

33. I describe this blockade in a piece I wrote for NACLA. See Frank-Vitale, "From Caravan to Exodus, from Migration to Movement." It also features in Pradilla's *Caravana*.

34. Kleinman, *Adventure Capital*, 8.

35. Frank-Vitale, "From Caravan to Exodus, from Migration to Movement."

36. Papadopoulos et al., *Escape Routes*; Nyers, "Migrant Citizenships and Autonomous Mobilities"; Rodríguez, "The Battle for the Border"; Olmos, "Racialized Im/Migration and Autonomy of Migration Perspectives"; Casas Cortés and Cobarrubias, "La autonomía de la migración"; Casas Cortes et al., "Riding Routes and Itinerant Borders."

37. Casas Cortes et al., "Riding Routes and Itinerant Borders," 895.

38. Cordero et al., *América Latina en movimiento*, 18; Mezzadra, "The Gaze of Autonomy"; Papadopoulos and Tsianos, "After Citizenship."

39. Mitropoulos, "Autonomy, Recognition, and Movement."

40. Papadopoulos et al., *Escape Routes*, 199.

41. Papadopoulos and Tsianos, "After Citizenship," 184.

42. See Casas Cortés and Cobarrubias, "La autonomía de la migración," for a thorough genealogy of the autonomy of migration framework.

43. Mezzadra, "The Gaze of Autonomy," 121.

44. Mezzadra, "The Gaze of Autonomy," 137.

45. Papadopoulos et al., *Escape Routes*, 209.

46. Papadopoulos and Tsianos, "After Citizenship," 188.

47. Núñez-Chaim et al., "Caravanas migrantes y el régimen de control fronterizo en México en Tiempos pandémicos," 2.

48. Franz, "Contesting the Place of Protest in Migrant Caravans," 183; Cuéllar, "Waterproofing the State."

49. Cuéllar, "Waterproofing the State."

50. Franz, "Contesting the Place of Protest in Migrant Caravans," 183.

51. Barragán, "México disuelve las caravanas migrantes para evitar que lleguen a la frontera con Estados Unidos"; Clemente, "Disuelven caravanas migrantes que esperaban documentos en Chiapas"; Domínguez, "Seis caravanas migrantes no llegaron a EU en tres meses."

52. Villalever and Schütze, "Caravanas Migrantes as Counter Strategies against Violence and (Im)Mobility"; Arriola Vega, "'Migration Crisis' and Migrant Caravans (October 2018–January 2019) in Mexico."

53. Clemente, "Muchos venezolanos en caravana ahora que México pide visa."

Conclusion

1. De Genova, "Afterword. Deportation: The Last Word?," 262.
2. Khosravi, "Introduction," 2.
3. Khosravi, "Introduction," 12.
4. Khosravi, "Introduction," 4.
5. De Genova, "Migrant 'Illegality' and Deportability in Everyday Life."
6. Rosas, "Grief and Border-Crossing Rage," 122.
7. El-Shaarawi and Razsa, "Movements upon Movements," 108.
8. Ticktin, "Borders," 144; emphasis in original.

References

Abu-Lughod, Lila. "Do Muslim Women Really Need Saving? Anthropological Reflections on Cultural Relativism and Its Others." *American Anthropologist* 104, no. 3 (September 1, 2002): 783–90.

Ahmed, Azam. "Inside Gang Territory in Honduras: 'Either They Kill Us or We Kill Them.'" *The New York Times*, May 4, 2019. https://www.nytimes.com/interactive/2019/05/04/world/americas/honduras-gang-violence.html.

Åkesson, Lisa. "Making Migrants Responsible for Development: Cape Verdean Returnees and Northern Migration Policies." *Africa Spectrum* 46, no. 1 (2011): 61–83.

Amnesty International. "Father Alejandro Solalinde Guerra—Mexico." 2010. http://www.amnesty.ie/node/1768.

Amnesty International. "Honduras: Zero Tolerance . . . for Impunity: Extrajudicial Executions of Children and Youths since 1998." Amnesty International, February 25, 2003. https://www.refworld.org/reference/countryrep/amnesty/2003/en/33152.

Amnesty International. "Mexico: Migrants' Rights Defender at Risk: José Alberto Donis Rodríguez." November 16, 2010. https://www.amnesty.org/en/documents/amr41/084/2010/en/.

Anderson, Jill. "'Tagged as a Criminal': Narratives of Deportation and Return Migration in a Mexico City Call Center." *Latino Studies* 13, no. 1 (March 2015): 8–27. https://doi.org/10.1057/lst.2014.72.

Andrews, Abigail Leslie. *Banished Men: How Migrants Endure the Violence of Deportation*. University of California Press, 2023.

Angulo-Pasel, C. "The Journey of Central American Women Migrants: Engendering the Mobile Commons." *Mobilities* 13, no. 6 (2018): 894–909. https://doi.org/10.1080/17450101.2018.1498225.

Arce, Alberto. *Blood Barrios: Dispatches from the World's Deadliest Streets.* Translated by John Washington and Daniela Ugaz. Zed Books, 2018.

Aretxaga, Begoña. *Shattering Silence: Women, Nationalism, and Political Subjectivity in Northern Ireland.* Princeton University Press, 1997.

Arriola Vega, Luis Alfredo. "'Migration Crisis' and Migrant Caravans (October 2018–January 2019) in Mexico: An Analysis from Contemporary Academic Publications." In *Crises and Migration: Critical Perspectives from Latin America*, edited by Enrique Coraza de los Santos and Luis Alfredo Arriola Vega. Springer International Publishing, 2022. https://doi.org/10.1007/978-3-031-07059-4_3.

Auyero, Javier, and María Fernanda Berti. *In Harm's Way: The Dynamics of Urban Violence.* Princeton University Press, 2015.

Babb, Florence E. "Feminist Anthropology." In *Theory in Social and Cultural Anthropology: An Encyclopedia*, edited by R. Jon McGee and Richard L. Warms. SAGE Publications, 2013. http://dx.doi.org/10.4135/9781452276311.n81.

Bachmann, Ingrid. "Photojournalist Accuses Mexican Immigration Agents of Robbery." *LatAm Journalism Review*, July 20, 2010. https://latamjournalismreview.org/articles/photojournalist-accuses-mexican-immigration-agents-of-robbery/.

Balaguera, Martha, and Alfonso Gonzales. "On the Migrant Trail, a Refugee Movement Emerges." *NACLA Report on the Americas*, January 29, 2018. https://nacla.org/blog/2018/01/29/migrant-trail-refugee-movement-emerges.

Barragán, Almudena. "México disuelve las caravanas migrantes para evitar que lleguen a la frontera con Estados Unidos." *El País México*, November 28, 2024. https://elpais.com/mexico/2024-11-28/mexico-disuelve-las-caravanas-migrantes-para-evitar-que-lleguen-a-la-frontera-con-estados-unidos.html.

Basch, Linda, Nina Glick Schiller, and Cristina Blanc-Szanton. *Nations Unbound: Transnational Projects, Postcolonial Predicaments and Deterritorialized Nation-States.* Routledge, 1994.

Bassols Batalla, Ángel. *Caravana de hombres libres: La huelga de Nueva Rosita y Cloete.* Editorial E-A, 1951.

Berger Cardoso, Jodi, Erin Randle Hamilton, Néstor Rodríguez, Karl Eschbach, and Jacqueline Hagan. "Deporting Fathers: Involuntary Transnational

Families and Intent to Remigrate among Salvadoran Deportees." *International Migration Review* 50, no. 1 (2016): 197–230. https://doi.org/10.1111/imre.12106.

Berry, Maya J., Claudia Chávez Argüelles, Shanya Cordis, Sarah Ihmoud, and Elizabeth Velásquez Estrada. "Toward a Fugitive Anthropology: Gender, Race, and Violence in the Field." *Cultural Anthropology* 32, no. 4 (2017): 537–65. https://doi.org/10.14506/ca32.4.05.

Besteman, Catherine. "Representing Violence and 'Othering' Somalia." *Cultural Anthropology* 11, no. 1 (1996): 120–33.

Bleichmar, Javier. "Deportation as Punishment: A Historical Analysis of the British Practice of Banishment and Its Impact on Modern Constitutional Law." *Georgetown Immigration Law Journal* 14, no. 1 (September 22, 1999): 115.

Boehm, Deborah. *Returned: Going and Coming in an Age of Deportation.* University of California Press, 2016.

Boehm, Deborah. "US-Mexico Mixed Migration in an Age of Deportation: An Inquiry into the Transnational Circulation of Violence." *Refugee Survey Quarterly* 30, no. 1 (March 1, 2011): 1–21. https://doi.org/10.1093/rsq/hdq042.

Boss, Pauline. *Ambiguous Loss: Learning to Live with Unresolved Grief.* Harvard University Press, 2000.

Bourgois, Philippe. "The Continuum of Violence in War and Peace: Post-Cold War Lessons from El Salvador." In *Violence in War and Peace: An Anthology,* edited by Nancy Scheper-Hughes and Philippe Bourgois. Blackwell Publishing, 2003.

Brenneman, Robert. *Homies and Hermanos: God and Gangs in Central America.* Oxford University Press, 2011.

Brotherton, David C., and Luis Barrios. *Banished to the Homeland.* Columbia University Press, 2011. https://doi.org/10.7312/brot14934.

Brotherton, David C., and Luis Barrios. "Displacement and Stigma: The Social-Psychological Crisis of the Deportee." *Crime, Media, Culture* 5, no. 1 (2009): 29–55. https://doi.org/10.1177/1741659008102061.

Bruneau, Thomas, Lucía Dammert, and Elizabeth Skinner. *Maras: Gang Violence and Security in Central America.* University of Texas Press, 2011.

Carlsen, Laura. "Armoring NAFTA: The Battleground for Mexico's Future." *NACLA Report on the Americas.* 2008. https://www.tandfonline.com/doi/abs/10.1080/10714839.2008.11722261.

Carter, Jon Horne. "Gothic Sovereignty: Gangs and Criminal Community in a Honduran Prison." *South Atlantic Quarterly* 113, no. 3 (July 1, 2014): 475–502. https://doi.org/10.1215/00382876-2692155.

Carter, Jon Horne. *Gothic Sovereignty: Street Gangs and Statecraft in Honduras.* University of Texas Press, 2022.

Carter, Jon Horne. "Revolution Betrayed." In *Behind the Migrant Caravan: Ethnographic Updates from Central America.* Hot Spots, Fieldsights, 2019. https://culanth.org/fieldsights/revolution-betrayed.

Casas Cortés, Maribel, and Sebastian Cobarrubias. "La autonomía de la migración: Una perspectiva alternativa sobre la movilidad humana y los controles migratorios." *Empiria: Revista de Metodología de Ciencias Sociales*, no. 46 (2020): 65–92.

Casas Cortés, Maribel, Sebastian Cobarrubias, and John Pickles. "Riding Routes and Itinerant Borders: Autonomy of Migration and Border Externalization." *Antipode* 47, no. 4 (September 2015): 894–914. https://doi.org/10.1111/anti.12148.

Castillo Ramírez, Guillermo. "Autonomía de las migraciones: De la producción política de fronteras a las luchas migrantes." *Migraciones Internacionales* 14 (April 15, 2023). https://doi.org/10.33679/rmi.v1i1.2573.

Centro Nacional de Información del Sector Social (CENISS). "Hondureños Retornados." Sistema Integral de Atención al Migrante Retornado (SIAMIR), 2020.

Charles, Christopher A. D. "The Reintegration of Criminal Deportees in Society." *Dialectical Anthropology* 34, no. 4 (2010): 501–11.

Chávez, Karma R. "Understanding Migrant Caravans from the Place of Place Privilege." *Departures in Critical Qualitative Research* 8, no. 1 (March 1, 2019): 9–16. https://doi.org/10.1525/dcqr.2019.8.1.9.

Clemente, Edgar H. "Disuelven caravanas migrantes que esperaban documentos en Chiapas." *La Jornada*, January 18, 2025. https://www.jornada.com.mx/noticia/2025/01/18/estados/disuelven-caravanas-migrantes-que-esperaban-documentos-en-chiapas-8939.

Clemente, Edgar H. "Muchos venezolanos en caravana ahora que México pide visa." *Los Angeles Times*, June 9, 2022.

Clifford, James. "Anthropology and/as Travel." *Etnofoor* 9, no. 2 (1996): 5–15.

Colín, Alfredo Islas. "Caravanas de migrantes y refugiados en México." *Barataria: Revista Castellano-Manchega de Ciencias Sociales* 25 (November 1, 2019): 131–46. https://doi.org/10.20932/barataria.v0i25.492.

Collyer, Michael. "Deportation and the Micropolitics of Exclusion: The Rise of Removals from the UK to Sri Lanka." *Geopolitics* 17, no. 2 (2012): 276–92. https://doi.org/10.1080/14650045.2011.562940.

Comisión de Derechos Humanos de la Ciudad de México (CDHDF). "Presenta el reportero Irineo Mújica imágenes de agresiones sufridas a manos de agentes de migración." August 11, 2010. https://cdhcm.org.mx/2010/08 /boletin-2262010/.

Contreras, Monica. "Caravana de Dignidad y Conciencia Wixárika avanza con paso firme hacia la CDMX." *Zona Docs*, May 17, 2022. https://www .zonadocs.mx/2022/05/17/caravana-de-dignidad-y-conciencia-wixarika -avanza-con-paso-firme-hacia-la-cdmx/.

Cook Heffron, Laurie. "'Salía de uno y me metí en otro': Exploring the Migration-Violence Nexus Among Central American Women." *Violence Against Women* 25, no. 6 (May 1, 2019): 677-702. https://doi.org/10.1177/1077801218797473.

Cordero, Blanca, Sandro Mezzadra, and Amarela Varela Huerta. *América Latina en movimiento: Migraciones, límites a la movilidad y sus desbordamientos*. Traficantes de Sueños, 2019.

Cortés, Almudena. "Gender-Based Violence and Border: Central American Migrants in Mexico Heading to the US." *European Review of Latin American and Caribbean Studies*, no. 105 (April 1, 2018): 39. https://doi.org/10.18352 /erlacs.10321.

Coutin, Susan Bibler. "Being En Route." *American Anthropologist* 107, no. 2 (2005): 195-206.

Coutin, Susan Bibler. "Confined Within: National Territories as Zones of Confinement." *Political Geography* 29, no. 4 (May 2010): 200-208. https:// doi.org/10.1016/j.polgeo.2010.03.005.

Coutin, Susan Bibler. "Deportation Studies: Origins, Themes and Directions." *Journal of Ethnic and Migration Studies* 41, no. 4 (March 21, 2015): 671-81. https://doi.org/10.1080/1369183X.2014.957175.

Coutin, Susan Bibler. *Exiled Home: Salvadoran Transnational Youth in the Aftermath of Violence*. Duke University Press, 2016.

Coutin, Susan Bibler. "Falling Outside: Excavating the History of Central American Asylum Seekers." *Law & Social Inquiry* 36, no. 3 (2011): 569-96.

Coutin, Susan Bibler. *Nations of Emigrants: Shifting Boundaries of Citizenship in El Salvador and the United States*. Cornell University Press, 2007.

Cuéllar, Jorge E. "Waterproofing the State: Migration, River-Borders, and Ecologies of Control." *Comparative American Studies: An International Journal* 18, no. 1 (January 2, 2021): 59-74. https://doi.org/10.1080/14775700 .2021.1872765.

Cuneo, C. Nicholas, Kara E. Huselton, Nathan C. Praschan, Altaf Saadi, and Matthew G. Gartland. "What Counts as 'Safe'? Exposure to Trauma and Violence Among Asylum Seekers from the Northern Triangle." *Health Affairs* 40, no. 7 (July 1, 2021): 1135–44. https://doi.org/10.1377/hlthaff .2021.00082.

Dako-Gyeke, Mavis, and Richard Baffo Kodom. "Deportation and Re-Integration: Exploring Challenges Faced by Deportee Residents in the Nkoranza Municipality, Ghana." *Journal of International Migration and Integration* 18, no. 4 (November 1, 2017): 1083–1103. https://doi.org/10.1007/s12134-017-0526-0.

Daniel, E. Valentine. *Charred Lullabies: Chapters in an Anthropology of Violence.* Princeton University Press, 1996.

Das, Veena, and Arthur Kleinman. Introduction to *Violence and Subjectivity,* edited by Veena Das, Arthur Kleinman, Mamphela Ramphele, and Pamela Reynolds. University of California Press, 2000.

Davis, Dána-Ain. "Border Crossings: Intimacy and Feminist Activist Ethnography in the Age of Neoliberalism." In *Feminist Activist Ethnography: Counterpoints to Neoliberalism in North America,* edited by Christa Craven and Dána-Ain Davis. Lexington Books, 2013.

De Genova, Nicholas. "Afterword. Deportation: The Last Word?" In *After Deportation: Ethnographic Perspectives,* edited by Shahram Khosravi. Springer, 2018.

De Genova, Nicholas. "Migrant 'Illegality' and Deportability in Everyday Life." *Annual Review of Anthropology* 31 (2002): 419–47.

De Genova, Nicholas. "Spectacles of Migrant 'Illegality': The Scene of Exclusion, the Obscene of Inclusion." *Ethnic and Racial Studies* 36, no. 7 (2013): 1180–98. https://doi.org/10.1080/01419870.2013.783710.

De Genova, Nicholas, and Nathalie Peutz, eds. *The Deportation Regime: Sovereignty, Space, and the Freedom of Movement.* Duke University Press, 2010.

De León, Jason. "The Efficacy and Impact of the Alien Transfer Exit Programme: Migrant Perspectives from Nogales, Sonora, Mexico." *International Migration* 51, no. 2 (April 1, 2013): 10–23. https://doi.org/10.1111/imig.12062.

De León, Jason. *The Land of Open Graves: Living and Dying on the Migrant Trail.* University of California Press, 2015.

Diario La Prensa. "Guerra entre diez bandas genera violencia en Choloma." August 2018. https://www.laprensa.hn/sucesos/1209586-410/homicidios-muertes-asesinatos-choloma-honduras-bandas_criminales-guerra-.

Dingeman-Cerda, Katie. "Segmented Re/Integration: Divergent Post-Deportation Trajectories in El Salvador." *Social Problems* 65, no. 1 (February 1, 2018): 116–34. https://doi.org/10.1093/socpro/spw049.

Dingeman-Cerda, Katie, and Susan Bibler Coutin. "The Ruptures of Return: Deportation's Confounding Effects." In *Punishing Immigrants: Policy, Politics, and Injustice*, edited by Charis E. Kubrin, Marjorie S. Zatz, and Ramiro Martínez. New York University Press, 2012.

Dingeman-Cerda, Katie, and Rubén G. Rumbaut. "Unwelcome Returns: The Alienation of the New American Diaspora in Salvadoran Society." In *The New Deportations Delirium: Interdisciplinary Responses*, edited by Daniel Kanstroom and M. Brinton Lykes. New York University Press, 2015.

Doering-White, John, and Alejandra Díaz De León. "The Shelter Multiple: How Humanitarianisms Hang Together at a Mexican Non-Governmental Migrant Shelter." *Journal of Ethnic and Migration Studies*, December 9, 2023, 1–19. https://doi.org/10.1080/1369183X.2023.2290449.

Doering-White, John, Amelia Frank-Vitale, and Jason De León. "Chapter 4: Central America." In *Fatal Journeys*, vol. 3, pt. 2: *Improving Data on Missing Migrants*. International Organization for Migration, 2017.

Domínguez, Pedro. "Seis caravanas migrantes no llegaron a EU en tres meses." *Milenio*, December 18, 2024. https://www.milenio.com/politica/seis -caravanas-migrantes-no-llegaron-a-eu-en-tres-meses.

Donato, Katharine M., Brandon Wagner, and Evelyn Patterson. "The Cat and Mouse Game at the Mexico-U.S. Border: Gendered Patterns and Recent Shifts." *International Migration Review* 42, no. 2 (July 1, 2008): 330–59.

Dreby, Joanna. "The Burden of Deportation on Children in Mexican Immigrant Families." *Journal of Marriage and Family* 74, no. 4 (August 1, 2012): 829–45. https://doi.org/10.1111/j.1741-3737.2012.00989.x.

Drotbohm, Heike. "On the Durability and the Decomposition of Citizenship: The Social Logics of Forced Return Migration in Cape Verde." *Citizenship Studies* 15, no. 3–4 (June 1, 2011): 381–96. https://doi.org/10.1080/13621025 .2011.564790.

Drotbohm, Heike, and Ines Hasselberg. "Deportation, Anxiety, Justice: New Ethnographic Perspectives." *Journal of Ethnic and Migration Studies* 41, no. 4 (March 21, 2015): 551–62. https://doi.org/10.1080/1369183X.2014 .957171.

Drybread, K. "Writing About Violence." In *Writing Anthropology: Essays on Craft and Commitment*, edited by Carole McGranahan. Duke University Press, 2020.

Economist. "Analysing Juan Orlando Hernández's Disputed Election Victory in Honduras." December 5, 2017. https://www.economist.com/the-americas /2017/12/05/analysing-juan-orlando-hernandezs-disputed-election-victory -in-honduras.

El País. "ONU apoyará programas de reinserción de migrantes retornados."
September 25, 2018. http://www.elpais.hn/2018/09/25/onu-apoyara
-programas-de-reinsercion-de-migrantes-retornados/.

El-Shaarawi, Nadia, and Maple Razsa. "Movements upon Movements: Refugee
and Activist Struggles to Open the Balkan Route to Europe." In *After Utopia*.
Routledge, 2021.

Elvira. Documentary. Multicom, 2009. https://multicom.tv/library/elvira.

"Elvira's Song: Tribute to Elvira Arellano and Her Son Saul." Chicago, 2007.
https://www.youtube.com/watch?v=Vzan1afn1MI.

Euraque, Darío A. *Reinterpreting the Banana Republic: Region and State in
Honduras, 1870–1972*. University of North Carolina Press, 1997.

Farmer, Paul. "An Anthropology of Structural Violence." *Current Anthropology*
45, no. 3 (2004): 305–25. https://doi.org/10.1086/382250.

Feldman, Allen. "Ethnographic States of Emergency." In *Fieldwork Under Fire:
Contemporary Studies of Violence and Culture*. University of California Press,
1996.

Feldman, Allen. *Formations of Violence: The Narrative of the Body and Political
Terror in Northern Ireland*. University of Chicago Press, 1991.

Ferrer, Mauricio. "Madres centroamericanas estiman en 70 mil los migrantes
desaparecidos en México." *La Jornada*, December 2013.

FitzGerald, David Scott. "Remote Control of Migration: Theorising Territoriality,
Shared Coercion, and Deterrence." *Journal of Ethnic and Migration Studies* 46,
no. 1 (January 2, 2020): 4–22. https://doi.org/10.1080/1369183X.2020.1680115.

Flotte, Nakay R. "Transmigrations: Central American Trans Queer Mobility,
Detention, and Return." PhD dissertation, Harvard University, 2021.

Fonseca, Ana, Laurence Hart, and Susanne Klink. "Reintegration: Effective
Approaches." International Organization for Migration, 2015.

Frank-Vitale, Amelia. "'Better in Jail There Than Dead Here': Deportation and
(Social) Death in Honduras." In *Migration and Mortality: Social Death,
Dispossession, and Survival in the Americas*, edited by Jamie Longazel and
Miranda Cady Hallett. Temple University Press, 2021.

Frank-Vitale, Amelia. "From Caravan to Exodus, from Migration to Movement." *NACLA Report on the Americas*, November 20, 2018. https://dev
.nacla.org/news/2018/11/26/caravan-exodus-migration-movement

Frank-Vitale, Amelia. "'Fui Migrante y Me Hospedaron': The Catholic Church's
Responses to Violence Against Central American Migrants in Mexico." In
*Religious Responses to Violence: Human Rights in Latin America Past and
Present*, edited by Alexander Wilde. University of Notre Dame Press, 2015.

Frank-Vitale, Amelia. "Rolling the Windows Up: On (Not) Researching Violence and Strategic Distance." *Geopolitics* 26, no. 1 (January 5, 2021): 139–58. https://doi.org/10.1080/14650045.2019.1662396.

Frank-Vitale, Amelia. "Writer's Block." Taking Note: Complexities and Ambiguities in Writing Ethnographic Fieldnotes. American Ethnologist website, August 26, 2022. https://americanethnologist.org/online-content/collections/taking-note/writers-block/.

Frank-Vitale, Amelia, and Jesse Hoffnung-Garskof. "Honduras, Gangs, and Asylum Law." *Latin American Perspectives* 52, no. 2 (March 1, 2025): 105–24. https://doi.org/10.1177/0094582X251321833.

Frank-Vitale, Amelia, and Juan Martínez d'Aubuisson. "The Generation of the Coup: Honduran Youth at Risk and of Risk." *Journal of Latin American and Caribbean Anthropology* 25, no. 4 (2020): 552–68. https://doi.org/10.1111/jlca.12512.

Frank-Vitale, Amelia, and Juan Martínez d'Aubuisson. "On Covering San Pedro Sula and Why Global Media Outlets Will Always Dangerously Get It Wrong." *Latino Rebels*, May 24, 2019. https://www.latinorebels.com/2019/05/24/sanpedrosulamedia/.

Frank-Vitale, Amelia, and Margarita Núñez Chaim. "'Lady Frijoles': Las caravanas centroamericanas y el poder de la hipervisibilidad de la migración indocumentada." *EntreDiversidades: Revista de Ciencias Sociales y Humanidades* 7, no. 1 (2020): 37–61. https://doi.org/10.31644/ED.V7.N1.2020.A02.

Frank-Vitale, Amelia, and Arelí Palomo Contreras. "Caravan Migrant Roots." *Linea84: Periodismo Etnográfico y Acción Comunitaria*, May 11, 2019. https://www.linea84.org/single-post/2019/05/11/Caravan-Migrant-Roots.

Franz, Margaret. "Contesting the Place of Protest in Migrant Caravans." *First Amendment Studies* 54, no. 2 (July 2, 2020): 181–89. https://doi.org/10.1080/21689725.2020.1837648.

Fuller, Norma, ed. *Difícil ser hombre: Nuevas masculinidades latinoamericanas.* Fondo Editorial de la PUCP, 2020.

Fundación para la Educación Ricardo Ernesto Maduro Andreu (FEREMA). "Educación: Una deuda pendiente. Informe de progreso educativo Honduras." FEREMA; Inter-American Dialogue; Universidad Pedagógica Nacional Francisco Morazán; Programa de Capacidades LAC Reads, USAID, 2017.

Funes, Eduin. "Representantes de la ASJ habrían recomendado 'reestructurar' Salud y Educación." *Tiempo Digital*, May 1, 2019. https://tiempo.hn/representantes-asj-reestructurar-salud-educacion/.

Galán, Arturo Alfaro. "Levanta fotoperiodista huelga de hambre frente al INM en precario estado de salud." *La Jornada de Oriente*, August 3, 2010. https://www.lajornadadeoriente.com.mx/2010/08/03/puebla/jus105.php.

Galemba, Rebecca B. "'He Used to Be a Pollero': The Securitisation of Migration and the Smuggler/Migrant Nexus at the Mexico-Guatemala Border." *Journal of Ethnic and Migration Studies* 44, no. 5 (2018): 870–86. https://doi.org/10.1080/1369183X.2017.1327803.

Gallagher, Janice. "The Last Mile Problem: Activists, Advocates, and the Struggle for Justice in Domestic Courts." *Comparative Political Studies* 50, no. 12 (October 1, 2017): 1666–98. https://doi.org/10.1177/0010414016688001.

Galtung, Johan. "Violence, Peace, and Peace Research." *Journal of Peace Research* 6, no. 3 (September 1, 1969): 167–91. https://doi.org/10.1177/002234336900600301.

Gandini, Luciana. "Las 'oleadas' de las caravanas migrantes y las cambiantes respuestas gubernamentales: Retos para la política migratoria." *Caravanas Migrantes: Las Respuestas de México, Opinión Técnica Sobre Temas de Relevancia Nacional*, Serie 08, January 1, 2019.

Gandini, Luciana, Alethia Fernández de la Reguera, and Juan Carlos Narváez Gutiérrez. *Caravanas*. UNAM, Secretaría de Desarrollo Institucional, 2020.

García, María Cristina. *Seeking Refuge: Central American Migration to Mexico, the United States, and Canada*. University of California Press, 2006.

Garibo García, María Georgina, and Tristan P. Call. "Caravanas de personas migrantes como expresiones contradictorias de tácticas de sobrevivencia y prácticas de subjetivación política." *EntreDiversidades: Revista de Ciencias Sociales y Humanidades* 7, no. 2 (2020): 59–93.

Geertz, Clifford. "Deep Hanging Out." *New York Review of Books*, October 22, 1998.

Geglia, Beth. "The Roots of the National Strike in Honduras: An Interview with Bayron Rodríguez Pineda." *NACLA Report on the Americas*, June 10, 2019. https://nacla.org/news/2019/06/10/roots-national-strike-honduras-interview-bayron-rodr%C3%ADguez-pineda.

Gibney, Matthew J. "Is Deportation a Form of Forced Migration?" *Refugee Survey Quarterly* 32, no. 2 (June 1, 2013): 116–29. https://doi.org/10.1093/rsq/hdt003.

Giroux, Henry A. "Neoliberalism and the Death of the Social State: Remembering Walter Benjamin's Angel of History." *Social Identities* 17, no. 4 (July 1, 2011): 587–601. https://doi.org/10.1080/13504630.2011.587310.

Golash-Boza, Tanya. *Deported: Immigrant Policing, Disposable Labor, and Global Capitalism*. New York University Press, 2015.

Golash-Boza, Tanya. "Forced Transnationalism: Transnational Coping Strategies and Gendered Stigma Among Jamaican Deportees." *Global Networks* 14, no. 1 (2014): 63–79. https://doi.org/10.1111/glob.12013.

Golash-Boza, Tanya. "'Negative Credentials,' 'Foreign-Earned' Capital, and Call Centers: Guatemalan Deportees' Precarious Reintegration." *Citizenship Studies* 20, no. 3–4 (May 18, 2016): 326–41. https://doi.org/10.1080/13621025.2016.1158357.

Golash-Boza, Tanya, and Yajaira Ceciliano-Navarro. "Life After Deportation." *Contexts* 18, no. 2 (May 1, 2019): 30–35. https://doi.org/10.1177/1536504219854715.

Golash-Boza, Tanya, and Pierrette Hondagneu-Sotelo. "Latino Immigrant Men and the Deportation Crisis: A Gendered Racial Removal Program." *Latino Studies* 11, no. 3 (September 1, 2013): 271–92. https://doi.org/10.1057/lst.2013.14.

Gómez Johnson, Cristina, and Fernanda Espinosa Moreno. "Transformaciones en las migraciones contemporáneas en México (2000–2019): Acercamiento a las violencias y solicitudes de refugio." *Estudios Políticos*, no. 58 (August 2020): 17–44. https://doi.org/10.17533/udea.espo.n58a02.

Goodman, Adam. *The Deportation Machine: America's Long History of Expelling Immigrants*. Princeton University Press, 2020.

Gordillo-García, Johan. "Social Movements and Political-Emotional Communities: An Approach from the Movement for Peace with Justice and Dignity in Mexico." *Social Movement Studies* 24, no. 2 (May 26, 2023): 239–56. https://doi.org/10.1080/14742837.2023.2216646.

Gramajo Bauer, Lizbeth del Rosario. "Dos crisis que explican las dinámicas migratorias más recientes en los tres países del norte de Centroamérica." *REMHU: Revista Interdisciplinar da Mobilidade Humana* 28, no. 60 (2020): 33–50.

Grillo, Ioan. *El Narco: Inside Mexico's Criminal Insurgency*. Bloomsbury Press, 2012.

Gutiérrez Rivera, Lirio. *Territories of Violence: State, Marginal Youth, and Public Security in Honduras*. Palgrave Macmillan, 2013.

Gutmann, Matthew C. "Introduction: Discarding Manly Dichotomies in Latin America." In *Changing Men and Masculinities in Latin America*. Duke University Press, 2003.

Gutmann, Matthew. "Remarking the Unmarked: An Anthropology of Masculinity Redux." *Annual Review of Anthropology* 52 (October 21, 2023): 55–72. https://doi.org/10.1146/annurev-anthro-052721-041915.

Gutmann, Matthew C., and Mara Viveros Vigoya. "Masculinities in Latin America." In *Handbook of Studies on Men and Masculinities*. SAGE Publications, 2005.

Hagan, Jacqueline, Karl Eschbach, and Néstor Rodríguez. "U.S. Deportation Policy, Family Separation, and Circular Migration." *International Migration Review* 42, no. 1 (2008): 64–88.

Hagan, Jacqueline, Joshua Wassink, and Brianna Castro. "A Longitudinal Analysis of Resource Mobilisation Among Forced and Voluntary Return Migrants in Mexico." *Journal of Ethnic and Migration Studies* 45, no. 1 (2019): 170.

Heidbrink, Lauren. *Migranthood: Youth in a New Era of Deportation*. Stanford University Press, 2020.

Herrera, Jack. "Trump's Gains with Pennsylvania Latinos Are Real. Maybe Enough to Withstand 'Island of Garbage.'" *Politico*, November 4, 2024. https://www.politico.com/news/magazine/2024/11/04/latinos-decide -election-pennsylvania-00186534.

Herrera, Vienna. "Femicide in Honduras: Women Dismissed by Their Own Government." *Contra Corriente*, August 8, 2020. https://contracorriente.red /en/2020/08/08/femicide-in-honduras-women-dismissed-by-their-own- government/.

Hiemstra, Nancy. "Geopolitical Reverberations of US Migrant Detention and Deportation: The View from Ecuador." *Geopolitics* 17, no. 2 (April 1, 2012): 293–311. https://doi.org/10.1080/14650045.2011.562942.

Hill Maher, Kristen. "Globalized Social Reproduction: Women Migrants and the Citizenship Gap." In *People Out of Place: Globalization, Human Rights and the Citizenship Gap*, edited by Alison Brysk and Gershon Shafir, 144–66. Taylor & Francis Group, 2004.

Holmer, Georgia, and Adrian Shtuni. "Returning Foreign Fighters and the Reintegration Imperative." Special Report. United States Institute of Peace, March 2017.

Horton, Sarah B. "From 'Deportability' to 'Denounce-ability': New Forms of Labor Subordination in an Era of Governing Immigration Through Crime." *PoLAR: Political and Legal Anthropology Review* 39, no. 2 (2016): 312–26. https://doi.org/10.1111/plar.12196.

Igarapé Institute. "Homicide Monitor." 2025. http://homicide.igarape.org/.

Innocente Escamilla, Yuri Arón. "Usos políticos del sufrimiento en el vía crucis del migrante, Ixtepec, Oaxaca." *Relaciones: Estudios de Historia y Sociedad* 40, no. 157 (March 2019): 33–52. https://doi.org/10.24901/rehs.v40i57.339.

Irwin, Robert McKee. "The Migrant Knowledge of a Caravanero." In *Migrant Feelings, Migrant Knowledge: Building a Community Archive*, edited by Robert McKee Irwin. University of Texas Press, 2022.

Johnson, Richard L., and Murphy Woodhouse. "Securing the Return: How Enhanced US Border Enforcement Fuels Cycles of Debt Migration." *Antipode* 50, no. 4 (September 1, 2018): 976–96. https://doi.org/10.1111/anti.12386.

Kanstroom, Daniel. *Aftermath: Deportation Law and the New American Diaspora*. Oxford University Press, 2014.

Khosravi, Shahram. Introduction to *After Deportation: Ethnographic Perspectives*, edited by Shahram Khosravi. Springer, 2018.

Kleinman, Arthur. "The Violences of Everyday Life: The Multiple Forms and Dynamics of Social Violence." In *Violence and Subjectivity*, edited by Veena Das, Arthur Kleinman, Mamphela Ramphele, and Pamela Reynolds. University of California Press, 2000.

Kleinman, Arthur, and Joan Kleinman. "The Appeal of Experience; The Dismay of Images: Cultural Appropriations of Suffering in Our Times." In *Social Suffering*, edited by Arthur Kleinman, Veena Das, and Margaret M. Lock. University Of California Press, 1997.

Kleinman, Julie. *Adventure Capital: Migration and the Making of an African Hub in Paris*. University of California Press, 2019.

Kofman, Eleonore. "Gendered Migrations, Social Reproduction and the Household in Europe." *Dialectical Anthropology* 38, no. 1 (March 1, 2014): 79–94. https://doi.org/10.1007/s10624-014-9330-9.

Kovic, Christine, and Patty Kelly. "Migrant Bodies as Targets of Security Policies: Central Americans Crossing Mexico's Vertical Border." *Dialectical Anthropology* 41, no. 1 (March 1, 2017): 1–11. https://doi.org/10.1007/s10624-017-9449-6.

Leutert, Stephanie. *Migrant Protection Protocols: Implementation and Consequences for Asylum Seekers in Mexico, PRP 218*. LBJ School of Public Affairs, 2020. https://doi.org/10.26153/tsw/8999.

Librado Luna, Daniel. *A 70 años la caravana minera de 1951 de Nueva Rosita a la Capital en busca de justicia*. Instituto Nacional de Estudios Históricos de las Revoluciones de México, 2021.

López, William D. *Separated: Family and Community in the Aftermath of an Immigration Raid*. Johns Hopkins University Press, 2019.

Malkki, Liisa. "National Geographic: The Rooting of Peoples and the Territorialization of National Identity Among Scholars and Refugees." *Cultural*

Anthropology 7, no. 1 (1992): 24–44. https://doi.org/10.1525/can.1992.7
.1.02a00030.

Marchand, Marianne H. "The Caravanas de Migrantes Making Their Way
North: Problematising the Biopolitics of Mobilities in Mexico." *Third World
Quarterly* 42, no. 1 (January 2, 2021): 141–61. https://doi.org/10.1080/014365
97.2020.1824579.

Mariscal, Ángeles. "'Ojalá nos acompañaran todo el camino': Migrantes que
viajan en caravana." *Expansión*, January 8, 2011. https://expansion.mx
/nacional/2011/01/08/ojala-nos-acompanaran-todo-el-camino-migrantes
-que-viajan-en-caravana.

Mariscal Nava, Dulce María, and Eduardo Torre Cantalapiedra. "Batallando
con fronteras: Estrategías migratorias en tránsito de participantes en
caravanas de migrantes." *Estudios Fronterizos*, no. 21 (2020).

Martínez, Carlos. *Juntos, todos juntos: Crónica del primer intento colectivo de
saltar la frontera estadounidense*. Pepitas de Calabaza, 2019.

Martínez, Daniel E., Jeremy Slack, and Ricardo D. Martínez-Schuldt. "Repeat
Migration in the Age of the 'Unauthorized Permanent Resident': A Quantita-
tive Assessment of Migration Intentions Postdeportation." *International
Migration Review* 52, no. 4 (December 1, 2018): 1186–1217. https://doi.org
/10.1177/0197918318767921.

Martínez, Óscar. "Los coyotes domados." *El Faro*, March 24, 2014. http://www
.salanegra.elfaro.net/es/201403/cronicas/15101/Los-coyotes-domados.htm.

Martínez, Oscar, and Juan José Martínez d'Aubuisson. *The Hollywood Kid: The
Violent Life and Violent Death of an MS-13 Hitman*. Verso, 2019.

Martínez d'Aubuisson, Juan. "Poor 'Hood, Mean 'Hood: The Violent History of
Rivera Hernández, Honduras." *InSight Crime*, December 9, 2015. https://
insightcrime.org/investigations/gang-history-rivera-hernandez-honduras/.

Martínez d'Aubuisson, Juan. *El que tenga miedo a morir que no nazca: Retrato de
San Pedro Sula, Honduras, una de las ciudades más homicidas del mundo*.
Planeta, 2025.

Martínez Hernández-Mejía, Iliana. *Reflexiones sobre la caravana migrante*.
ITESO, 2018.

McDonald, Kate. "Imperial Mobility: Circulation as History in East Asia Under
Empire." *Transfers* 4, no. 3 (Winter 2014): 68–87.

Mckenzie, Sean, and Cecilia Menjívar. "The Meanings of Migration, Remittances and Gifts: Views of Honduran Women Who Stay." *Global Networks* 11,
no. 1 (January 1, 2011): 63–81. https://doi.org/10.1111/j.1471-0374.2011
.00307.x.

McLean, Lisa. "A Question That Has No End: The Politics of Life and Death in the Search for Disappeared Migrants in Mexico." *Citizenship Studies* 24, no. 8 (November 16, 2020): 994–1009. https://doi.org/10.1080/13621025.2020 .1769027.

Mejía, Oscar Alfonso. "Race in Trans and Queer Migration: Arcoíris 17's Contesting of Colonial Legacies." In *The Routledge Handbook of Ethnicity and Race in Communication*. Routledge, 2023. https://doi.org/10.4324/9780367748586-17.

Menjívar, Cecilia. *Enduring Violence: Ladina Women's Lives in Guatemala*. University of California Press, 2011.

Menjívar, Cecilia, and Shannon Drysdale Walsh. "The Architecture of Feminicide: The State, Inequalities, and Everyday Gender Violence in Honduras." *Latin American Research Review* 52, no. 2 (2017): 221–40.

Mercado, Kevin. "Menores retornados tienen oportunidad de reinserción." *Diario La Prensa*, April 2, 2018. https://www.laprensa.hn/honduras /1165770-410/menores-retornados-oportunidad-reinsercion-hondure-os.

Mezzadra, Sandro. "The Gaze of Autonomy: Capitalism, Migration and Social Struggles." In *The Contested Politics of Mobility*. Routledge, 2010.

Miroff, Nick. "The Murder Capital of the World." *Washington Post*, December 27, 2011. http://www.washingtonpost.com/world/the-murder-capital-of -the-world/2011/12/26/gIQAehQKJP_graphic.html.

Mitropoulos, Angela. "Autonomy, Recognition, and Movement." In *Constituent Imagination: Militant Investigations, Collective Theorization*, edited by Stephen Shukaitis, David Graeber, and Erika Biddle. AK Press, 2007.

Montes, Veronica. "Fleeing Home: Notes on the Central American Caravan in Its Transit to Reach the US–Mexico Border." *Latino Studies* 17, no. 4 (December 1, 2019): 532–39. https://doi.org/10.1057/s41276-019- 00214-x.

Moreno, Hiram. "Pide caravana reconocer como grupo vulnerable a migrantes." *La Jornada* (Chahuites, Oaxaca), January 9, 2011. https://www .jornada.com.mx/2011/01/09/politica/008n1pol.

Moslimani, Mohamad, Luis Noe-Bustamante, and Sono Shah. "Facts on Hispanics of Honduran Origin in the United States, 2021." Pew Research Center, August 16, 2023. https://www.pewresearch.org/race-and-ethnicity /fact-sheet/us-hispanics-facts-on-honduran-origin-latinos/.

Muñoz Martínez, Hepzibah. "The Politics of Scale, Place, and Mobility in the Mexican Peace Movement, 2006–2012." *Canadian Journal of Latin American and Caribbean Studies / Revue Canadienne des Études Latino-Américaines et Caraïbes* 40, no. 2 (2015): 157–75.

Nazario, Sonia. "How the Most Dangerous Place on Earth Got Safer." *The New York Times*, August 11, 2016. https://www.nytimes.com/2016/08/14/opinion /sunday/how-the-most-dangerous-place-on-earth-got-a-little-bit-safer.html.

Nazario, Sonia. "Someone Is Always Trying to Kill You." *The New York Times*, April 5, 2019. https://www.nytimes.com/interactive/2019/04/05/opinion /honduras-women-murders.html.

Neumann, Rachel. "We Make the Road by Walking: Lessons from the Zapatista Caravan." *Monthly Review*, June 2001. https://doi.org/10.14452/MR-053- 02-2001-06_6.

Novelo, Victoria. "Pequeñas historias de grandes momentos de la vida de los mineros del carbón de Coahuila." *Estudios Sociológicos* 12, no. 36 (1994): 533-56.

Núñez-Chaim, Margarita, Amarela Varela-Huerta, and Valentina Glockner. "Caravanas migrantes y el régimen de control fronterizo en México en tiempos pandémicos: El caso de la caravana de los 50 días." *Textos y Contextos* 1, no. 26 (April 6, 2023): e3703. https://doi.org/10.29166/tyc.v1i26.3703.

Nyers, Peter. "Migrant Citizenships and Autonomous Mobilities." *Migration, Mobility, & Displacement* 1, no. 1 (May 27, 2015). https://doi.org/10.18357 /mmd11201513521.

Observatorio Nacional de la Violencia. "Boletín especial sobre homicidios en Honduras, 2019." Edición especial no. 83. Instituto Universitario en Democracia, Paz y Seguridad (IUDPAS), February 2020.

O'Leary, Anna Ochoa. "In the Footsteps of Spirits: Migrant Women's Testimo-nios in a Time of Heightened Border Enforcement." In *Human Rights Along the US-Mexico Border: Gendered Violence and Insecurity*. University of Arizona Press, 2009.

O'Leary, Anna Ochoa. "Mujeres en el cruce: Remapping Border Security Through Migrant Mobility." *Journal of the Southwest* 51, no. 4 (Winter 2009): 523-42.

O'Leary, Anna Ochoa. "Of Coyotes, Crossings, and Cooperation: Social Capital and Women's Migration at the Margins of the State." *Research in Economic Anthropology* 32 (2012): 133-60.

Olivo Diaz López, Maria-Jesus. "Relocating Morolica: Vulnerability and Resilience in Post-Mitch Honduras." ProQuest Dissertations Publishing, 2002.

Olmos, Daniel. "Racialized Im/Migration and Autonomy of Migration Perspectives: New Directions and Opportunities." *Sociology Compass* 13, no. 9 (2019): e12729. https://doi.org/10.1111/soc4.12729.

Olson, Jared. "How an Emergency Declaration Deepened Honduras's Crime Crisis." *Al Jazeera*, August 15, 2025. https://www.aljazeera.com/news /longform/2025/8/15/how-an-emergency-declaration-deepened-hondurass-crime-crisis.

Ordóñez, Ronald. "Analfabetismo, un problema viejo con nuevos actores en Honduras." *Proceso Digital*, October 22, 2022. https://proceso.hn /analfabetismo-un-problema-viejo-con-nuevos-actores-en-honduras/.

Oviedo, Douglas. *Caravaneros*. Festina Publicaciones, 2020.

Papadopoulos, Dimitris, Niamh Stephenson, and Vassilis Tsianos. *Escape Routes: Control and Subversion in the Twenty-First Century*. Pluto Press, 2008. https://doi.org/10.2307/j.ctt183q4b2.

Papadopoulos, Dimitris, and Vassilis Tsianos. "After Citizenship: Autonomy of Migration, Organisational Ontology and Mobile Commons." *Citizenship Studies* 17, no. 2 (April 1, 2013): 178–96. https://doi.org/10.1080/13621025.201 3.780736.

París Pombo, María Dolores, and Verónica Montes. "Visibilidad como estrategia de movilidad: El éxodo centroamericano en México (2018–2019)." *EntreDiversidades: Revista de Ciencias Sociales y Humanidades*, January 1, 2020.

Petrozziello, Allison J. "Feminised Financial Flows: How Gender Affects Remittances in Honduran–US Transnational Families." *Gender & Development* 19, no. 1 (March 1, 2011): 53–67. https://doi.org/10.1080/13552074.2011 .554022.

Peutz, Nathalie. "Embarking on an Anthropology of Removal." *Current Anthropology* 47, no. 2 (April 1, 2006): 217–41.

Pine, Adrienne. "Forging an Anthropology of Neoliberal Fascism." *Public Anthropologist* 1, no. 1 (January 22, 2019): 20–40. https://doi.org/10.1163 /25891715-00101003.

Pine, Adrienne. *Working Hard, Drinking Hard: On Violence and Survival in Honduras*. University of California Press, 2008.

Pradilla, Alberto. *Caravana: Cómo el éxodo centroamericano salió de la clandestinidad*. Debate, 2019.

Rabasa, José. *Writing Violence on the Northern Frontier: The Historiography of Sixteenth-Century New Mexico and Florida and the Legacy of Conquest*. Duke University Press, 2000.

Rainsford, Cat. "Honduras Police Purge May Be Derailed by Alternative Agenda." *InSight Crime*, July 26, 2019. https://www.insightcrime.org/news /brief/honduras-police-purge-derailed-alternative-agenda/.

Redacción. "Escuadrón militar de ejecuciones arbitrarias en la FNAMP y sicariato desde la PMOP." *Reporteros de Investigación*, July 12, 2022. https:// reporterosdeinvestigacion.com/2022/07/12/escuadron-militar-de -ejecuciones-arbitrarias-en-la-fnamp-y-sicariato-desde-la-pmop/.

Reichman, Daniel. *The Broken Village: Coffee, Migration, and Globalization in Honduras*. ILR Press, 2011.

Rho, María Gabriela. "Ciudadanía y luchas migrantes: Debates desde la autonomía de las migraciones." *Revista Reflexiones* 100, no. 2 (December 2021): 188–207. https://doi.org/10.15517/rr.v100i2.43440.

Rivera Hernández, Raúl Diego. "Making Absence Visible: The Caravan of Central American Mothers in Search of Disappeared Migrants." *Latin American Perspectives* 44, no. 5 (September 1, 2017): 108–26. https://doi .org/10.1177/0094582X17706905.

Rizzo Lara, Rosario de la Luz. "La Caminata del Migrante: A Social Movement." *Journal of Ethnic and Migration Studies* 47, no. 17 (December 13, 2021): 3891–3910. https://doi.org/10.1080/1369183X.2021.1940111.

Rockefeller, Stuart Alexander. "'Flow.'" *Current Anthropology* 52, no. 4 (2011): 557–78. https://doi.org/10.1086/660912.

Rodkey, Evin. "Disposable Labor, Repurposed: Outsourcing Deportees in the Call Center Industry." *Anthropology of Work Review* 37, no. 1 (2016): 34–43. https://doi.org/10.1111/awr.12083.

Rodríguez, Néstor. "The Battle for the Border: Notes on Autonomous Migra- tion, Transnational Communities, and the State." *Social Justice* 23, no. 3 (65) (1996): 21–37.

Rosaldo, Renato. "Anthropology and 'the Field.'" Paper presented at confer- ence held at Stanford University and UC Santa Cruz, February 18–19, 1994.

Rosas, Gilberto. "Grief and Border-Crossing Rage." *Anthropology and Human- ism* 46, no. 1 (2021): 114–28. https://doi.org/10.1111/anhu.12328.

Rosas, Xavier. "Paso a paso hacia la Paz: Luchando por los derechos humanos de inmigrantes." *Lado B*, July 27, 2011. https://www.ladobe.com.mx/2011/07 /paso-a-paso-hacia-la-paz-luchando-por-los-derechos-humanos-de- inmigrantes/.

Ruiz Soto, Ariel G., and María Jesús Mora. "El lado olvidado de la deportación: El costo de ignorar los retos de reintegración de los retornados." Migration Policy Institute, April 15, 2025. https://www.migrationpolicy.org/news /retos-de-reintegracion.

Rutherford, Danilyn. "Toward an Anthropological Understanding of Masculini- ties, Maleness, and Violence: Wenner-Gren Symposium Supplement 23."

Current Anthropology 62, no. S23 (February 2, 2021): S1-4. https://doi
.org/10.1086/712484.

Salazar Parreñas, Rhacel. *Servants of Globalization: Women, Migration, and
Domestic Work*. Stanford University Press, 2001.

Sanchez, Gabriella. "Portrait of a Human Smuggler: Race, Class, and
Gender Among Facilitators of Irregular Migration on the US–Mexico
Border." In *Race, Criminal Justice, and Migration Control*. Oxford
University Press, 2018. https://doi.org/10.1093/oso/9780198814887.003
.0003.

Sanchez, Gabriella. "Women and Migrant Smuggling Facilitation in the United
States." In *Critical Insights on Irregular Migration Facilitation: Global
Perspectives*, edited by Gabriella Sanchez and Luigi Achilli. European
University Institute, 2019.

Scarnato, Jenn Miller. "Deportation Meets Development: A Case Study
of Return Migration in Guatemala." *Migration and Development* 8,
no. 2 (May 4, 2019): 192–206. https://doi.org/10.1080/21632324.2018
.1500004.

Scheper-Hughes, Nancy. *Death Without Weeping: The Violence of Everyday Life in
Brazil*. University of California Press, 1993.

Scheper-Hughes, Nancy, and Philippe Bourgois, eds. *Violence in War and Peace:
An Anthology*. Blackwell Publishing, 2003.

Schmidt, Leigh Anne, and Stephanie Buechler. "'I Risk Everything Because I
Have Already Lost Everything': Central American Female Migrants Speak
Out on the Migrant Trail in Oaxaca, Mexico." *Journal of Latin American
Geography* 16, no. 1 (April 1, 2017): 139.

Schuster, Liza, and Nassim Majidi. "Deportation Stigma and Re-Migration."
Journal of Ethnic and Migration Studies 41, no. 4 (March 21, 2015): 635–52.
https://doi.org/10.1080/1369183X.2014.957174.

Schuster, Liza, and Nassim Majidi. "What Happens Post-Deportation? The
Experience of Deported Afghans." *Migration Studies* 1, no. 2 (July 1, 2013):
221–40. https://doi.org/10.1093/migration/mns011.

Shorack, Marna, Elizabeth G. Kennedy, and Amelia Frank-Vitale. "A State of
Mistrust." *NACLA Report on the Americas* 52, no. 4 (October 1, 2020): 404–9.
https://doi.org/10.1080/10714839.2021.1840168.

Silva, Fernando. "Cristina y Josiris en Honduras, el país al que regresó la desaparición forzada." *Contra Corriente*, October 23, 2024. https://contracorriente
.red/2024/10/23/cristina-y-josiris-en-honduras-el-pais-al-que-regreso-la
-desaparicion-forzada/.

Skurski, Julie, and Fernando Coronil. "Introduction: States of Violence and the Violence of States." In *States of Violence*, edited by Julie Skurski and Fernando Coronil. University of Michigan Press, 2006.

Slack, Jeremy. *Deported to Death: How Drug Violence Is Changing Migration on the US-Mexico Border*. University of California Press, 2019.

Soberanes, Rodrigo. "La PGR identifica 60 cuerpos encontrados en San Fernando, Tamaulipas." *CNN México*, September 20, 2012. http://mexico.cnn.com/nacional/2012/09/20/la-pgr-identifica-60-cuerpos-encontrados-en-san-fernando-tamaulipas.

Solís Vega, Cristina. *Culturas del cuidado en transición: Espacios, sujetos e imaginarios en una sociedad de migración*. Editorial Uoc, 2009.

Spear, Joanna. "Disarmament, Demobilization, Reinsertion and Reintegration in Africa." In *Ending Africa's Wars: Progressing to Peace*, edited by Oliver Furley and Roy May. Routledge, 2006.

Speed, Shannon. "A Dreadful Mosaic: Rethinking Gender Violence through the Lives of Indigenous Women Migrants." *Gendered Perspectives on International Development*, no. 304 (June 1, 2014): 78.

Spivak, Gayatri. "Can the Subaltern Speak?" In *Marxism and the Interpretation of Culture*, edited by Cary Nelson and Lawrence Grossberg. Macmillan, 1988.

Stahler-Sholk, Richard. "Globalization and Social Movement Resistance: The Zapatista Rebellion in Chiapas, Mexico." *New Political Science* 23, no. 4 (December 1, 2001): 493–516. https://doi.org/10.1080/07393140120099606.

Stephen, Lynn. "Gendered Violence and Indigenous Mexican Asylum Seekers: Expert Witnessing as Ethnographic Engagement." *Anthropological Quarterly* 91, no. 1 (May 26, 2018): 325–63. https://doi.org/10.1353/anq.2018.0010.

Stephen, Lynn. "Los Nuevos Desaparecidos y Muertos: Immigration, Militarization, Death, and Disappearance on Mexico's Borders." In *Security Disarmed: Critical Perspectives on Gender, Race, and Militarization*, edited by Sandra Morgen, Barbara Sutton, and Julie Novkov. Rutgers University Press, 2008.

Swedenburg, Ted. "With Genet in the Palestinian Field." In *Violence in War and Peace: An Anthology*, edited by Nancy Scheper-Hughes and Philippe Bourgois. Blackwell Publishing, 2003.

Tavernise, Sabrina. "Reading, Pa., Knew It Was Poor. Now It Knows Just How Poor." *The New York Times*, September 27, 2011. https://www.nytimes.com/2011/09/27/us/reading-pa-tops-list-poverty-list-census-shows.html.

Thangaraj, Stanley. "Masculinities." *Feminist Anthropology* 3, no. 2 (2022): 254–62. https://doi.org/10.1002/fea2.12104.

Theidon, Kimberly. "Conclusions: Reflections on the Women, Peace, and Security Agenda." In *Gender Violence in Peace and War*, edited by Victoria Sanford, Katerina Stefatos, and Cecilia M. Salvi. Rutgers University Press, 2016.

Theidon, Kimberly. "'Terror's Talk: Fieldwork and War.'" *Dialectical Anthropology* 26, no. 1 (2001): 19.

Theidon, Kimberly. "Transitional Subjects: The Disarmament, Demobilization and Reintegration of Former Combatants in Colombia." *International Journal of Transitional Justice* 1, no. 1 (March 1, 2007): 66–90. https://doi.org/10.1093/ijtj/ijm011.

Ticktin, Miriam. "Borders: A Story of Political Imagination." *Borderlands Journal* 21, no. 1 (January 1, 2022): 138–70. https://doi.org/10.21307/borderlands-2022-007.

Torre Cantalapiedra, Eduardo. *Caravanas: Sus protagonistas ante las políticas migratorias*. Colef, 2021.

TRAC. "Asylum Denial Rates Continue to Climb." Transactional Records Access Clearinghouse (TRAC), October 28, 2020. https://trac.syr.edu/immigration/reports/630/.

Trevizo, Dolores. "Dispersed Communist Networks and Grassroots Leadership of Peasant Revolts in Mexico." *Sociological Perspectives* 45, no. 3 (2002): 285–315. https://doi.org/10.1525/sop.2002.45.3.285.

Truong, Thanh-Dam. "Gender, International Migration and Social Reproduction: Implications for Theory, Policy, Research and Networking." *Asian and Pacific Migration Journal* 5, no. 1 (March 1, 1996): 27–52. https://doi.org/10.1177/011719689600500103.

Tsing, Anna. *Friction: An Ethnography of Global Connection*. Princeton University Press, 2005.

Tsing, Anna. "The Global Situation." *Cultural Anthropology* 15, no. 3 (2000): 327–60.

UNESCO. "Honduras: Education and Literacy." Institute of Statistics, United Nations Educational, Scientific, and Cultural Organization, 2019. http://uis.unesco.org/en/country/hn.

US Department of State. "Mérida Initiative." 2008. http://www.state.gov/j/inl/merida/.

US Government Accountability Office (GAO). "Central America: USAID Assists Migrants Returning to Their Home Countries, but Effectiveness of Reintegration Efforts Remains to Be Determined." December 7, 2018.

Varela Huerta, Amarela. "'Luchas migrantes': Un nuevo campo de estudio para la sociología de los disensos." *Andamios* (Mexico City) 12, no. 28 (August 11, 2015): 145. https://doi.org/10.29092/uacm.v12i28.37.

Varela Huerta, Amarela. "México, de 'frontera vertical' a 'país tapón': Migrantes, deportados, retornados, desplazados internos, y solicitantes de asilo en México." *Iberofórum: Revista de Ciencias Sociales de la Universidad Iberoamericana*, Año XIV, no. 27 (2019): 49–76.

Varela Huerta, Amarela. "La trinidad perversa de la que huyen las fugitivas centroamericanas: Violencia feminicida, violencia de estado y violencia de mercado." *Debate Feminista* 53 (May 1, 2017): 1–17. https://doi.org/10.1016/j.df.2017.02.002.

Varela Huerta, Amarela, and Lisa McLean. "Caravanas de migrantes en México: Nueva forma de autodefensa y transmigración." *Revista CIDOB d'Afers Internacionals*, no. 122 (2019): 163–86.

Vargas Carrasco, Felipe de Jesús. "El vía crucis del migrante: Demandas y membresía." *Trace* (Mexico City), no. 73 (2018): 117–33.

Velasco Ortiz, Laura, and Rafael Alonso Hernández López. "Salir de las sombras: La visibilidad organizada en las caravanas de migrantes centroamericanas." In *Caravanas migrantes y desplazamientos colectivos en la frontera México-Estados Unidos*, edited by Camilo Contreras Delgado, María Dolores París Pombo, and Laura Velasco Ortiz. El Colegio de la Frontera Norte, 2021.

Velásquez Estrada, R. Elizabeth. "Intersectional Justice Denied: Racist Warring Masculinity, Negative Peace, and Violence in Post-Peace Accords El Salvador." *American Anthropologist* 124, no. 1 (2022): 39–52. https://doi.org/10.1111/aman.13680.

Vigh, Henrik. "Crisis and Chronicity: Anthropological Perspectives on Continuous Conflict and Decline." *Ethnos* 73, no. 1 (March 1, 2008): 5–24. https://doi.org/10.1080/00141840801927509.

Villalever, Ximena Alba, and Stephanie Schütze. "Caravanas Migrantes as Counter Strategies Against Violence and (Im)Mobility." In *Forced Migration Across Mexico: Organized Violence, Migrant Struggles, and Life Trajectories*, edited by Ximena Alba Villalever, Stephanie Schütze, Ludger Pries, and Oscar Calderón Morillón. Routledge, Taylor & Francis Group, 2024.

Viveros Vigoya, Mara. "Contemporary Latin American Perspectives on Masculinity." In *Changing Men and Masculinities in Latin America*. Duke University Press, 2003.

Vogt, Wendy. "The Arterial Border: Negotiating Economies of Risk and Violence in Mexico's Security Regime." *International Journal of Migration and Border Studies* 3, no. 2-3 (2017): 192-207. https://doi.org/10.1504/IJMBS.2017.083244.

Vogt, Wendy. "Dirty Work, Dangerous Others: The Politics of Outsourced Immigration Enforcement in Mexico." *Migration and Society* 3, no. 1 (June 1, 2020): 50-63. https://doi.org/10.3167/arms.2020.111404.

Vogt, Wendy. *Lives in Transit: Violence and Intimacy on the Migrant Journey.* University of California Press, 2018.

Walters, William. "Deportation, Expulsion, and the International Police of Aliens." *Citizenship Studies* 6, no. 3 (September 1, 2002): 265-92. https://doi.org/10.1080/1362102022000011612.

Walters, William. "Expulsion, Power, Mobilisation." *Radical Philosophy*, no. 203 (December 1, 2018): 33.

Willers, Susanne. "Migration and Reproductive Strategies of Central American Women in Transit Through Mexico." *Journal of Family Studies* 24, no. 1 (January 2, 2018): 59-75. https://doi.org/10.1080/13229400.2017.1398102.

Wiltberger, Joseph. "Beyond Remittances: Contesting El Salvador's Developmentalist Migration Politics." *Journal of Latin American and Caribbean Anthropology* 19, no. 1 (March 1, 2014): 41-62. https://doi.org/10.1111/jlca.12065.

Wimmer, Andreas, and Nina Glick Schiller. "Methodological Nationalism, the Social Sciences, and the Study of Migration: An Essay in Historical Epistemology." *International Migration Review* 37, no. 3 (Fall 2003): 576-610.

Wolf, Sonja. *Mano Dura: The Politics of Gang Control in El Salvador.* University of Texas Press, 2017.

Zecena, Ruben. "Migrating Like a Queen: Visuality and Performance in the Trans Gay Caravan." *Women's Studies Quarterly* 47, no. 3 (2019): 99-118.

Zilberg, Elana. "Fools Banished from the Kingdom: Remapping Geographies of Gang Violence between the Americas (Los Angeles and San Salvador)." *American Quarterly* 56, no. 3 (2004): 759-79. https://doi.org/10.1353/aq.2004.0048.

Zilberg, Elana. *Space of Detention: The Making of a Transnational Gang Crisis Between Los Angeles and San Salvador.* Duke University Press, 2011.

Index

Note: Page numbers followed by "fig." indicate figures; page numbers followed by "table" indicate tables; page numbers followed by "map" indicate maps.

[237]

Chico, 53–54, 56–57, 58
Chiquimula, Guatemala 87
Chirizos, 194–95n18, 197–98n4
Choloma, Honduras 18, 19, 48, 50–51, 53, 77, 83, 110, 118–19, 163
Christian missions, 35
church foundations, US-based, 110
CIA (Central Intelligence Agency), 35, 198n14
circulation(s), 88–93, 132–33, 157, 168; as analytic in anthropology, 89; ethnography of, 88; language of, 151, 152–53; relationality and, 89; as researcher, 163; theories of, 205n45; thinking "otherwise," 170–73
Circumvention of Lawful Pathways Rule (CLP), 81, 82
citizenship, 8, 200–201n2; challenge to idea of, 90, 156, 158, 166, 167; rights and privileges of, 75, 200–201n2
Coahuila, Mexico, 141–42
Coatzacoalcos, Veracruz, Mexico, 140
cocaine, 6, 46, 64
Cofamipro, Comité de Familiares de Migrantes de El Progreso, Yoro (Committee of Families of Migrants of El Progreso, Yoro), 144
Cofradía, Honduras 48
Cold War: end of, 18, 45, 78; US counterinsurgency operations in Central America during, 5–6, 194n7
collective mobility tactics, 91, 157, 158
Colombia, 46, 82
colonias. See neighborhoods
Comité de Diálogo del Éxodo—the Exodus Dialogue Committee, 152
constancias, 161–62
containment, 71; micropolitics of, 5; shift to, 82–83, 84; spaces of, 67, 159
Copán, Honduras, 5

corruption, 91, 102, 149
Coutin, Susan Bibler, 89–90, 107
COVID-19 pandemic, 84, 86–87, 195n25
coyotes, 83
criminal convictions, 73, 75, 203n14
criminalization, 62, 79, 93, 96, 98, 112–20, 164, 168, 201n6; gendered, 30; of poverty, 115; racialized, 30; of urban poor, 69; of youth, 47–48, 117–18
criminal justice system, 31, 203n18
criminal law, 202–3n13
Cuéllar, Jorge, 158

daily life, 7, 12–13, 29, 45, 67, 96, 164, 167, 200n39; ethnography of, 12, 14
Danlí, Honduras, 177
Darién Gap, 82, 204n40
De Genova, Nicholas, 165
De León, Jason, 203–4n21
deportability: begins at home, 88–93; carceral quality of, 90
deportados. See deportees
deportation(s), 1, 59–61, 92, 133, 136, 164, 169; as administrative fix, 4; anthropology of, 163–70; becoming circulation, 84 (see also circulation(s)); changes in mid-1990s, 4; changing experience of, 69; as civil procedure, 203n14; compared to exile and banishment, 4, 8, 69, 72–75; deportation data, 185–86t., 194n10; "deportation machine," 74; deportation regime, 90, 91, 168; difficulty of conceptualizing, 14; as disciplining mechanism for undocumented labor, 202–3n13; ethnography of, 12–18; etymological origins of, 74; experience of, 68–69, 72–73; as

deportation(s) *(continued)*
  form of forced migration, 75; future
    of, 167; governmentality of, 72–73;
    of immigrants with legal status, 4;
    implications of, 8; importance of
    ethnographic approach to, 14; as
    important social phenomenon, 7;
    increasing number of, 163;
    marginalization and, 163–64;
    masking of violence inherent in,
    127–28; mass, 169; of men, 29;
    methodological challenges of
    ethnographic approach, 14–15; of
    minors, 16; multiple, 5, 60–61,
    90–91, 157, 165; new era of, 74–75,
    78–84, 167–70; ordinariness of,
    3–5, 14–15, 27, 68–69, 98; violence
    of, 9, 72, 73, 75, 169–70, 203–
    4n21; visibility under second
    Trump administration, 9;
    voluntary, 70
deportation studies, 8, 72–74, 92–93,
    106–8
deportee processing centers, 15–16,
    76, 89, 94–96, 161–62; Honduran
    government suspension of NGO
    access to, 15–16, 18
deportees, 1, 3–4, 12, 29, 59–63, 66–72;
    criminalization of, 79; dangers
    faced by, 73; de facto foreignness
    of, 201–2n7; education and, 97–105;
    entrepreneurship and, 106–12;
    experience of, 7–8; frequent, 5, 15,
    32–33, 67, 90–91; gang culture and,
    45; in Guatemala, 201n6; inter-
    views of, 1, 3, 16–17; masculinities
    and, 29–30; as "new American
    diaspora," 73; reintegration of,
    201–2n7, 201n6, 202n10; remigra-
    tion of, 203–4n21; ubiquity of in
    Honduras, 14–15

derecho a migrar, 142, 152, 158–60,
    167, 168–69. *See also* right to
    migrate
detention, 70, 83, 84, 88–89, 92,
    132–33, 164, 203–4n21.
deterrence, 80, 85, 97, 160
Dingeman-Cerda, Katie, 107, 202n10
dirty war era, continuation of
    extrajudicial "enforcement" from,
    47–48
disappearances (migrant), 143–44
discrimination, structural, 96
displacement, 40–41, 49, 51–63, 78,
    87, 92, 132–33, 164, 167
División Policial Anti Maras y
    Pandillas Contra el Crimen
    Organizado (Anti-Gang and
    Organized Crime Police Division)
    (DIPAMPCO), 207n30
Dominican Republic: deportees in,
    201–2n7; deportees to, 107–8
Doña Licha, 25–28, 112–14
Doris, 32
Dreby, Joanna, 202n12
Drotbohm, Heike, 202n12
drug trafficking, 6, 46, 64. *See also*
    cartels

Edita, 143–44
education, 90, 130; barriers to, 105;
    deportees and, 97–105; lack of
    access to, 110; (re)integration and,
    96, 97–105, 108; reintegration into
    educational system, 101
El Barretal, Tijuana, Mexico 131
el barrio, 44
El Combo Que No Se Deja, 194–
    95n18, 197–98n4
El Progreso, Yoro, Honduras, 143
El Salvador, 5, 10, 144; criminalization
    in, 98; deportation of gang-in-

volved youth from, 73–74; deportation studies and, 73–74; deported gang members from, 88; deportees in, 202n10; gangs and gang culture exported from the United States in, 45; immigrants from, 4; migrants from, 9; migration patterns and, 7

El-Shaarawi, Nadia, 133, 172

El Trébol, San Pedro Sula, Honduras 41, 43, 97

emplacement, 40–41

employment, 70, 90

encierro, 50, 71–72, 77. *See also* enclosure

enclosure, condition of, 50, 51–52, 71

entrepreneurship, 105; deportees and, 106–12; migrant return and reintegration, 96

entrepreneurship programs, 108–12, 129–30

Eric, 61–63

Estadio Benito Juárez, Tijuana, Mexico 131, 170

Estefani, 56

ethnographic research: methodological challenges, 14–15; vs. statistics, 7–8

ethnography: basics of, 18–20; as being present, 14; of circulation, 88; as cultivating serendipity, 14, 163; of deportation, 12–18; meaning of, 13–14; on post-deportation context, 166, 167

Euraque, Darío, 45

Evangelical Lutheran Church, 109, 110

exclusion, 88, 90, 93, 96, 110, 126, 128, 165, 167

exile, 61, 69, 72–75, 169

exodus, 7, 13, 146, 152–53

export agriculture, 45–46

externalization, 8–9, 79, 80–82, 84, 93, 139–40, 154, 154–55, 160, 168, 194n10; strategy of, 82

extortion, 65, 110, 118–19, 174, 198n6

extrajudicial "enforcement," 47–48

Ezra, 85–88, 91–92, 159

Facebook messenger, 60, 85, 163

Faith in Action (Fe en Acción, or FeAc), 15, 85, 116, 130, 134, 146; expulsion of, 6; Return and Rebuild Program (Programa de Retornar y Reconstruir, or Pro-R), 15, 16–18, 86, 104–5, 108–9, 110–12, 206n9

families: family separations, 9, 84–85, 202n12; mixed-status, 169; reconnecting, 17; transnational, 202n12

fascism, neoliberal, 115

Feldman, Allan, 55

femicide, 53, 54–55

feminist scholarship: feminist epistemology, 29–30; on men and masculinities, 29–30

field notes, 1, 20, 21–25, 41–43, 63–65, 103–4, 112–14, 170–73

FitzGerald, David, 84

Flaco, 120–27

foreign aid, 18, 96

Franklin, 110–12, 127, 129

Franz, Margaret, 158

freedom of transit, 143, 151–52, 167

fronteras internas, 34–65. *See also* internal borders

Fuerza Nacional Anti-Maras y Pandillas (National Anti-Gang Force) (FNAMP), 207n30

futurity, 170–71, 172

gang control, 24–27, 33, 59, 87, 89, 110–11; boundaries and, 38–40, 70, 103; geography of, 24–25, 38–40, 43, 48–51, 52, 70, 103; surveillance and, 60–61

gang-involved youth: deportation of, 73–74; prosecution of, 47

gang membership, 47, 120–27; prosecution for, 47

gangs, 6, 11–12, 24, 26, 27, 35, 36, 88, 118, 121, 194–95n18, 197–98n4; consolidation of after Hurricane Mitch, 46–47, 87; discipline imposed by, 125, 126–27; drug trafficking, 46; exported from the United States, 45; extortion and, 65, 110, 118, 119, 174; fledgling, 43–44; guilt by association with, 47; local absorbed by larger, 43–44; membership in, 42–43; police and, 124–25, 176; power shifts within, 49–50; surveillance by, 60–61; used by drug cartels, 46; war among, 123. *See also* maras; pandillas

gang violence, fears of, 86–87

Garifuna, 5, 30

gender, migration and, 31

gender-based violence, 23, 28, 29

geography, 167; of gang control, 70

Gibney, Michael, 75

girls, 26; gender-based violence and, 28; risk of homicide for, 54–55

Giroux, Henry, 115

Glockner, Valentina, 156–57

Gladys, 112–14, 117, 121

global north, 31, 154

Gloria, 60

Golash-Boza, Tanya, 201n6

Goodman, Adam, 74

governmentality, 200–201n2

governments, reintegration and, 106

graffiti, 22, 118, 121

Grimaldi, Grazzia, 197n45

group migration, 131–60

guardia nacional, 82

Guatemala, 5, 10, 82, 87–88, 144; agreement with United States, 79, 81; deportees in, 201–2n7, 201n6; migrants from, 4, 9, 78; migration patterns and, 7; military in, 159; reintegration in, 201n6

Guatemalan military, regional migration regime and, 87–88

Gutmann, Matthew, 29

haircuts, 47

Hasselberg, Ines, 202n12

HCH, 133–34

health care, 90, 102

Hector, 163

Heidbrink, Lauren, 203–4n21

Hemeteria, 143–44

Henry, 112–16, 127

Hermana Leticia, 145

Hermanos en El Camino, 207n30

Hernández Alvarado, Juan Orlando, 118; dubious reelection victory in 2017, 193n6; government of, 101, 102; imprisonment of, 6; as president of Congress, 119; protest movements against, 150; reelection campaign of, 16.

Hiemstra, Nancy, 203–4n21

Holy Week, 140, 142, 143

homicides, 10–11, 53, 70

Honduran government, 106, 195n23; agreement with US, 79, 81; disappeared migrants and, 144; discourse on migration and security, 16; education and, 101, 102, 105; migrant reintegration and, 95; reliance on US assistance, 45;

cartels and, 46; Kevin and, 59–61; Marlon and, 41–42; origins of, 6; police and, 65; Ramón and, 175–77. *See also* maras

mareros, 21, 44, 47, 64–65, 176, 177

marginalization, 40–41, 56, 96, 132–33, 163–64, 200n39

Maribel, 83–84

Mariela, 112–14

marijuana, 64, 72

Marlon, 41–48

Martínez d'Aubuisson, Juan, 44

masculinities, feminist scholarship on, 29–30

Matías Romero, Oaxaca, Mexico, 207–8n36

Matta Ballesteros, Juan, 46, 198n14

Maya civilization, 5

men, focus on, 25–30

Mennonites, 110

Mérida Initiative, 80

methodology, 18–21

Mexico, 13, 32–33, 144, 163, 202n12; Afro-Indigenous Garifuna population targeted in, 30; agreement with United States, 79–81; changes in, 79; criminalization in, 98; deportations from, 7, 9, 67; deportees in, 201–2n7; Guardia Nacional in, 159; harassment by police officers in, 66–67; immigration enforcement in, 79–80, 137, 139–40, 154, 156, 159, 194n10; immigration policy of, 136–37; Ley General de Población in, 137; migrants in, 7, 57–58, 71–72, 77, 82–84, 111–12, 125, 129–30, 133, 204n33; migrants' rights movement in, 136; migration-related research in, 18; as país tapón, or stopper country, 81, 82; "Plan Frontera Sur,"

80, 81, 156; police blockades in, 148–49, 149fig.; shelters in, 83, 142, 207–8n36; transit migration in, 9, 132, 139, 141; as "vertical" or "arterial" border, 81

Mexico City, Mexico, 141–42, 150, 209–10n22

Miami, Florida, 4

microenterprises, 105, 108–9, 110, 129

migrant caravans, 9, 13, 70, 81, 84, 91, 131–60, 170; in 2010, 135, 207–8n36; in 2011, 132, 140, 141, 208n3; in 2012, 132; in 2013, 132; in 2014, 132, 140–41; in 2016, 140–41; in 2018, 132, 133–34, 146–53, 208n4; in 2018–19, 145; arrival of, 133–40; author participation in, 9, 11, 132, 136, 138; history of, 132, 133; as idea and phenomenon, 131–60; as protest, 139, 140–45; scholarship on, 132, 144–45; since 2018, 144–45; as "transnational social movements," 144–45

Migrant Protection Protocols (Remain in Mexico), 81, 156

migrants: dangers for, 141; endurance and persistence of, 171–72; exploitation of, 141; fear of, 10; ideal, 28; "mutilated" by freight trains, 141; potential, 128–29; queer-identified, 141; stopped in Mexico, 79–80; targeted for murder, 10; violence against, 135, 137–38

migrants' rights movement, 134–38, 147–48. *See also* specific activists

migration, 59–63, 87, 92, 132–33, 164; as an act of hope, 170–71; bordering practices and, 156–57; distinct history of Honduran, 78–79; as exodus, 152–53; group, 131–60 (see also migrant caravans); hopeless

North American Free Trade Agreement (NAFTA), 80
Norwegian Refugee Council (NRC), 95
Nuñez Chaim, Margarita, 156–57

Oaxaca, Mexico, 82, 129–30, 135, 137–38, 147–48, 157map
Oaxaca City, Oaxaca, Mexico, 151
Occupy movement, 140
O. Henry (William Sydney Porter), 6
Olanchanos, 194–95n18
Olancho, Honduras, 109, 175, 197–98n4
Omar, 146, 150–51
opportunities, lack of access to, 56, 62
organized crime, 27, 44–45, 198n6
outsiderness, 23–25

país tapón, or stopper country, 81, 82
Pamela, 16–17
pandillas, 11, 12, 41–48, 53, 61, 197–98n4
pandilleros, 35, 47, 60, 120–27, 176; fleeing gang discipline, 125, 126–27; reintegration and, 126–27
Papadopolous, Dimitris, 155–56
participant observation, 18–20
"Paso a paso hacia la Paz" (Step by step toward Peace), 136
Pastor Luis, 34–37, 54, 176
patriarchy, violence of, 29
Pedro, 1
Peña Nieto, Enrique, 81, 140–41, 146, 149
Peutz, Nathalie, 14–15
Pine, Adrienne, 48, 115
"Plan Frontera Sur," 80, 81, 156
police, 21, 26, 45, 65, 82, 174; abuse by, 134–35; acting as middlemen in extortion schemes, 118–19;
anti-extortion, 118; dangers of speaking to, 59–60; gangs and, 124–25, 176; harassment by, 62, 66–67, 112–17; ineffectiveness of, 118–19; lack of respect shown by, 116–20; in Mexico, 66–67, 132, 134–35; military, 112–17; MS-13 and, 65; police blockades, 148–49, 149fig.; tactics of, 89; targeting by, 27, 28; USAID and, 121. See also policing
Policía Militar del Orden Público (PMOP), 119, 120fig. See also military police
policing, 22–23, 57, 59–60, 119; anti-immigrant, 30; logics of, 88; "mano dura," 47–48; methods of, 88; military involvement in, 119 (see also military police); policing models, 88; racism and, 66–67
post-deportation context, 96, 165, 166, 167
post-deportation studies, 106, 165
Potrerillos, Honduras 103–4
poverty, 56, 198n6; criminalization of, 115; framed as "danger," 23; as reason for migration, 10
power, 29; microdynamics of, 48–51; migration and, 154–55; mobility and, 12
precarity, 92–93
pretrial detention, 114, 124–25
Prevention Through Deterrence (PTD), 80, 83, 203–4n21
privilege, 23–24
Profe Juan, 38–39, 97–100, 101–3, 117–19, 127, 207n30
prosperity gospel, 110
protest movements, 140–42, 144, 153–54. See also migrant caravans
pseudonyms, 11–12

United States (continued)
threat" in, 28; counterinsurgency operations in Central America during Cold War, 5–6, 45; deportation from, 7, 59, 67, 73; doctors from, 35; externalization of immigration agenda, 80, 139–40, 154, 194n10; gangs and gang culture exported from, 45; immigration enforcement in, 79, 154; immigration policy of, 136; inner cities in, 22–23; migration to, 7, 71, 77, 127–28, 131–60; military bases of, 6; new era of deportation in, 167–70; regional migration regime and, 87–88; strategy of externalization, 82 (see also externalization); undocumented labor in, 202–3n13; war on drugs and, 46. *See also* US-Mexico border

urban poor, criminalization of, 69
urban youth, criminalization of, 62
urban youth culture, criminalization of, 47
US Agency for International Development (USAID), 34–35, 101, 102, 106, 109, 110, 161; police and, 121
US counterinsurgency operations, 5–6, 45
US Department of Homeland Security, 196n36, 206n6
US Drug Enforcement Agency (DEA), 198n14
US forces, 132
US immigration courts, 81
US-Mexico border, 131, 156, 171fig., 203–4n21; "crisis" at, 173; detention at, 83; ever-tightening enforcement at, 8–9; expanded policing of, 79; externalization of enforcement of,

80; Mexican police at, 132; US forces at, 132

Varela Huerta, Amarela, 81, 82, 156–57
Vatos Locos, 44, 194–95n18
Venezuelans, 160
Viacrucis, 140–42, 143, 145
Vigh, Henrik, 58
vigilante groups, 47, 194–95n18, 198n6
Villanueva, Honduras, 163
violence, 10, 53, 77, 132–33; contexts of, 23–24; of deportation, 72, 169–70, 203–4n21, 203n19; displacement due to, 48–52; drug-war related, 140; embedded in ordinariness of deportation, 5; environmental, 10; epidemic of, 163; essentialism of, 55; ever-present possibility of, 69; everyday, 51–59, 199–200n38, 200n39; gangs as stand-in for, 44–45; gender-based violence, 10; intentional, 203n19; kinds of, 200n39; against migrants, 135, 137–38; political, 10; pornography of, 55; rates in Honduras, 10–11; as reason for migration, 9–10; represented in writing, 55–56; social geography of, 34–65; structural, 10, 56–57; writing about, 55–56
Vista del Cielo, San Pedro Sula, Honduras 25–27, 28, 114, 115–16, 120–27, 130
vocational training, 109
voice notes, 20, 60, 170, 176

war on drugs, 46, 80, 140
"war on terror," 28
Wixárika, 209–10n22

women: care work and, 31–32; gender-based violence and, 23, 28; interventions by, 31–32; migration of, 28–29, 30; violence and, 54–55; in the workforce, 30–31

workplace raids, 9

World Health Organization, 10

writing process, 20–21

Yadira, 66–67, 68–69, 72

youths, 89; criminalization of, 47–48, 117–20; prosecuted for gang membership, 47. *See also* boys; girls

Zapatistas, 209–10n22

Zilberg, Elana, 74, 88–90

California Series in Public Anthropology

The California Series in Public Anthropology emphasizes the anthropologist's role as an engaged intellectual. It continues anthropology's commitment to being an ethnographic witness, to describing, in human terms, how life is lived beyond the borders of many readers' experiences. But it also adds a commitment, through ethnography, to reframing the terms of public debate—transforming received, accepted understandings of social issues with new insights, new framings.

SERIES EDITOR: IEVA JUSIONYTE (BROWN UNIVERSITY)

FOUNDING EDITOR: ROBERT BOROFSKY (HAWAII PACIFIC UNIVERSITY)

ADVISORY BOARD: CATHERINE BESTEMAN (COLBY COLLEGE), PHILIPPE BOURGOIS (UCLA), JASON DE LEÓN (UCLA), LAURENCE RALPH (PRINCETON UNIVERSITY), AND NANCY SCHEPER-HUGHES (UC BERKELEY)

1. *Twice Dead: Organ Transplants and the Reinvention of Death,* by Margaret Lock
2. *Birthing the Nation: Strategies of Palestinian Women in Israel,* by Rhoda Ann Kanaaneh (with a foreword by Hanan Ashrawi)
3. *Annihilating Difference: The Anthropology of Genocide,* edited by Alexander Laban Hinton (with a foreword by Kenneth Roth)
4. *Pathologies of Power: Health, Human Rights, and the New War on the Poor,* by Paul Farmer (with a foreword by Amartya Sen)
5. *Buddha Is Hiding: Refugees, Citizenship, the New America,* by Aihwa Ong
6. *Chechnya: Life in a War-Torn Society,* by Valery Tishkov (with a foreword by Mikhail S. Gorbachev)
7. *Total Confinement: Madness and Reason in the Maximum Security Prison,* by Lorna A. Rhodes
8. *Paradise in Ashes: A Guatemalan Journey of Courage, Terror, and Hope,* by Beatriz Manz (with a foreword by Aryeh Neier)
9. *Laughter Out of Place: Race, Class, Violence, and Sexuality in a Rio Shantytown,* by Donna M. Goldstein

Founded in 1893,
UNIVERSITY OF CALIFORNIA PRESS
publishes bold, progressive books and journals
on topics in the arts, humanities, social sciences,
and natural sciences—with a focus on social
justice issues—that inspire thought and action
among readers worldwide.

The UC PRESS FOUNDATION
raises funds to uphold the press's vital role
as an independent, nonprofit publisher, and
receives philanthropic support from a wide
range of individuals and institutions—and from
committed readers like you. To learn more, visit
ucpress.edu/supportus.

www.ingramcontent.com/pod-product-compliance
Lightning Source LLC
Chambersburg PA
CBHW032346280326
41935CB00008B/469